Certificate Paper C1

FUNDAMENTALS OF
MANAGEMENT ACCOUNTING

For assessments under the 2006
syllabus in 2008

Practice & Revision Kit

In this January 2008 new edition

- Banks of multiple choice questions and objective test questions on every syllabus area
- Answers with detailed feedback
- Two mock assessments
- Fully up to date as at 1 January 2008

BPP Learning Media's **i-Pass** product also supports this paper

LEARNING MEDIA

First edition June 2006
Second edition January 2008

ISBN 9780 7517 5180 2 (previous edition 0 7517 2652 4)

British Library Cataloguing-in-Publication Data
A catalogue record for this book
is available from the British Library

Published by

BPP Learning Media Ltd
BPP House, Aldine Place
London W12 8AA

www.bpp.com/learningmedia

Printed in Great Britain by
WM Print
45-47 Frederick Street
Walsall
WS2 9NE

We are grateful to the Chartered Institute of
Management Accountants for permission to reproduce
past examination questions. The answers to past
examination questions have been prepared by BPP
Learning Media Ltd.

Contents

Page

Revision

Revising with this Kit iv
Effective revision vi

The assessment

Assessment technique ix
Tackling multiple choice questions xi
Tackling objective test questions xii

Background

Current issues xiv
Useful websites xiv

Question and answer checklist/index xv

	Questions	Answers
Question practice		
Objective test questions	3	119
Assessment practice		
Mock assessment 1	225	239
Mock assessment 2	253	271

Review form & free prize draw

Revising with this Kit

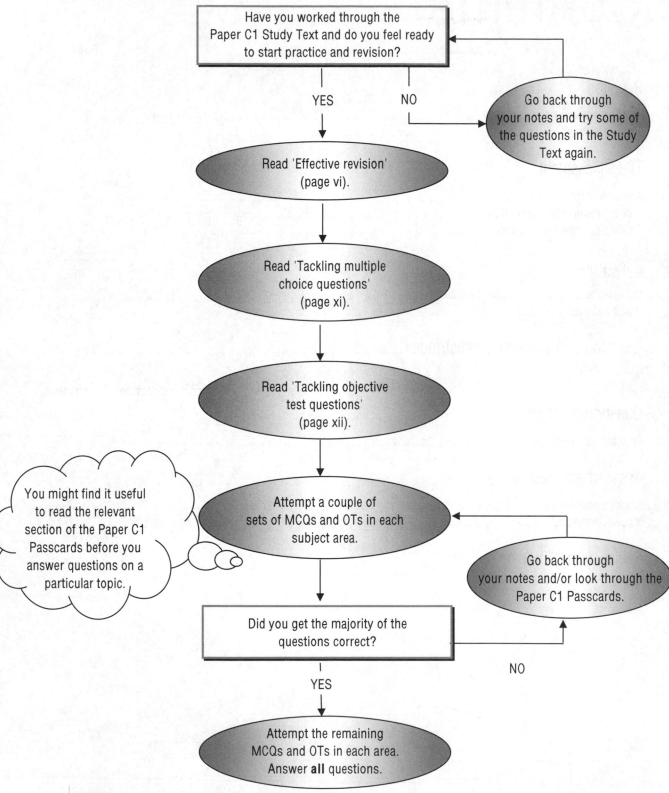

Have you worked through the
Paper C1 Study Text and do you feel ready
to start practice and revision?

YES   NO

Go back through
your notes and try some of
the questions in the Study
Text again.

Read 'Effective revision'
(page vi).

Read 'Tackling multiple
choice questions'
(page xi).

Read 'Tackling objective
test questions'
(page xii).

You might find it useful
to read the relevant
section of the Paper C1
Passcards before you
answer questions on a
particular topic.

Attempt a couple of
sets of MCQs and OTs in each
subject area.

Go back through
your notes and/or look through the
Paper C1 Passcards.

Did you get the majority of the
questions correct?

NO

YES

Attempt the remaining
MCQs and OTs in each area.
Answer **all** questions.

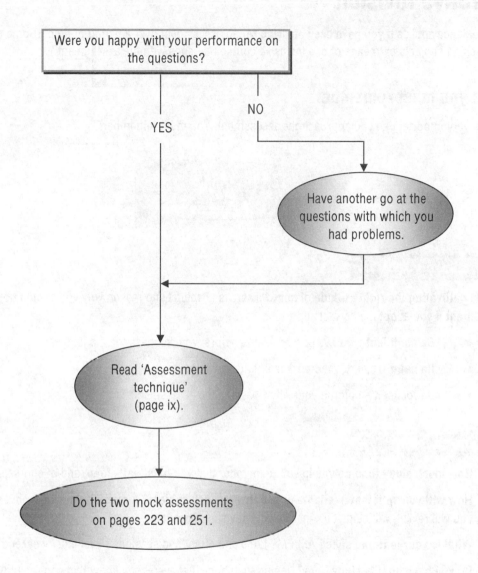

Were you happy with your performance on the questions?

YES

NO

Have another go at the questions with which you had problems.

Read 'Assessment technique' (page ix).

Do the two mock assessments on pages 223 and 251.

Effective revision

This guidance applies if you have been studying for an assessment over a period of time. (Some tuition providers are teaching subjects by means of one intensive course that ends with the assessment.)

What you must remember

Time is very important as you approach the assessment. You must remember:

> **Believe in yourself**
>
> **Use time sensibly**

Believe in yourself

Are you cultivating the right attitude of mind? There is absolutely no reason why you should not pass this **assessment** if you adopt the correct approach.

- **Be confident** – you've passed exams before, you can pass them again
- **Be calm** – plenty of adrenaline but no panicking
- **Be focused** – commit yourself to passing the assessment

Use time sensibly

1. **How much study time do you have?** Remember that you must **eat**, **sleep**, and of course, **relax**.

2. **How will you split that available time between each subject?** A revision timetable, covering what and how you will revise, will help you organise your revision thoroughly.

3. **What is your learning style?** AM/PM? Little and often/long sessions? Evenings/ weekends?

4. **Do you have quality study time?** Unplug the phone. Let everybody know that you're studying and shouldn't be disturbed.

5. **Are you taking regular breaks?** Most people absorb more if they do not attempt to study for long uninterrupted periods of time. A five minute break every hour (to make coffee, watch the news headlines) can make all the difference.

6. **Are you rewarding yourself for your hard work?** Are you leading a **healthy lifestyle?**

What to revise

Key topics

You need to spend **most time** on, and practise **lots of questions** on, topics that are likely to yield plenty of questions in your assessment.

You may also find certain areas of the syllabus difficult.

Difficult areas are

- Areas you find dull or pointless
- Subjects you highlighted as difficult when you studied them
- Topics that gave you problems when you answered questions or reviewed the material

DON'T become depressed about these areas; instead do something about them.

- Build up your knowledge by **quick tests** such as the quick quizzes in your BPP Learning Media Study Text and the batches of questions in the I-Pass CD ROM.

- Work carefully through **examples** and **questions** in the Text, and refer back to the Text if you struggle with questions in the Kit.

Breadth of revision

Make sure your revision covers all areas of the syllabus. Your assessment will test your knowledge of the whole syllabus.

How to revise

There are four main ways that you can revise a topic area.

Write it!

Read it!

Teach it!

Do it!

Write it!

Writing important points down will help you recall them, particularly if your notes are presented in a way that makes it easy for you to remember them.

Read it!

You should read your notes or BPP Learning Media Passcards actively, testing yourself by doing quick quizzes or Kit questions while you are reading.

Teach it!

Assessments require you to show your understanding. Teaching what you are learning to another person helps you practise explaining topics that you might be asked to define in your assessment. Teaching someone who will challenge your understanding, someone for example who will be taking the same assessment as you, can be helpful to both of you.

Do it!

Remember that you are revising in order to be able to answer questions in the assessment. Practising questions will help you practise **technique** and **discipline**, which can be crucial in passing or failing assessments.

1   Start your question practice by doing a couple of sets of objective test questions in a subject area. Note down the questions where you went wrong, try to identify why you made mistakes and go back to your Study Text for guidance or practice.

2   The **more questions** you do, the more likely you are to pass the assessment. However if you do run short of time:

- Make sure that you have done at least some questions from every section of the syllabus

- Look through the banks of questions and do questions on areas that you have found difficult or on which you have made mistakes

3   When you think you can successfully answer questions on the whole syllabus, attempt the **two mock assessments** at the end of the Kit. You will get the most benefit by sitting them under strict assessment conditions, so that you gain experience of the vital assessment processes.

- Managing your time
- Producing answers

BPP Learning Media's *Learning to Learn Accountancy* gives further valuable advice on how to approach revision. BPP Learning Media has also produced other vital revision aids.

- **Passcards** – Provide you with clear topic summaries and assessment tips

- **i-Pass CDs** – Offer you tests of knowledge to be completed against the clock

- **Success CDs** – Help you revise on the move

You can purchase these products by visiting www.bpp.com/cima

BPP
LEARNING MEDIA

Assessment technique

Format of the assessment

The assessment will contain 50 questions to be completed in 2 hours. The questions will be a combination of multiple choice questions and other types of objective test questions.

Passing assessments

Passing assessments is half about having the knowledge, and half about doing yourself full justice in the assessment. You must have the right approach to two things.

> **The day of the assessment**
>
> **Your time in the assessment room**

The day of the assessment

1   Set at least one **alarm** (or get an alarm call) for a morning assessment.

2   Have **something to eat** but beware of eating too much; you may feel sleepy if your system is digesting a large meal.

3   Allow plenty of **time to get to the assessment room**; have your route worked out in advance and listen to news bulletins to check for potential travel problems.

4   **Don't forget** pens and watch. Also make sure you remember **entrance documentation** and **evidence of identity**.

5   Put **new batteries** into your calculator and take a spare set (or a spare calculator).

6   **Avoid discussion** about the assessment with other candidates outside the assessment room.

Your time in the assessment room

1   **Listen carefully to the invigilator's instructions**

     Make sure you understand the formalities you have to complete.

2   **Ensure you follow the instructions on the computer screen**

     In particular ensure that you select the correct assessment (not every student does!), and that you understand how to work through the assessment and submit your answers.

3   Keep your eye on the time

In the assessment you will have to complete 50 questions in 120 minutes. That will mean that you have roughly 2½ minutes on average to answer each question. You will be able to answer some questions instantly, but others will require thinking about. If after a minute or so you have no idea how to tackle the question, leave it and come back to it later.

4   Label your workings clearly with the question number

This will help you when you check your answers, or if you come back to a question that you are unsure about.

5   Deal with problem questions

There are two ways of dealing with questions where you are unsure of the answer.

(a)   **Don't submit an answer.** The computer will tell you before you move to the next question that you have not submitted an answer, and the question will be marked as not done on the list of questions. The risk with this approach is that you run out of time before you do submit an answer.

(b)   **Submit an answer**. You can always come back and change the answer before you finish the assessment or the time runs out. You should though make a note of answers that you are unsure about, to ensure that you do revisit them later in the assessment.

6   Make sure you submit an answer for every question

When there are ten minutes left to go, concentrate on submitting answers for all the questions that you have not answered up to that point. You won't get penalised for wrong answers so take a guess if you're unsure.

7   Check your answers

If you finish the assessment with time to spare, check your answers before you sign out of the assessment. In particular revisit questions that you are unsure about, and check that your answers are in the right format and contain the correct number of words as appropriate.

BPP Learning Media's *Learning to Learn Accountancy* gives further valuable advice on how to approach the day of the assessment.

Tackling multiple choice questions

The MCQs in your assessment contain a number of possible answers. You have to **choose the option(s) that best answers the question**. The three incorrect options are called distracters. There is a skill in answering MCQs quickly and correctly. By practising MCQs you can develop this skill, giving you a better chance of passing the assessment.

You may wish to follow the approach outlined below, or you may prefer to adapt it.

Step 1 **Note down how long** you should allocate to each MCQ. For this paper you will be answering 50 questions in 120 minutes, so you will be spending on average just under two and a half minutes on each question. Remember however that you will not be expected to spend an equal amount of time on each MCQ; some can be answered instantly but others will take time to work out.

Step 2 **Attempt each question**. Read the question thoroughly.

You may find that you recognise a question when you sit the assessment. Be aware that the detail and/or requirement may be different. If the question seems familiar read the requirement and options carefully – do not assume that it is identical.

Step 3 Read the four options and see if one matches your own answer. Be careful with numerical questions, as the distracters are designed to match answers that incorporate **common errors**. Check that your calculation is correct. Have you followed the requirement exactly? Have you included every stage of a calculation?

Step 4 You may find that none of the options matches your answer.

- **Re-read the question** to ensure that you understand it and are answering the requirement

- **Eliminate any obviously wrong answers**

- **Consider which of the remaining answers** is the **most likely** to be correct and select the option

Step 5 If you are still unsure, **continue to the next question**. Likewise if you are nowhere near working out which option is correct after a couple of minutes, leave the question and come back to it later. Make a note of any questions for which you have submitted answers, but you need to return to later. The computer will list any questions for which you have not submitted answers.

Step 6 **Revisit questions** you are uncertain about. When you come back to a question after a break you often find you are able to answer it correctly straight away. If you are still unsure have a guess. You are not penalised for incorrect answers, so **never leave a question unanswered!**

Tackling objective test questions

What is an objective test question?

An objective test (**OT**) question is made up of some form of **stimulus**, usually a question, and a **requirement** to do something.

- **MCQs.** Read through the information on page (xi) about MCQs and how to tackle them.

- **True or false**. You will be asked if a statement is true or false.

- **Data entry**. This type of OT requires you to provide figures such as the correct figure for inventory valuation, or words to fill in a blank.

- **Multiple response.** These questions provide you with a number of options and you have to identify those that fulfil certain criteria.

- **Matching.** This OT question format could ask you to classify particular costs into one of a range of cost classifications provided, to match descriptions of variances with one of a number of variances listed, and so on.

OT questions in your assessment

CIMA is currently developing different types of OTs for inclusion in computer-based assessments. The timetable for introduction of new types of OTs is uncertain, and it is also not certain how many questions in your assessment will be MCQs, and how many will be other types of OT. Practising all the different types of OTs that this Kit provides will prepare you well for whatever questions come up in your assessment.

Dealing with OT questions

Again you may wish to follow the approach we suggest, or you may be prepared to adapt it.

Step 1   Work out **how long** you should allocate to each OT. Remember that you will not be expected to spend an equal amount of time on each one; some can be answered instantly but others will take time to work out.

Step 2   **Attempt each question**. Read the question thoroughly, and note in particular what the question says about the **format** of your answer and whether there are any **restrictions** placed on it (for example the number of words you can use).

    You may find that you recognise a question when you sit the assessment. Be aware that the detail and/or requirement may be different. If the question seems familiar read the requirement and options carefully – do not assume that it is identical.

Step 3   Read any options you are given and select which ones are appropriate. Check that your calculations are correct. Have you followed the requirement exactly? Have you included every stage of the calculation?

Step 4   You may find that you are unsure of the answer.

- Re-read the question to ensure that you understand it and are answering the requirement
- Eliminate any obviously wrong options if you are given a number of options from which to choose

Step 5   If you are still unsure, **continue to the next question**. Make a note of any questions for which you have submitted answers, but you need to return to later. The computer will list any questions for which you have not submitted answers.

Step 6   Revisit questions you are uncertain about. When you come back to a question after a break you often find you are able to answer it correctly straight away. If you are still unsure have a guess. You are not penalised for incorrect answers, so **never leave a question unanswered!**

Current issues

Feedback from students

Feedback from students sitting the CBAs has highlighted the following:

- A mix of £ and $ may be used
- Sales tax may be referred to as VAT
- Inventory may be referred to as stock
- Receivables may be referred to as debtors
- Payables may be referred to as creditors

Useful websites

The websites below provide additional sources of information of relevance to your studies for *Fundamentals of Management Accounting*.

- BPP   www.bpp.com

  For details of other BPP material for your CIMA studies

- CIMA   www.cimaglobal.com

  The official CIMA website

BPP))) LEARNING MEDIA

Question and Answer checklist/index

The headings in this checklist/index indicate the main topics of questions, but questions often cover several different topics.

		Page number	
		Question	Answer
Objective test questions			
1	Introduction to management accounting and costing I	3	119
2	Introduction to management accounting and costing II	5	120
3	Cost behaviour	7	121
4	Overheads costs – absorption costing I	10	123
5	Overheads costs – absorption costing II	12	125
6	Overheads costs – absorption costing III	15	128
7	Overheads costs – absorption costing IV	16	130
8	Overheads costs – absorption costing V	19	133
9	Inventory valuation I	22	134
10	Inventory valuation II	24	137
11	Breakeven analysis and limiting factor analysis I	27	140
12	Breakeven analysis and limiting factor analysis II	29	142
13	Breakeven analysis and limiting factor analysis III	33	145
14	Standard costing and variance analysis I	36	147
15	Standard costing and variance analysis II	38	150
16	Standard costing and varlance analysis III	41	153
17	Standard costing and variance analysis IV	44	155
18	Standard costing and variance analysis V	46	157
19	Standard costing and variance analysis VI	49	159
20	Budgeting I	51	161
21	Budgetlng II	53	163
22	Budgeting III	56	166
23	Budgeting IV	57	168
24	Budgeting V	60	169
25	Budgeting VI	63	173
26	Budgeting VII	66	177
27	Budgeting VIII	69	180
28	Cost bookkeeping I	72	183
29	Cost bookkeeping II	75	185
30	Cost bookkeeping III	78	187
31	Cost bookkeeping IV	80	189
32	Process costing I	84	191
33	Process costing II	86	194
34	Process costing III	89	197

35	Job, batch and contract costing I	91	200
36	Job, batch and contract costing II	93	202
37	Job, batch and contract costing III	96	205
38	Service costing	99	208

Mixed bank questions

39	Mixed bank I	101	210
40	Mixed bank II	104	212
41	Mixed bank III	107	215
42	Mixed bank IV	110	216
43	Mixed bank V	113	219

Mock assessment 1	225	239
Mock assessment 2	253	271

Objective test questions

1 Introduction to management accounting and costing I

1   A cost unit is

    A   the cost per hour of operating a machine
    B   the cost per unit of electricity consumed
    C   a unit of product or service in relation to which costs are ascertained
    D   a measure of work output in a standard hour

2   A cost centre is

    A   A unit of product or service in relation to which costs are ascertained
    B   An amount of expenditure attributable to an activity
    C   A production or service location, function, activity or item of equipment for which costs are accumulated
    D   A centre for which an individual budget is drawn up

3   Which of the following items might be a suitable cost unit within the accounts payable department of a company?

    (i)   Postage cost
    (ii)   Invoice processed
    (iii)   Supplier account

    A   Item (i) only
    B   Item (ii) only
    C   Item (iii) only
    D   Items (ii) and (iii) only

4   Prime cost is

    A   all costs incurred in manufacturing a product
    B   the total of direct costs
    C   the material cost of a product
    D   the cost of operating a department

5   Which of the following costs are part of the prime cost for a manufacturing company?

    A   Cost of transporting raw materials from the supplier's premises
    B   Wages of factory workers engaged in machine maintenance
    C   Depreciation of lorries used for deliveries to customers
    D   Cost of indirect production materials

6   Which of the following are direct expenses?

    (i)   The cost of special designs, drawing or layouts
    (ii)   The hire of tools or equipment for a particular job
    (iii)   Salesman's wages
    (iv)   Rent, rates and insurance of a factory

√ (A)   (i) and (ii)
B   (i) and (iii)
C   (i) and (iv)
D   (iii) and (iv)

7   Which of the following are indirect costs?

(i)   The depreciation of maintenance equipment
(ii)   The overtime premium incurred at the specific request of a customer
(iii)   The hire of a tool for a specific job

√ (A)   Item (i) only
B   Items (i) and (ii) only
C   Items (ii) and (iii) only
D   All of them

8   A company employs three drivers to deliver goods to its customers. The salaries paid to these drivers are:

A   a part of prime cost
B   a direct production expense
C   a production overhead
(D)   a selling and distribution overhead

The following information relates to questions 9 and 10

The overhead expenses of a company are coded using a five digit coding system, an extract from which is as follows:

Cost centre	Code no	Types of expense	Code no
Machining	10	Indirect materials	410
Finishing	11	Depreciation of production machinery	420
Packing	12	Indirect wages	430
Stores	13	Maintenance materials	440
Maintenance	14	Machine hire costs	450
		Depreciation of non-production equipment	460

The coding for the hire costs of a packing machine is 12450

9   The coding for the depreciation of maintenance equipment is

A   10460
B   14420
C   14440
(D)   14460

10   The coding for the issue of indirect materials issued from stores to the machining department is

    (A)   10410
    B   10440
    C   13410
    D   13440

2 Introduction to management accounting and costing II

1   Gross wages incurred in department 1 in June were $54,000. The wages analysis shows the following summary breakdown of the gross pay.

NB/ Only direct wages are the ordinary pay to direct workers plus their basic overtime pay.

	Paid to direct labour $	Paid to indirect labour $
Ordinary time	25,185	11,900
Overtime: basic pay	5,440	3,500
premium	1,360	875
Shift allowance	2,700	1,360
Sick pay	1,380	300
	36,065	17,935

What is the direct wages cost for department 1 in June?

    A $25,185
    B $30,625
    (C) $34,685
    D $36,065

2   Which of the following would be classed as indirect labour?

    A   A coach driver in a transport company
    B   Machine operators in a milk bottling plant
    (C)   A maintenance assistant in a factory maintenance department
    D   Plumbers in a construction company

3   Which of the following item(s) might be a suitable cost unit within the credit control department of a company?

    ☐ Telephone expense

    ☑ Cheque received and processed

    ☑ Customer account

4 Which one of the following would be classed as indirect labour?

- [ ] Machine operators in a company manufacturing washing machines
- [✓] A stores assistant in a factory store
- [ ] Plumbers in a construction company
- [✓] A committee in a firm of management consultants

NB Committee is administrative expenses.

5 A company has to pay a $1 per unit royalty to the designer of a product which it manufactures and sells.

The royalty charge would be classified in the company's accounts as a (tick the correct answer):

- [✓] Direct expense
- [ ] Production overhead
- [ ] Administrative overhead
- [ ] Selling overhead

6 Fixed costs are conventionally deemed to be (tick the correct answer):

- [ ] Constant per unit of activity
- [✓] Constant in total when activity changes
- [ ] Outside the control of management
- [ ] Unaffected by inflation

7 A cost centre is (tick the correct answer):

- [ ] a unit of output or service for which costs are ascertained
- [✓] a function or location for which costs are ascertained
- [ ] a segment of the organisation for which budgets are prepared
- [ ] an amount of expenditure attributable to a particular activity

8 Depreciation on production equipment is (tick all answers that are correct):

- [✓] Not a cash cost
- [✓] Part of production overheads
- [ ] Part of prime cost
- [ ] Always calculated using a machine-hour rate

9   A manufacturing firm has temporary production problems and overtime is being worked.

The amount of overtime premium contained in direct wages would normally be classed as which one of the following:

☐ Direct expenses

☑ Production overheads

☐ Direct labour costs

☐ Administrative overheads

10   The following information is available for product Zed for the month of January.

Production costs:

Variable $8 per unit
Fixed $12,000

The total production cost of producing 8,000 units of product Zed in January is $ 76,000 .

3 Cost behaviour

1 . Variable costs are conventionally deemed to

   Ⓐ   be constant per unit of output
   B   vary per unit of output as production volume changes
   C   be constant in total when production volume changes
   D   vary, in total, from period to period when production is constant

2   The following is a graph of cost against level of activity

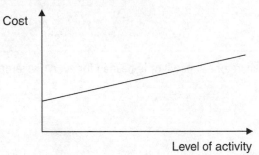

To which one of the following costs does the graph correspond?

   Ⓐ   Electricity bills made up of a standing charge and a variable charge
   B   Bonus payment to employees when production reaches a certain level
   C   Salesman's commissions payable per unit up to a maximum amount of commission
   D   Bulk discounts on purchases, the discount being given on all units purchased

The following information relates to questions 3 to 5

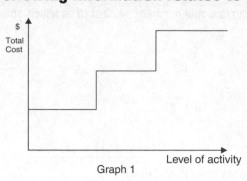

Graph 1

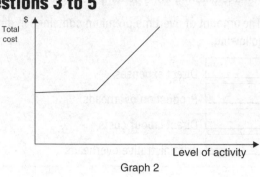

Graph 2

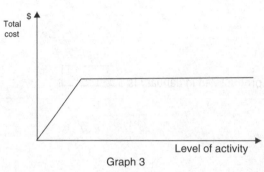

Graph 3

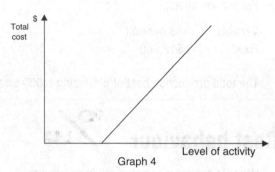

Graph 4

Which one of the above graphs depicts the costs described in questions 3 to 5?

3   Photocopier rental costs, where a fixed rental is payable up to a certain number of copies each period. If the number of copies exceeds this amount, a constant charge per copy is made for all subsequent copies during that period.

   A   Graph 1
   B   Graph 2
   C   Graph 3
   D   Graph 4

4   Supervisor salary costs, where one supervisor is needed for every five employees added to the staff.

   A   Graph 1
   B   Graph 2
   C   Graph 3
   D   Graph 4

5   Vehicle hire costs, where a constant rate is charged per mile travelled, up to a maximum monthly payment regardless of the miles travelled.

   A   Graph 1
   B   Graph 2
   C   Graph 3
   D   Graph 4

6   A production worker is paid a salary of $650 per month, plus an extra 5 cents for each unit produced during the month. This labour cost is best described as:

A   A variable cost
B   A fixed cost
C   A step cost
D   A semi-variable cost

7   The following data have been collected for four cost types – W, X, Y, Z – at two activity levels:

Cost type	Cost @ 100 units $	Cost @ 140 units $
W	8,000	10,560
X	5,000	5,000
Y	6,500	9,100
Z	6,700	8,580

Where V = variable, SV = semi-variable and F = fixed, assuming linearity, the four cost types W, X, Y and Z are respectively

	W	X	Y	Z
A	V	F	SV	V
B	SV	F	V	SV
C	V	F	V	V
D	SV	F	SV	SV

8   B Co has recorded the following data in the two most recent periods.

Total costs of production $	Volume of production Units
13,500	700
18,300	1,100

What is the best estimate of the company's fixed costs per period?

A $13,500
B $13,200
C $5,100
D $4,800

9   A hotel has recorded that the laundry costs incurred were $570 when 340 guests stayed for one night. They know that the fixed laundry cost is $400 per night. What is the variable laundry cost per guest-night (to the nearest cent)?

A $0.50
B $1.18
C $1.68
D   Impossible to calculate from the information available

10   A Co has recorded the following data for two recent periods.

	Transport costs $	Deliveries made
	9,680	840
	9,860	930

[handwritten: +180, +90, 1680, FC = 8000]

The transport costs for a particular period could be represented by:

A $10.60 × number of deliveries
B $11.52 × number of deliveries
C $8,000 – ($2 × number of deliveries)
Ⓓ $8,000 + ($2 × number of deliveries)

4 Overhead costs – absorption costing I *[handwritten: 7/10]*

1   A method of dealing with overheads involves spreading common costs over cost centres on the basis of benefit received. This is known as

A   overhead absorption
Ⓑ   overhead apportionment
C   overhead allocation
D   overhead analysis

2   The process of cost apportionment is carried out so that

A   costs may be controlled
B   cost units gather overheads as they pass through cost centres
C   whole items of cost can be charged to cost centres
Ⓓ   common costs are shared among cost centres

3   Which of the following statements about overhead absorption rates are true?

(i)   They are predetermined in advance for each period
✓ (ii)   They are used to charge overheads to products
(iii)   They are based on actual data for each period
(iv)   They are used to control overhead costs

Ⓐ   (i) and (ii) only
B   (i), (ii) and (iv) only
C   (ii), (iii) and (iv) only
D   (iii) and (iv) only

4   The following extract of information is available concerning the four cost centres of EG Co.

	Production cost centres			Service cost centre
	Machinery	Finishing	Packing	Canteen
Number of direct employees	7	6	2	–
Number of indirect employees	3	2	1	4
Overhead allocated and apportioned	$28,500	$18,300	$8,960	$8,400

[handwritten: 10, 8, 3, Total = 21]

BPP)))
LEARNING MEDIA

The overhead cost of the canteen is to be re-apportioned to the production cost centres on the basis of the number of employees in each production cost centre. After the re-apportionment, the total overhead cost of the packing department, to the nearest $, will be

    Ⓐ $1,200   RTQ!

    B $9,968

    C $10,080

    Ⓓ $10,160

The following information relates to questions 5 and 6

Budgeted information relating to two departments in JP Co for the next period is as follows.

Department	Production overhead $	Direct material cost $	Direct labour cost $	Direct labour hours	Machine hours
1	27,000	67,500	13,500	2,700	45,000
2	18,000	36,000	100,000	25,000	300

Individual direct labour employees within each department earn differing rates of pay, according to their skills, grade and experience.

---

5   What is the most appropriate production overhead absorption rate for department 1?

    A   40% of direct material cost

    B   200% of direct labour cost

    C $10 per direct labour hour

    Ⓓ $0.60 per machine hour

---

6   What is the most appropriate production overhead absorption rate for department 2?

    A   50% of direct material cost   NB Dep is labour intensive so a direct

    B   18% of direct labour cost   labour-hour rate would be most

    Ⓒ $0.72 per direct labour hour   appropriate.

    Ⓓ $60 per machine hour

The following information relates to questions 7 and 8

The pharmacy in a busy hospital uses pre-determined rates for absorbing total overheads, based on the budgeted number of prescriptions to be handled. A rate of $7 per prescription has been calculated, and the following overhead expenditures have been estimated at two activity levels.

Total overheads $	Number of prescriptions
97,000	13,000 VC=4
109,000	16,000

7   Based on the data above, what is the estimated level of fixed overheads?

    A $39,000
    (B) $45,000
    C $48,000
    D $91,000

8   Based on the data above, what was the budgeted level of activity in prescriptions to be handled?

    A   13,000
    (B)   15,000
    C   16,000
    D   30,333

9   Which of the following bases of apportionment would be **most** appropriate for apportioning heating costs to production cost centres?

    (A)   Floor space occupied (square metres)
    (B)   Volume of space occupied (cubic metres)
    C   Number of employees
    D   Labour hours worked

[handwritten note: NB for heating, use cubic metres.]

10   In the context of overhead analysis, what is meant by reciprocal servicing?

    A   Where only one service cost centre exists which provides services to all production cost centres

    B   Where two service cost centres provide service for all production departments but not for each other

    (C)   Where two or more service cost centres provide service for production departments and for each other

    D   Where two or more service cost centres provide service to only some production departments and not for each other

5 Overhead costs – absorption costing II

1   Which of the following statements about predetermined overhead absorption rates are true?

    (i)   Using a predetermined absorption rate avoids fluctuations in unit costs caused by abnormally high or low overhead expenditure or activity levels

    (ii)   Using a predetermined absorption rate offers the administrative convenience of being able to record full production costs sooner

    (iii) Using a predetermined absorption rate avoids problems of under/over absorption of overheads because a constant overhead rate is available.

    A   (i) and (ii) only
    B   (i) and (iii) only
    C   (ii) and (iii) only
    D   All of them

2   Over-absorbed overheads occur when

    A   absorbed overheads exceed actual overheads
    B   absorbed overheads exceed budgeted overheads
    C   actual overheads exceed budgeted overheads
    D   budgeted overheads exceed absorbed overheads

3   A company absorbs overheads on machine hours which were budgeted at 11,250 with overheads of $258,750. Actual results were 10,980 hours with overheads of $254,692.

    Overheads were

    A   under absorbed by $2,152
    B   over absorbed by $4,058
    C   under absorbed by $4,058
    D   over absorbed by $2,152

The following information relates to questions 4 and 5

Budgeted labour hours	8,500
Budgeted overheads	$148,750
Actual labour hours	7,928
Actual overheads	$146,200

4   Based on the data given above, what is the labour hour overhead absorption rate?

    A $17.20 per hour
    B $17.50 per hour
    C $18.44 per hour
    D $18.76 per hour

5   Based on the data given above, what is the amount of under-/over-absorbed overhead?

    A $2,550 under-absorbed overhead
    B $2,550 over-absorbed overhead
    C $7,460 over-absorbed overhead
    D $7,460 under-absorbed overhead

6   Edison has the following data relating to overheads.

	Budget	Actual
Fixed overheads	$15,000	$14,000
Direct labour hours	20,000	19,500

    Overheads are absorbed on the basis of labour hours.

Which of the following statements is true?

A   Overheads will be under absorbed by $1,000 due to the lower than expected expenditure.

B   Overheads will be under absorbed by $1,000 due to the unexpected decrease in labour hours.

C   Overheads will be under absorbed by $625 due to lower than expected expenditure and lower than expected labour hours.

D   Overheads will be over absorbed by $625 due to lower than expected expenditure offset by lower than expected labour hours.

7   The budgeted absorption rate for variable production overhead in department X is $2.50 per direct labour hour and for fixed overhead is $4 per direct labour hour. Actual direct labour hours worked fell short of budget by 1,000 hours. If expenditures were as expected for variable and fixed overheads, the total under-absorbed overhead for the period would be:

A $0
B $2,500
C $4,000
D $6,500

8   The production overhead of department D is absorbed using a machine hour rate. Budgeted production overheads for the department were $280,000 and the actual machine hours were 70,000. Production overheads were under absorbed by $9,400.

If actual production overheads were $295,000 what was the overhead absorption rate per machine hour (to the nearest cent)?

A $4.00
B $4.08
C $4.21
D $4.35

The following information relates to questions 9 and 10

A company has the following actual and budgeted data for year 4.

	Budget	Actual
Production	8,000 units	9,000 units
Variable production overhead per unit	$3	$3
Fixed production overheads	$360,000	$432,000
Sales	6,000 units	8,000 units

Overheads are absorbed using a rate per unit, based on budgeted output and expenditure.

9   The production overhead absorbed during year 4 was

A $384,000
B $405,000
C $432,000
D $459,000

10   Production overhead was

A   under absorbed by $27,000
B   under absorbed by $72,000
C   under absorbed by $75,000
D   over absorbed by $27,000

6 Overhead costs – absorption costing III

1   Overhead apportionment is used to (tick the correct answer):

☐ Charge whole items of costs to cost centres

☐ Charge cost units with an appropriate share of overheads

☐ Charge whole items of costs to cost units

☐ Spread common costs over cost centres

☐ Ensure budgeted overheads are not exceeded

2   A company absorbs overheads on the basis of machine hours. In a period, actual machine hours were 22,435, actual overheads were $496,500 and there was over absorption of $64,375.

The budgeted overhead absorption rate was $☐ per machine hour (to the nearest $).

3   A firm had opening inventories of 33,480 units and closing inventories of 25,920 units. Profits using marginal costing were $228,123 and using absorption costing were $203,931.

The fixed overhead absorption rate per unit (to the nearest cent) was $☐

4   Budgeted overheads $690,480
     Budgeted machine hours   15,344
     Actual machine hours   14,128
     Actual overheads $679,550

Based on the data above, the machine hour absorption rate is (to the nearest $) $☐ per machine hour.

5   Budgeted overheads $690,480
    Budgeted machine hours   15,344
    Actual machine hours   14,128
    Actual overheads $679,550

    Overhead for the period was [   ] absorbed by $ [   ]

---

6   Budgeted overheads for a period were $338,000. In the event, actual labour hours and overheads were 12,560 hours and $344,000 respectively.

    If there was under absorption of $17,440, the number of labour hours budgeted was [   ] hours .

---

7   In a period, opening inventories were 825 units and closing inventories 1,800 units. The profit based on marginal costing was $50,400 and profit using absorption costing was $60,150.

    The fixed overhead absorption rate per unit (to the nearest $) is $ [   ]

---

8   A company absorbs overheads on machine hours which were budgeted at 14,400 with budgeted overheads of $316,800. Actual results were 14,100 hours with overheads of $338,400.

    Overheads were [   ] absorbed by $ [   ]

---

9   The following data relate to the overhead expenditure of a contract decorators at two activity levels.

    Square metres painted   12,750   15,100
    Overheads $73,950 $83,585

    The estimate of the overheads if 13,800 square metres are to be painted is $ [   ]

---

10 A firm absorbs overheads on labour hours. In one period 8,200 hours were worked, actual overheads were $109,000 and there was $14,000 over-absorption.

    The overhead absorption rate per hour was $ [   ] (to the nearest $)

---

7 Overhead costs – absorption costing IV

10 / Learn
10 formulae

1   A vehicle repair company recovers overheads on the basis of labour hours. Budgeted overheads were $615,000 and actual labour hours were 48,225. Overheads were over recovered by $35,000.

    If actual overheads were $640,150 the budgeted overhead absorption rate per hour was $ [   ] (to the nearest $)

2   When opening inventories were 8,500 litres and closing inventories 6,750 litres, a firm had a profit of $27,400 using marginal costing.

Q   Assuming that the fixed overhead absorption rate was $2 per litre, the profit using absorption costing would

be $ [   ]

---

3 | | |
    |---|---|
    | Actual overheads | $496,980 |
    | Actual machine hours | 16,566 |
    | Budgeted overheads | $475,200 |

    Based on the data above, and assuming that the budgeted overhead absorption rate was $32 per hour, the

    number of machine hours (to the nearest hour) budgeted to be worked was [14,850] hours.

---

4 | | |
    |---|---|
    | Actual overheads | $496,980 |
    | Actual machine hours | 16,566 |
    | Budgeted overheads | $475,200 |

    Based on the data above and assuming that the budgeted overhead absorption rate was $32 per hour:

    The overhead for the period was [over] absorbed by $ [33,132]

---

5 | | |
    |---|---|
    | Budgeted machine hours | 17,000 |
    | Actual machine hours | 21,250 |
    | Budgeted overheads | $85,000 |
    | Actual overheads | $110,500 |

    Based on the data above:

    The machine hour absorption rate is $ [5] per hour.

---

6 | | |
    |---|---|
    | Budgeted machine hours | 17,000 |
    | Actual machine hours | 21,250 |
    | Budgeted overheads | $85,000 |
    | Actual overheads | $110,500 |

    The overhead for the period was [under] absorbed by $ [4250]

---

7   An overhead absorption rate is used to (tick the correct answer):

    [   ] Share out common costs over benefiting cost centres

    [   ] Find the total overheads for a cost centre

    [✓] Charge overheads to products

    [   ] Control overheads

---

8   Y Co absorbs overheads on the basis of standard labour hours. The overhead absorption rate for the period
     has been based on budgeted overheads of $165,000 and 55,000 standard labour hours.

     During the period, overheads of $180,000 were incurred and 60,000 standard labour hours were produced.

     Which of the following statements is/are correct?

☐	Overhead was $15,000 over absorbed
☐	Overhead was $15,000 under absorbed
☑	No under or over absorption occurred

---

9   The Management Accountant of X Co is preparing the budgeted overhead analysis sheet for the year 20X7/8.
     The company has two production cost centres (Machining and Assembly) and two service departments
     (Stores and Maintenance). The directly attributable production overheads have already been allocated to the
     cost centres but other costs need to be apportioned. A section of the template being used by the
     Management Accountant and other information is shown below.

Overhead Analysis Sheet 20X7/X8
(all values in $)

		Departments				
Costs	Basis of apportionment	Machining	Assembly	Stores	Maintenance	Total
Various	Allocated	1,105,000	800,000	90,000	350,000	2,345,000
Rent	Area occupied		A			750,000
Personnel department	E B		C			60,000
Equipment depreciation		D				200,000

Other information:

	Departments			
	Machining	Assembly	Stores	Maintenance
Employees	75	210	25	40
Area occupied (square metres)	10,000	6,000	3,000	1,000
Cost of equipment $	1,200,000	150,000	50,000	200,000
Machine hours	500,000	50,000		
Direct labour hours	30,000	120,000		

The items that would be entered on the overhead analysis sheet in the boxes A, B, C and D are:

A $225,000

B Employees

C $6,000

D 150,000

---

10   X Co uses a standard absorption costing system. For the year 20X0/1, X Co recorded the following information:

	Assembly department	
	Budget	Actual
Output (units)	30,000	35,000
Overheads ($)	2,400,000	2,900,000 2,800,000
Direct labour cost ($)	960,000	1,000,000
Direct labour hours	120,000	145,000
Machine hours	80,000	100,000

Complete the following statement:

At the end of the year, the overheads absorbed in the Assembly department were under absorbed by

$ 100,000

---

8 Overhead costs – absorption costing V

10/10

1   The following data is available for department X for the latest period.

Budgeted production overhead	$165,000
Actual production overhead	$165,000
Budgeted machine hours	60,000
Actual machine hours	55,000

Which of the following statements is correct?

A   No under or over-absorption of overhead occurred
B   Overhead was $13,750 under-absorbed
C   Overhead was $27,500 under-absorbed
D   Overhead was $27,500 over-absorbed

---

2   A cost centre uses a direct labour hour rate to absorb overheads. Data for the latest period are as follows:

Budgeted overhead	$25,760
Actual overhead	$23,592
Actual direct labour hours	4,925
Overhead under absorbed	$937

How many direct labour hours were budgeted to be worked during the period?

A   4,925
B   5,378
C   5,600
D   This cannot be calculated from the information provided

---

3   Which of the following situations will always result in under absorption of overheads?

A   Budgeted overheads are higher than the actual overheads incurred
B   Actual overheads incurred are higher than the absorbed overheads
C   Actual production volume is lower than budgeted production volume
D   Actual overheads incurred are higher than the budgeted overheads

---

4   A call centre recovers overheads on the basis of the number of calls made. Budgeted overheads for the latest period were $112,530 but actual overhead expenditure amounted to $107,415.

During the period 68,200 calls were made and overhead was under recovered by $5,115.

The overhead absorption rate per call made was $ ⎡ 1.5 ⎤

---

5   Data for department Y for the latest period was as follows.

Budgeted direct labour hours   12,300
Actual direct labour hours   11,970
Production overhead absorption rate $2.60 per direct labour hour
Production overhead under absorbed $5,670

The actual production overhead incurred during the period was $ ⎡ 36792 ⎤

---

6   Based on 98,400 budgeted direct labour hours for the period, a cost centre's overhead absorption rate is $12.15 per direct labour hour.

The actual direct labour hours worked during the period amounted to 101,235 and the actual overhead expenditure incurred was $807,033.

What was the under or over absorbed overhead for the period (to the nearest $)?

A $388,527 under absorbed
B $388,527 over absorbed
C $422,972 under absorbed
D $422,972 over absorbed

---

7   The following data are available for department P for March.

	Machine hours	Production overhead $
Budget	51,150	190,960
Actual	58,305	194,350

Production overheads are absorbed on the basis of machine hours. The production overhead for March is (to the nearest $):

A $27,209 under absorbed
B $27,209 over absorbed
C $23,128 under absorbed
D $23,128 over absorbed

---

8   The following data are available for department L for June.

	Labour hours	Production overhead
		$
Budget	4,755	347,115
Actual	6,310	310,710

The production overhead absorption rate per labour hour to the nearest cent for June is $ 73

---

9   The following data are available for the machining department for March.

	Machine hours	Production overhead
		$
Budget	17,050	95,480
Actual	19,500	99,820

Production overheads are absorbed on the basis of machine hours. The production overhead for March is:

A $4,340 under absorbed
B $4,340 over absorbed
C $9,380 under absorbed
D $9,380 over absorbed

---

10   The following data are available for the blasting department for March.

	Labour hours	Production overhead
		$
Budget	1,910	53,480
Actual	2,674	66,850

The production overhead absorption rate per labour hour for March is:

A $20
B $25
C $28
D $35

9 Inventory valuation I

1   A company makes regular purchases of a particular packaging material. The price of this material has been increasing steadily during the latest period, and this trend is likely to continue into the foreseeable future. Which of the following methods will produce the lowest closing inventory valuation?

A   First in, first out (FIFO)
B   Last in, first out (LIFO)
C   Next in, first out (NIFO)
D   Average price

2   In a period of continual price inflation for material purchases

A   the LIFO method will produce lower profits than the FIFO method, and lower closing inventory values

B   the LIFO method will produce lower profits than the FIFO method, and higher closing inventory values

C   the FIFO method will produce lower profits than the LIFO method, and lower closing inventory values

D   the FIFO method will produce lower profits than the LIFO method, and higher closing inventory values

3   A firm uses the First In First Out (FIFO) system for pricing inventory issues. During a period, product costs were overstated and profits understated. This meant that during the period, prices were:

A   falling
B   unchanged
C   rising slowly
D   rising rapidly

4   A firm has a high level of inventory turnover and uses the FIFO (First In First Out) issue pricing system. In a period of rising purchase prices, the closing inventory valuation is

A   close to current purchase prices
B   based on the prices of the first items received
C   much lower than current purchase price
D   the average of all goods purchased in the period

The following information relates to questions 5 and 6

G Co makes the following purchases and sales.

1 January	Purchases	4,000 units for $10,000
31 January	Purchases	1,000 units for $2,000
15 February	Sales	3,000 units for $13,000
28 February	Purchases	1,500 units for $3,750
14 March	Sales	500 units for $1,200

5   At 31 March which of the following closing inventory valuations using FIFO is correct?

A $8,000
B $7,500
C $7,000
D $6,500

6   At 31 March which of the following closing inventory valuations using LIFO is correct?

A $6,500
B $7,000
C $7,500
D $8,000

7   With all average price systems where it is required to keep prices up to date, the average price must be re-calculated

A   each time an issue is made
B   each accounting period
C   each time a purchase is made
D   each time a purchase is made at a different price to the average price

The following information relates to questions 8 and 9

Inventory item 2362 X

Date		Units	Receipts Price per unit $	Value $	Units	Issues Price per unit $	Value $
1 June	Opening inventory	100	5.00	500			
3 June	Receipts	300	4.80	1,440			
5 June	Issues				220		
12 June	Receipts	170	5.20	884			
24 June	Issues				300		

8   Using the weighted average price method of inventory valuation, the cost of the materials issued on 5 June was

A $1,056
B $1,067
C $1,078
D $1,100

9   Using the weighted average price method of inventory valuation, the value of closing inventory on 30 June was

     A $248
     B $250
     C $251
     D $260

10   A wholesaler buys and resells a range of items, one of which is the Kay. Each Kay is resold for $3 per unit and opening inventory for June was 400 units valued at $1.80 per unit. The wholesaler purchased a further 600 units on 10 June for $2.10 per unit, and sold 800 units on 25 June. What gross profit would be recorded for the sale of Kays during June, using either the FIFO or the LIFO method of inventory valuation?

	FIFO gross profit	LIFO gross profit
A	$780	$840
B	$960	$720
C	$840	$780
D	$1,560	$1,620

10 Inventory valuation II

1   A wholesaler had opening inventory of 300 units of product Emm valued at $25 per unit at the beginning of January. The following receipts and sales were recorded during January.

Date	2 Jan	12 Jan	21 Jan	29 Jan
		400		
Issues	250		200	75

The purchase cost of receipts was $25.75 per unit. Using a weighted average method of valuation, calculate the value of closing inventory at the end of January.

     A $11,550
     B $4,492
     C $4,192
     D $9,550

2   Dee Co had an opening inventory value of $7,500 (300 units valued at $25 each) on 1 June. The following receipts and issues were recorded during June.

8 June	Receipts	220 units	$40 per unit
15 June	Issues	180 units	
16 June	Issues	100 units	
21 June	Receipts	120 units	$48 per unit
25 June	Issues	60 units	
28 June	Receipts	180 units	$55 per unit

The company currently uses the LIFO method for costing inventory but is thinking of changing to FIFO. If the company changed from LIFO to FIFO, how would the profits be affected?

A   Profits would increase by $4,080

B   Profits would decrease by $4,080

C   Profits would increase by $7,500

D   Profits would decrease by $7,500

---

3   In a period of rising prices, which of the following will be true with a first in first out (FIFO) system of pricing inventory issues?

| ✓ | Product costs are overstated and profits understated |

| | Product costs are overstated and profits overstated |

| | Product costs are understated and profits understated |

| ✓ | Product costs are understated and profits overstated |

---

4   600 units of component J, valued at a price of $15.50, were in inventory on 1 May. The following receipts and issues were recorded during May.

3 May	Received	800 units @ $17.20 per unit
13 May	Received	700 units @ $18.10 per unit
25 May	Issued	1,700 units

Using the LIFO method, the total value of the issues on 25 May was $ _____.

---

5   XYZ Co had an opening inventory value of $880 (275 units valued at $3.20 each) on 1 April.

The following receipts and issues were recorded during April.

8 April	Receipts	600 units	$3.00 per unit
15 April	Receipts	400 units	$3.40 per unit
30 April	Issues	900 units	

Using the FIFO method, the total value of the issues on 30 April is $ _____

---

6   A company uses a First In First Out (FIFO) system for pricing inventory issues. During a period, product costs were overstated and profits were understated. This meant that during the period, prices were:

| | Rising |

| ✓ | Falling |

---

7   2,400 units of component C, valued at a price of $6 each, were in inventory on 1 March. The following receipts and issues were recorded during March.

3 March	Received	4,000 units @ $6.20 per unit
12 March	Received	2,000 units @ $6.86 per unit
23 March	Issued	5,100 units

Using the weighted average price method of inventory valuation, the total value of the components remaining in inventory on 23 March was $ _____

---

8   2,400 units of component C, valued at a price of $6 each, were in inventory on 1 March. The following receipts and issues were recorded during March.

3 March	Received	4,000 units @ $6.20 per unit
12 March	Received	2,000 units @ $6.86 per unit
23 March	Issued	5,100 units

Using the FIFO method of inventory valuation, the total value of the components issued on 23 March was

$ _____ (to the nearest $)

---

9   2,400 units of component C, valued at a price of $6 each, were in inventory on 1 March.

The following receipts and issues were recorded during March.

3 March	Received	4,000 units @ $6.20 per unit
12 March	Received	2,000 units @ $6.86 per unit
23 March	Issued	5,100 units

Using the LIFO method of inventory valuation, the total value of the components issued on 23 March was $

_____

---

10   P Co had an opening inventory value of $2,640 (300 units valued at $8.80 each) on 1 April. The following receipts and issues were recorded during April:

10 April	Receipt	1,000 units	$8.60 per unit
23 April	Receipt	600 units	$9.00 per unit
29 April	Issues	1,700 units	

Using the LIFO method, the total value of the issues on 29 April was $ _____ (to the nearest $)

---

11 Breakeven analysis and limiting factor analysis I

1   Which of the following statements is/are correct?

    (i)   The incremental cost of buying a larger quantity of material might be a negative cost, which is a cost reduction

    (ii)   If a company reduces its selling price by 20% so that sales volume increases by 25%, total profit will remain unchanged

    (iii)   A direct cost need not be a variable cost, but might be a fixed cost

    A   (i) only
    B   (i) and (ii) only
    C   (ii) and (iii) only
    D   (i) and (iii) only

2   A company makes a single product and incurs fixed costs of $30,000 per month. Variable cost per unit is $5 and each unit sells for $15. Monthly sales demand is 7,000 units. The breakeven point in terms of monthly sales units is:

    A   2,000 units
    B   3,000 units
    C   4,000 units
    D   6,000 units

3   A company manufactures a single product for which cost and selling price data are as follows.

Selling price per unit	$12
Variable cost per unit	$8
Fixed costs per month	$96,000
Budgeted monthly sales	30,000 units

The margin of safety, expressed as a percentage of budgeted monthly sales, is (to the nearest whole number):

    A   20%
    B   25%
    C   73%
    D   125%

The following information relates to questions 4 to 6

Information concerning K Co's single product is as follows.

	$ per unit
Selling price	6.00 6.6
Variable production cost	1.20 1.32
Variable selling cost	0.40
Fixed production cost	4.00 5
Fixed selling cost	0.80

Budgeted production and sales for the year are 10,000 units.

QUESTIONS

4   What is the company's breakeven point, to the nearest whole unit?

   A   8,000 units
   B   8,333 units
   C   10,000 units
   D   10,909 units

5   How many units must be sold if K Co wants to achieve a profit of $11,000 for the year?

   A   2,500 units
   B   9,833 units
   C   10,625 units
   D   13,409 units

6   It is now expected that the variable production cost per unit and the selling price per unit will each increase by 10%, and fixed production costs will rise by 25%.

What will be the new breakeven point, to the nearest whole unit?

   A   8,788 units
   B   11,600 units
   C   11,885 units
   D   12,397 units

7   A Co makes a single product which it sells for $10 per unit. Fixed costs are $48,000 per month and the product has a contribution to sales ratio of 40%.

In a month when actual sales were $140,000, A Co's margin of safety, in units, was

   A   2,000
   B   12,000
   C   14,000
   D   20,000

8   A single product company has a contribution to sales ratio of 40%. Fixed costs amount to $90,000 per annum.

The number of units required to break even is

   A   36,000
   B   150,000
   C   225,000
   D   impossible to calculate without further information

9   Z plc makes a single product which it sells for $16 per unit. Fixed costs are $76,800 per month and the product has a contribution to sales ratio of 40%. In a period when actual sales were $224,000, Z plc's margin of safety, in units, was

C:6.4   *BEP: 192,000*

    A   2,000   *12,000 units.*
    B   12,000   *14,000 units.*
    C   14,000
    D   32,000

---

10   A company's breakeven point is 6,000 units per annum. The selling price is $90 per unit and the variable cost is $40 per unit. What are the company's annual fixed costs?

    A $120
    B $240,000
    C $300,000
    D $540,000

---

12 Breakeven analysis and limiting factor analysis II

1   E Co manufactures a single product, P. Data for the product are as follows.

	$ per unit
Selling price	20
Direct material cost	4
Direct labour cost	3
Variable production overhead cost	2
Variable selling overhead cost	1
Fixed overhead cost	5
Profit per unit	5

The profit/volume ratio for product P is

    A   25%
    B   50%
    C   55%
    D   60%

The following information relates to questions 2 to 4

W Co sells one product for which data is given below:

	$ per unit
Selling price	10
Variable cost	6
Fixed cost	2

The fixed costs are based on a budgeted level of activity of 5,000 units for the period.

2   How many units must be sold if W Co wishes to earn a profit of $6,000 for one period?

    A   1,500
    B   1,600
    C   4,000
    D   8,000

---

3   What is W Co's margin of safety for the budget period if fixed costs prove to be 20% higher than budgeted?

    A   29%
    B   40%
    C   50%
    D   66⅔%

---

4   If the selling price and variable cost increase by 20% and 12% respectively by how much must sales volume change compared with the original budgeted level in order to achieve the original budgeted profit for the period?

    A   24.2% decrease
    B   24.2% increase
    C   39.4% decrease
    D   39.4% increase

---

5   B Co manufactures and sells a single product, with the following estimated costs for next year.

	Unit cost	
	100,000 units of output	150,000 units of output
	$	$
Direct materials	20.00	20.00
Direct labour	5.00	5.00
Production overheads	10.00	7.50
Marketing costs	7.50	5.00
Administration costs	5.00	4.00
	47.50	41.50

Fixed costs are unaffected by the volume of output.

B Co's management think they can sell 150,000 units per annum if the sales price is $49.50.

The breakeven point, in units, at this price is

    A   36,364
    B   90,000
    C   101,020
    D   225,000

---

6   X Co generates a 12 per cent contribution on its weekly sales of $280,000. A new product, Z, is to be
     introduced at a special offer price in order to stimulate interest in all the company's products, resulting in a 5
     per cent increase in weekly sales of the company's other products. Product Z will incur a variable unit cost
     of $2.20 to make and $0.15 to distribute. Weekly sales of Z, at a special offer price of $1.90 per unit, are
     expected to be 3,000 units.

     The effect of the special offer will be to increase the company's weekly profit by:

     A $330
     B $780
     C $12,650
     D $19,700

7

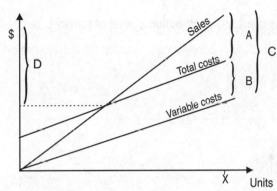

     In the above breakeven chart, the contribution at level of activity x can be read as:

     A   distance A (Profit)
     B   distance B (fixed costs)
     C   distance C
     D   distance D

8   Which of the following statements about profit/volume graphs are correct?

     (i)   The profit-volume line starts at the origin

     (ii)   The profit-volume line crosses the x axis at the breakeven point

     (iii) Any point on the profit-volume line above the x axis indicates the profit (as measured on the vertical
            axis) at that level of activity

     A   (i) and (ii) only
     B   (ii) and (iii) only
     C   (i) and (iii) only
     D   All of them

9

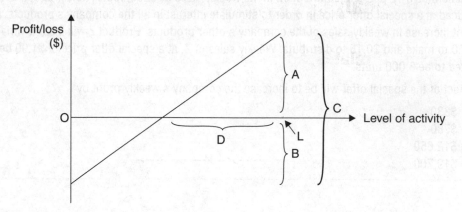

In the above profit-volume chart, the contribution at level of activity L can be read as:

A   distance A Profit
B   distance B Fixed cost
C   distance C
D   distance D MoS (units)

10

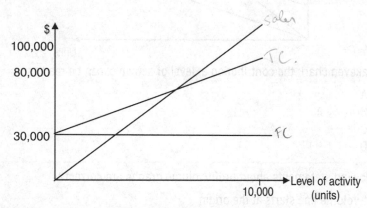

The above breakeven chart has been drawn for R Co's single product. Which of the following statements about the product are correct?

(i)   The product's selling price is $10 per unit
(ii)   The product's variable cost is $8 per unit
(iii)   The product incurs fixed costs of $30,000 per period
(iv)   The product earns a profit of $70,000 at a level of activity of 10,000 units

A   (i), (ii) and (iii) only
B   (i) and (iii) only
C   (i), (iii) and (iv) only
D   (iii) and (iv) only

13 Breakeven analysis and limiting factor analysis III ⁶/₁₀ R

The following graph relates to questions 1 and 2

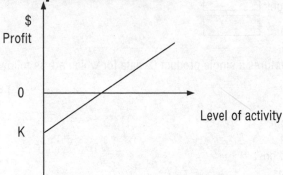

1   Point K on the graph indicates the value of:

✓

☐ Semi-variable cost

☐ Total cost

☐ Variable cost

☑ Fixed cost

2   This graph is known as a:

✓

☐ Conventional breakeven chart

☐ Contribution breakeven chart

☐ Semi-variable cost chart

☑ Profit volume chart

NB
✓ Fixed costs + profit = Contribution

3   A company's single product has a contribution to sales ratio of 20%. The unit selling price is $12. In a
    period when fixed costs were $48,000 the profit earned was $5,520.

K

Direct wages were 30% of total variable costs, and so the direct wages cost for the period was $ [57,600]   58,152

4   A company manufactures three products, details of which are as follows.

	Product J $ per unit	Product K $ per unit	Product L $ per unit
Selling price	140	122	134
Direct materials ($2/kg)	22	14	26
Other variable cost	84	72	51
Fixed cost	20	26	40

NB Key here is the
contribution per kg!

Contribution: 34   36   57
                                        4.38
C/kg: 3.09   5.14

In a period when direct material is restricted in supply, the ranking of the products in terms of the most profitable use of the material is:

First: product ☐ L

Second: product ☐ K

Third: product ☐ J

---

5   Windy Co manufactures a single product Q, data for which are as follows.

NB Profit/volume ratio is another term used to describe the contribution/sales ratio.

	$ per unit
Selling price	60
Direct material cost	14
Direct labour cost	12
Variable overhead cost	19
Fixed overhead cost	11
Profit	4

The profit/volume ratio for product Q is ☐ 7 % (to the nearest percent)

---

6   Which of the following situations, each considered separately, will cause the slope of the line on a profit/volume chart to decrease?

☐ ✓   An increase in the direct material cost per unit

☐ ✓   An increase in the trade discount per unit sold

☐   An increase in the fixed cost incurred per period

☐ ✓   An increase in the royalty payable per unit

7

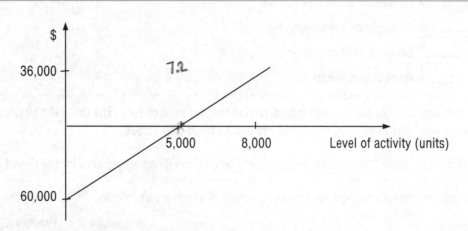

The above profit-volume chart has been drawn for S Co's single product. Which of the following statements about the product is/are correct?

☑ The product incurs fixed costs of $60,000 per period

☑ The product earns a contribution of $12 per unit

☐ The product's selling price is $4.50 per unit

8   Which of the following statements about traditional breakeven charts is/are correct? RTQ

☑ The fixed costs are depicted by a straight line parallel to the vertical axis

☑ The sales revenue line passes through the origin

☑ The total cost line cuts the vertical axis at the point which is equal to the period fixed costs

☐ The breakeven point is the point where the sales revenue line crosses the fixed cost line

9   H Company sells product V, for which data is as follows.

	$ per unit	
Selling price	108	118.8
Variable cost	73	78.11

Period fixed costs amount to $196,000, and the budgeted profit is $476,000 per period. Contribution 35   40.69

If the selling price and variable cost per unit increase by 10% and 7% respectively, the sales volume will

need to ⟦ fall ⟧ to ⟦ 16515 ⟧ units in order to achieve the original budgeted profit for the period.

10 A company makes a single product for which standard cost details are as follows.

	$ per unit	Required
Direct material ($8 per litre) 9L	72	18,000L
Direct labour ($7 per hour) 7	49	14,000hrs
Production overhead	56	
Total production cost	177	

The product is perishable and no Inventories are held.

Demand for next period will be 2,000 units but only 16,000 litres of material and 15,000 hours of labour will be available. The limiting factor(s) next period will be:

☑ Material

☐ Labour

14 Standard costing and variance analysis I

1 JC Co operates a bottling plant. The liquid content of a filled bottle of product T is 2 litres. During the filling process there is a 30% loss of liquid input due to spillage and evaporation. The standard price of the liquid is $1.20 per litre. The standard cost of the liquid per bottle of product T, to the nearest cent, is

- A $2.40
- B $2.86
- C $3.12
- D $3.43

2 The operations to produce a unit of product L require 9 active hours. Budgeted idle time of 10% of total hours paid for is to be incorporated into the standard times for all products. The wage rate is $4 per hour. The standard labour cost of one unit of product L is:

- A $10.00
- B $36.00
- C $39.60
- D $40.00

3 What is a standard hour?

- A   An operating hour in which there are no exceptional events, eg machine breakdowns
- B   An hour during which only standard units are made
- C   The amount of work achievable in an hour, working at standard efficiency levels
- D   An hour during which only standard hourly rates are paid to labour

4 Wood Co manufactures garden sheds, garden tables and workbenches. In order to monitor trends in productivity they measure output in terms of standard hours. Actual results for the first week of October are shown below.

	Units produced	Standard time per unit	Actual time taken
		hours	hours
Sheds	270	1.2	330
Tables	80	0.7	50
Workbenches	140	1.0	135

The number of standard hours produced was

- A   490
- B   515
- C   520
- D   1,421

5   Extracts from P Co's records for last month are as follows.

	Budget	Actual
Production	7,000 units	7,200 units
Direct material cost	$42,000	$42,912

What is the total direct material cost variance?

A $288 (F)
B $288 (A)
C $912 (A)
D $1,200 (F)

6 pu

should : 43,200

used

---

6   The standard cost information for SC Co's single product shows the standard direct material content to be 4 litres at $3 per litre.

Actual results for May were:

Production   1,270 units
Material used   5,000 litres at a cost of $16,000

All of the materials were purchased and used during the period. The direct material price and usage variances for May are:

	Material price	Material usage
A	$1,000 (F)	$240 (F)
B	$1,000 (A)	$240 (F)
C	$1,000 (F)	$240 (A)
D	$1,000 (A)	$256 (F)

Material usage

Actual 1270   should 5080
                 Actual 5000

The following information relates to questions 7 and 8

T Co uses a standard costing system, with its material inventory account being maintained at standard cost. The following details have been extracted from the standard cost card in respect of direct materials:

8 kg @ $0.80/kg = $6.40 per unit

Budgeted production in April was 850 units.

The following details relate to actual materials purchased and issued to production during April when actual production was 870 units:

Materials purchased	8,200 kg costing $6,888
Materials issued to production	7,150 kg

---

7   The direct material price variance for April was

should : 6960 kg
did : 7150 kg

A $286 (A)
B $286 (F)
C $328 (A)
D $328 (A)

---

8   The direct material usage variance for April was

     A $152 (F)   6960
     B $152 (A)   7150
     C $159.60 (A)
     D $280 (A)

9   ABC Co uses standard costing. It purchases a small component for which the following data are available.

Actual purchase quantity	6,800 units	std: 5780
Standard allowance for actual production	5,440 units	cost.
Standard price	85 cent/unit	
Purchase price variance (adverse)	($544)	

What was the actual purchase price per unit?

     A   75c
     B   77c
     C   93c
     D   95c

10   In a period, 11,280 kilograms of material were used at a total standard cost of $46,248. The material usage variance was $492 adverse.

What was the standard allowed weight of material for the period?   NB If variance is adverse, standard useage is less than actual useage.

     A   10,788 kgs   4.1   120
     B   11,160 kgs
     C   11,280 kgs
     D   11,400 kgs

15 Standard costing and variance analysis II   8/10

1   Extracts from L Co's records for November are as follows.

	Budget	Actual	
Production	9,840 units	9,600 units	
Direct labour cost	$39,360	$43,200	38400

What is the total direct labour cost variance?

     A $960 (F)
     B $3,840 (A)
     C $4,800 (F)
     D $4,800 (A)

2 S Co has extracted the following details from the standard cost card of one of its products.

Direct labour   4.5 hours @ $6.40 per hour

During March, S Co produced 2,300 units of the product and incurred direct wages costs of $64,150. The actual hours worked were 11,700.

RTQ!

The direct labour rate and efficiency variances were

	Rate	Efficiency	
	$	$	
A	10,730 (F)	8,640 (F)	74480
B	10,730 (F)	8,640 (A)	64150
C	10,730 (A)	8,640 (A)	
D	10,730 (F)	7,402 (A)	

3 Z Co uses a standard costing system and has the following labour cost standard in relation to one of its products.

4 hours skilled labour @ $6.00 per hour $24.00

During October, 3,350 of these products were made which was 150 units less than budgeted. The labour cost incurred was $79,893 and the number of direct labour hours worked was 13,450.

The direct labour variances for the month were

	Rate	Efficiency
A	$807 (F)	$297 (A)
B	$807 (F)	$300 (A)
C	$807 (F)	$3,300 (A)
D	$807 (A)	$300 (F)

Rate – shald 80,700
Did 79,893

Effy Shald 13400 / 13450

The following information relates to questions 4 to 6

Barney Co expected to produce 200 units of its product, the Bone, in 20X3. In fact 260 units were produced. The standard labour cost per unit was $70 (10 hours at a rate of $7 per hour). The actual labour cost was $18,600 and the labour force worked 2,200 hours although they were paid for 2,300 hours.

4 What is the direct labour rate variance for Barney Co in 20X3?

A	$400 (A)
B	$2,500 (F)
C	$2,500 (A)
D	$3,200 (A)

Actual 2300   Shald 16,100
Did 18,600

5 What is the direct labour efficiency variance for Barney Co in 20X3?

A	$400 (F)
B	$2,100 (F)
C	$2,800 (A)
D	$2,800 (F)

Shald : 260 × 10 = 2,600
Did : = 2,200
400
400 × 7 = 2800

NB use the actual hours worked here for this.

Actual 260 units   Shald = 2600   Did = 2,200

6   What is the idle time variance?

(handwritten: 2100 / 2800)

    A $700 (F)
    B $700 (A)
    C $809 (A)
    D $809 (F)

The following information relates to questions 7 and 8

R Co uses a standard costing system. The budget for one of its products for September includes direct labour cost (based on 4 hours per unit) of $117,600. During September 3,350 units were made which was 150 units less than budgeted. The direct labour cost incurred was $111,850 and the number of direct labour hours worked was 13,450.

7   The direct labour rate variance for the month was

    A $710 (F)
    B $1,130 (F)
    C $1,130 (A)
    D $5,750 (A)

(handwritten: Budget: 3500 units / £8.40ph × 4hrs / £33.60 p/unit   Should: 112,980 / Did: 111,850)

8   The direct labour efficiency variance for the month was

    A $415.80 (A)
    B $420.00 (A)
    C $420.00 (F)
    D $710.00 (F)

(handwritten: Should: 13400 / Did: 13450)

9   During a period 17,500 labour hours were worked at a standard cost of $6.50 per hour. The labour efficiency variance was $7,800 favourable.

How many standard hours were produced?

(handwritten: 113,750)

    A   1,200
    B   16,300
    C   17,500
    D   18,700

(handwritten: 1200)

10   In a period 12,250 units were made and there was a favourable labour efficiency variance of $11,250. If 41,000 labour hours were worked and the standard wage rate was $6 per hour, how many standard hours (to two decimal places) were allowed per unit?

    A   3.19
    B   3.35
    C   3.50
    D   6.00

(handwritten: 1875 hours diff.)

16 Standard costing and variance analysis III

The following information relates to questions 1 to 3

Extracts from V Co's records for June are as follows.

	Budget	Actual
Production	520 units	560 units
Variable production overhead cost	$3,120	$4,032
Labour hours worked	1,560	2,240

1   The variable production overhead total variance for June is:

    A $240 (A)
    B $672 (A)
    C $672 (F)
    D $912 (A)

2   The variable production overhead expenditure variance for June is:

    A $448 (F)
    B $448 (A)
    C $672 (A)
    D $912 (A)

3   The variable production overhead efficiency variance for June is:

    A $1,008 (A)
    B $1,120 (A)
    C $1,120 (F)
    D $1,360 (A)

The following information relates to questions 4 and 5

The standard variable production overhead cost of product B is as follows.

4 hours at $1.70 per hour = $6.80 per unit

During period 3 the production of B amounted to 400 units. The labour force worked 1,690 hours, of which 30 hours were recorded as idle time. The variable overhead cost incurred was $2,950.

4   The variable production overhead expenditure variance for period 3 was

    A $77 (A)
    B $128 (A)
    C $128 (F)
    D $230 (A)

5   The variable production overhead efficiency variance for period 3 was

    A $102 (F)
    B $102 (A)
    C $105 (A)
    D $153 (A)

The following data are given for questions 6 and 7 below

Trafalgar Co budgets to produce 10,000 units of product D12, each requiring 45 minutes of labour. Labour is charged at $20 per hour, and variable overheads at $15 per labour hour. During September 20X3, 11,000 units were produced. 8,000 hours of labour were paid at a total cost of $168,000. Variable overheads in September amounted to $132,000.

6   What is the correct labour efficiency variance for September 20X3?

    A $5,000 (A)
    B $5,000 (F)
    C $5,250 (F)
    D $10,000 (A)

7   What is the correct variable overhead expenditure variance for September 20X3?

    A $3,750 (F)
    B $4,125 (F)
    C $12,000 (A)
    D $12,000 (F)

The following data are given for sub-questions 8 and 9

X40 is one of many items produced by the manufacturing division. Its standard cost is based on estimated production of 10,000 units per month. The standard cost schedule for one unit of X40 shows that 2 hours of direct labour are required at $15 per labour hour. The variable overhead rate is $6 per direct labour hour. During April, 11,000 units were produced; 24,000 direct labour hours were worked and charged; $336,000 was spent on direct labour; and $180,000 was spent on variable overheads.

8   The direct labour rate variance for April is

    A $20,000 (F)
    B $22,000 (F)
    C $24,000 (A)
    D $24,000 (F)

9   The variable overhead efficiency variance for April is

A $12,000 (A)
B $12,000 (F)
C $15,000 (A)
D $15,000 (F)

10   In order to indicate to managers the trend and materiality of variances, B Co expresses them as percentages as in the following examples.

	July %	August %	September %	October %	November %
Material usage variance as a percentage of standard total production cost	3 (F)	2 (A)	6 (A)	10 (A)	12 (A)
Material price variance as a percentage of standard cost of material used	1 (A)	2 (A)	7 (F)	8 (F)	9 (F)

(A) denotes an adverse variance; (F) denotes a favourable variance

The following statements relate to recent operational events.

Statement

1   In September the buyer located a new supplier who charged a lower price than the previous supplier. The material was found to be of low quality, however, leading to a high level of waste.

2   The general trend is that all direct material variances are becoming more significant and are likely to be worthy of management attention.

3   A change in the bonus payment scheme has improved the productivity of labour, who are now processing material more effectively.

Which of the statements is or are consistent with the results shown?

A   Statements 1 and 2 only
B   Statements 1 and 3 only
C   Statements 2 and 3 only
D   Statement 2 only

6/10

17 Standard costing and variance analysis IV

1   Which of the following would help to explain an adverse direct material price variance?

√ (i)   The material purchased was of a higher quality than standard
√ (ii)   A reduction in the level of purchases meant that expected bulk discounts were forgone
  (iii) The standard price per unit of direct material was unrealistically high

A   All of them
B   (i) and (ii) only
C   (ii) and (iii) only
D   (i) and (iii) only

2   Which of the following would help to explain a favourable direct labour efficiency variance?

✗ (i)   Employees were of a lower skill level than specified in the standard
√ (ii)   Better quality material was easier to process
√ (iii) Suggestions for improved working methods were implemented during the period

A   All of them
B   (i) and (ii) only
C   (ii) and (iii) only
D   (i) and (iii) only

3   Which of the following is not a reason for an idle time variance?

A   Wage rate increase
B   Machine breakdown
C   Non-availability of material
D   Illness or injury to worker

4   Which of the following would help to explain a favourable direct material usage variance?

√ (i)   The material purchased was of a higher quality than standard
√ (ii)   Losses due to evaporation were less than expected
  (iii) Activity levels were lower than budget therefore less material was used

A   All of them
B   (i) and (ii) only
C   (ii) and (iii) only
D   (i) and (iii) only

5   Which of the following would help to explain a favourable direct labour rate variance?

√ (i)   Employees were of a lower grade than standard
√ (ii)   The standard hourly rate of pay was set unrealistically high
√ (iii) A pay increase which had been anticipated in the budget was not awarded

A   All of them
B   (i) and (ii) only
C   (ii) and (iii) only
D   (i) and (iii) only

PTQ   Labour efficiency vs labour rate!

44

The following information relates to questions 6 and 7

Put the reasons for variances listed below into the correct place in the tables.

Machine breakdown
Defective material
More economical use of non-material resources
Wage rate increase
Unforeseen discounts received
Lack of training of production workers

6

Variance	Favourable	Unfavourable
(a) Material price	Unforeseen discounts received	
(b) Material usage		Defective material
(c) Labour rate		Wage rate increase

7

Variance	Favourable	Unfavourable
(a) Labour efficiency	Mo	Lack of training
(b) Variable overhead expenditure	More economical use of non-material	
(c) Idle time		Machine breakdown

8   A company revises its standards at the beginning of each year. Because of inflation, it sets its standard price for materials at the estimated price level for the middle of the year. During one control period early in the year, a fairly large favourable direct materials price variance was reported. Which of the following would help to explain this variance?

   (i)   The control period was early in the year
   (ii)   Direct materials were purchased in greater bulk than usual
   (iii) Discounts were taken from suppliers for early settlement of invoices

   A   All of them
   B   (i) and (ii) only
   C   (ii) and (iii) only
   D   (i) and (iii) only

NB Early settlement discounts are a financial matter and do not affect the actual purchase price of materials.

9   The following variances are extracted from the monthly management accounts of SG Co.

Direct material total variance $800 (A)
Direct material usage variance $1,200 (F)

Which of the following statements are consistent with these variances?

(i)   High quality material was purchased, which led to a lower level of quality control rejects of completed output

(ii)   Rapid inflation affected the price of the company's raw material so efforts were made to reduce the quantity of material used per unit of output

A   (i) only
B   (ii) only
C   (i) and (ii)
D   Neither of the statements is consistent with the variances

---

10   Which of the following would help to explain an adverse variable production overhead efficiency variance?

(i)   Employees were of a lower skill level than specified in the standard
(ii)   Unexpected idle time resulted from a series of machine breakdowns
(iii)   Poor quality material was difficult to process

A   All of them
B   (i) and (ii) only
C   (ii) and (iii) only
D   (i) and (iii) only

NB/ Production overhead efficiency variance is the same as a direct labour efficiency variance.
① Variable overheads are incurred during active hours only.

---

18 Standard costing and variance analysis V

1   In a period 4,800 units were made and there was an adverse labour efficiency variance of $26,000. Workers were paid $8 per hour, total wages were $294,800 and there was a nil rate variance.

3250 hrs too many

Standard hours per unit = ☐ 7

---

2   Spendthrift Co purchased 6,850 kgs of material at a total cost of $32,195. The material price variance was $1,370 adverse.

The standard price per kg was $ ☐ 4.5 (to the nearest cent)

---

3   Rainbow Co has prepared the following standard cost information for one unit of product Orange.

Direct materials	2kg @ $13/kg	$26.00
Direct labour	3.3 hours @ $4/hour	$13.20
Fixed overheads	4 hours @ $2.50	$10.00

Actual results for the period were recorded as follows:

Production	4,820 units
Materials – 9,720 kg	$121,500
Labour – 15,800 hours	$66,360
Fixed overheads	$41,700

(handwritten) NB

(handwritten) ① Material price: kg × price per kg
(handwritten) ② Material usage: units used difference × standard cost price.

All of the materials were purchased and used during the period.

The direct material price and usage variances are:

			Favourable	Adverse
Material price	$ 3820 (to the nearest $) *4860*	✓	*✓*
Material usage	$ 80 (to the nearest $) *1040*		✓

(handwritten cross marks: + at left, ✓)

---

4   Rainbow Co has prepared the following standard cost information for one unit of product Orange.

Direct materials	2kg @ $13/kg	$26.00
Direct labour	3.3 hours @ $4/hour	$13.20
Fixed overheads	4 hours @ $2.50	$10.00

Actual results for the period were recorded as follows:

Production	4,820 units
Materials – 9,720 kg	$121,500
Labour – 15,800 hours	$66,360
Fixed overheads	$41,700

(handwritten) Rate: Should: 63,200   Did: 66,360
(handwritten) Efficiency: Should: 15,906   Did: 15,800

The direct labour rate and efficiency variances are:

		Favourable	Adverse
Labour rate	$ 3160		✓
Labour efficiency	$ 424	✓	

(handwritten) Labour rate:
(handwritten) Actual: 15,800   Should: 53,140
(handwritten) Did: 66,360
(handwritten) 14,220 hrs.

5   Standard cost data for ED Co's single product is as follows.

	$ per unit
Direct labour, 1 hour at $7 per hour	7
Variable production overhead	3
Fixed production overhead	4

The fixed production overhead absorption rate is based on budgeted monthly production of 2,000 units. Overheads are assumed to be related to direct labour hours of active working.

Actual results for June

Production output	1,800 units
	$
Direct wages paid – 1,600 hours	12,000
Variable production overhead	6,000
Fixed production overhead	8,200

A machine breakdown resulted in 200 hours of idle time during June.

The idle time variance was $ ☐ adverse/favourable(delete as necessary).

---

6   Tweenie Co has a standard direct labour cost of $18 for a single unit of production. The standard wage is $9 per hour.

During June, 1,100 units were produced. Direct labour was paid for 2,400 hours at a total cost of $20,400.

	Favourable	Adverse
The direct labour rate variance for June was $ 1200	✓	☐

---

7   Tweenie Co has a standard direct labour cost of $18 for a single unit of production. The standard wage rate is $9 per hour.

During June, 1,100 units were produced. Direct labour was paid for 2,400 hours at a total cost of $20,400.

	Favourable	Adverse
The direct labour efficiency variance for June was $ 1800	☐	✓

---

8   Which of the following variances would be shown in an operating statement prepared under a standard marginal costing system (tick all that are correct)?   NB/All of them.

☐ ✓ Variable overhead efficiency variance

☐ ✓ Variable overhead expenditure variance

☐ ✓ Fixed overhead expenditure variance

---

9   Sunshine Co has a standard ingredients cost of $14 for a single unit of production. The standard ingredient price is $7 per litre.

During May 856 units were produced. The ingredients cost was $12,376 for a total of 1,820 litres.

	Favourable	Adverse
The ingredients usage variance for May was $ 108	☐	✓

---

10 Sunshine Co has a standard ingredients cost of $14 for a single unit of production. The standard ingredient price is $7 per litre. During May 856 units were produced. The ingredients cost was $12,376 for a total of 1,820 litres.

		Favourable	Adverse
The ingredients price variance for May was $	.364	✓	✓

19 Standard costing and variance analysis VI ⁶⁄₁₀ R

The following information relates to questions 1 and 2

KD Co uses a standard marginal costing system. Actual and budgeted results for year 4 are shown below.

	Actual	Budget
	$	$
Sales revenue	204,120 *189,000*	180,000
Variable cost	136,700	120,000
Contribution	67,420	60,000
Fixed overhead	38,000	40,000
Profit	29,420	20,000

The management accountant has established that during year 4 the average unit sales price was 8% higher than standard.

1 By how much did actual sales volume exceed budgeted sales volume, as a percentage of the budgeted sales quantities?   5 %

		Favourable	Adverse
2 What is the sales volume variance for year 4? $	2000	✓	

3 Extracts from Drizzle Co's records from last period are as follows.

NB/ Use production overhead cost per labour hours worked.

	Budget	Actual
Production	1,925 units	2,070 units
Variable production overhead cost	$13,475	$13,455
Labour hours worked	3,850	2,990

The variable production overhead expenditure variance for last period is

		Favourable	Adverse
$	1035	✓	

4 Kiwi Co has a standard ingredient cost of $28 for an individual unit of production. The standard ingredient cost is $14 per litre. During June 312 units were produced. The ingredient cost was $4,972 for 350 litres.

		Favourable	Adverse
The ingredient price variance for June was $	72		✓

5   A company manufactures a single product. The standard selling price is $70. The monthly budgeted contribution is $6,900, based on selling 230 units. In April the actual sales revenue was $15,200, when 200 units were sold.

The sales price variance in April was $ [1200] favourable/adverse (delete as necessary).

The sales volume contribution variance in April was $ [1200] favourable/adverse (delete as necessary).

The following information relates to questions 6 and 7

M Co sells product L. An extract from its budget for the four-week period ended 28 October 20X1 shows that it planned to sell 500 units at a unit price of $300, which would give a C/S ratio of 30%.

Annual sales were 521 units at an average selling price of $287. The actual C/S ratio averaged 26%.

6   The sales price variance (to the nearest $1) was

A $6,773 (A)
B $6,500 (A)
C $6,500 (F)
D $6,773 (F)

7   The sales volume contribution variance (to the nearest $1) was

A $1,890 (F)
B $1,808 (F)
C $1,638 (F)
D $1,567 (F)

8   Information on standard rates of pay would be provided by:

☐ A trade union
☐ A purchasing manager
☑ A production manager
☐ A personnel manager
☐ A work study manager

9   The following data relate to work in the finishing department.

Basic daily pay   8 hours × $6 per hour
Standard time allowed to finish one unit   12 minutes
Premium bonus payable at the basic rate   50% of time saved

On a particular day an employee finishes 50 units. His gross pay for the day will be [54] (to the nearest $)

LEARNING MEDIA

10   An employee is paid according the following differential piecework scheme,

Weekly output	Rate of pay per unit
Units	$
1–25	2.30
26–40	2.40
41 and above	2.60

(handwritten: 410, + 57.5)

with only the additional units qualifying for the higher rates. In addition he receives a guaranteed weekly

wage of $420. In a week when he produces 28 units, his gross wage will be $ `484.7`

(handwritten: 7/10)

20 Budgeting I

1   Which of the following may be considered to be objectives of budgeting?

(i)   Co-ordination
(ii)   Communication
(iii)   Expansion
(iv)   Resource allocation

A   All of them
B   (i), (ii) and (iv)
C   (ii), (iii) and (iv)
D   (ii) and (iv)

2   Which of the following would probably **not** be contained in a budget manual?

A   A timetable for budget preparation
B   The production cost budget
C   An organisation chart
D   Specimen budgetary control reports

(handwritten: NB/ the budget manual provides guidelines and information about the budget process.)

3   A master budget comprises

A   the budgeted income statement
B   the budgeted cash flow, budgeted income statement and budgeted balance sheet
C   the budgeted cash flow
D   the entire set of budgets prepared

4   What does the statement 'sales is the principal budget factor' mean?

A   Sales is the largest item in the budget
B   The level of sales will determine the level of cash at the end of the period
C   The level of sales will determine the level of profit at the end of the period
D   The company's activities are limited by the level of sales it can achieve

5   Which of the following is **not** a functional budget?

A   Production budget
B   Distribution cost budget
C   Selling cost budget
(D)   Cash budget

6   Which of the following tasks would usually be carried out first in the budgetary planning process?

+ (A)   Identify the principal budget factor
B   Establish the level of sales demand
C   Calculate the predetermined overhead absorption rate
(D)   Establish the organisation's long term objectives

NB first establish the long-term objectives.

7   If a company has no production resource limitations, in which order would the following budgets be prepared?

1   Material usage budget   4   Finished goods inventory budget
2   Sales budget   5   Production budget
3   Material purchase budget   6   Material inventory budget

A   5, 4, 1, 6, 3, 2
(B)   2, 4, 5, 1, 6, 3
C   2, 4, 5, 1, 3, 6
(D)   2, 5, 4, 1, 6, 3

NB

8   In a situation where there are no production resource limitations, which of the following items of information must be available for the production budget to be completed?

(i)   Sales volume from the sales budget
(ii)   Material purchases from the purchases budget
(iii)   Budgeted change in finished goods inventory
(iv)   Standard direct labour cost per unit

A   (i), (ii) and (iii)
B   (i), (iii) and (iv)
(C)   (i) and (iii)
D   All of them

9   When preparing a production budget, the quantity to be produced equals

A   sales quantity + opening inventory of finished goods + closing inventory of finished goods
(B)   sales quantity − opening inventory of finished goods + closing inventory of finished goods
C   sales quantity − opening inventory of finished goods − closing inventory of finished goods
D   sales quantity + opening inventory of finished goods − closing inventory of finished goods

sales : 40
opinv : 20
clinv : 5

Production : 25

LEARNING MEDIA

10   The quantity of material in the material purchases budget is greater than the quantity of material in the material usage budget. Which of the following statements can be inferred from this situation?

    A   Wastage of material occurs in the production process
√ B   Finished goods inventories are budgeted to increase
    C   Raw materials inventories are budgeted to increase
    D   Raw materials inventories are budgeted to decrease

21 Budgeting II

 9/10

1   PQ Co plans to sell 24,000 units of product R next year. Opening inventory of R is expected to be 2,000 units and PQ Co plans to increase inventory by 25 per cent by the end of the year. How many units of product R should be produced next year?

500 + 24,000

    A   23,500 units
    B   24,000 units
    C   24,500 units
    D   30,000 units

2   Each unit of product Alpha requires 3 kg of raw material. Next month's production budget for product Alpha is as follows.

Opening inventories:

Raw materials	15,000 kg
Finished units of Alpha	2,000 units
Budgeted sales of Alpha	60,000 units

60,000 units → 60,000 kg
− 8,000 kg
+ 3,000 kg

Planned closing inventories:

| Raw materials | 7,000 kg |
| Finished units of Alpha | 3,000 units |

The number of kilograms of raw materials that should be purchased next month is:

    A   172,000
    B   175,000
    C   183,000
    D   191,000

3   Budgeted sales of X for December are 18,000 units. At the end of the production process for X, 10% of production units are scrapped as defective. Opening inventories of X for December are budgeted to be 15,000 units and closing inventories will be 11,400 units. All inventories of finished goods must have successfully passed the quality control check. The production budget for X for December, in units is:

    A   12,960
    B   14,400
    C   15,840
    D   16,000

18,000
+ 2,000
− 3600

4   PR Co manufactures a single product, M. Budgeted production output of product M during August is 200 units. Each unit of product M requires 6 labour hours for completion and PR Co anticipates 20 per cent idle time. Labour is paid at a rate of $7 per hour. The direct labour cost budget for August is

    A $6,720
    B $8,400
    C $10,080
    D $10,500

5   Each unit of product Echo takes five direct labour hours to make. Quality standards are high, and 8% of units are rejected after completion as sub-standard. Next month's budgets are as follows.

Opening inventories of finished goods	3,000 units
Planned closing inventories of finished goods	7,600 units
Budgeted sales of Echo	36,800 units

All inventories of finished goods must have successfully passed the quality control check.

What is the direct labour hours budget for the month?

    A   190,440 hours
    B   207,000 hours
    C   223,560 hours
    D   225,000 hours

6   A Local Authority is preparing a cash budget for its refuse disposal department. Which of the following items would NOT be included in the cash budget?

    A   Capital cost of a new collection vehicle
    B   Depreciation of the refuse incinerator
    C   Operatives' wages
    D   Fuel for the collection vehicles

7   The following details have been extracted from the receivables collection records of C Co.

Invoices paid in the month after sale	60%
Invoices paid in the second month after sale	25%
Invoices paid in the third month after sale	12%
Bad debts	3%

Invoices are issued on the last day of each month.
Customers paying in the month after sale are entitled to deduct a 2% settlement discount.

Credit sales values for June to September are budgeted as follows.

June	July	August	September
$35,000	$40,000	$60,000	$45,000

The amount budgeted to be received from credit sales in September is

    A $46,260
    B $49,480
    C $50,200
    D $50,530

8   BDL plc is currently preparing its cash budget for the year to 31 March 20X8. An extract from its sales
     budget for the same year shows the following sales values.

	$
March	60,000
April	70,000
May	55,000
June	65,000

40% of its sales are expected to be for cash. Of its credit sales, 70% are expected to pay in the month after
sale and take a 2% discount; 27% are expected to pay in the second month after the sale, and the remaining
3% are expected to be bad debts.

The value of sales receipts to be shown in the cash budget for May 20X7 is

A $60,532
B $61,120
C $66,532
D $86,620

The following information relates to questions 9 and 10

Each unit of product Zeta requires 3 kg of raw material and 4 direct labour hours. Material costs $2 per kg and the
direct labour rate is $7 per hour.

The production budget for Zeta for April to June is as follows.

	April	May	June
Production units	7,800	8,400	8,200

9   Raw material opening inventories are budgeted as follows.

	April	May	June
	3,800 kg	4,200 kg	4,100 kg

The closing inventory budgeted for June is 3,900 kg

Material purchases are paid for in the month following purchase. The figure to be included in the cash
budget for June in respect of payments for purchases is:

A $25,100
B $48,800
C $50,200
D $50,600

10   Wages are paid 75% in the month of production and 25% in the following month. The figure to be included
     in the cash budget for May in respect of wages is:

A $222,600
B $231,000
C $233,800
D $235,200

22 Budgeting III

8/10

1 A principal budget factor is:

- [ ] The factor on which total annual expenditure is highest
- [ ] The factor with the highest unit cost
- [✓] A factor which limits the activities of an undertaking
- [ ] A factor common to all budget centres
- [ ] A factor controllable by the manager of the budget centre

2 Which one of these costs would *not* be included in the cash budget of a travel company?

- [✓] Depreciation of computer terminals
- [ ] Commission paid to travel agents
- [ ] Capital cost of a new computer
- [ ] Advertising expenses

3 A carpet fitting firm estimates that it will take 3,520 actual active hours to carpet an office block. Unavoidable interruptions and lost time are estimated to take 20% of the operatives' time. If the wage rate is $7 per hour, the budgeted labour cost is $ ⌊ 30,800 ⌋ (to the nearest $)

4 A job requires 4,590 actual labour hours for completion and it is anticipated that there will be 10% idle time. If the wage rate is $8 per hour, the budgeted labour cost for the job is $ ⌊ 40,800 ⌋ (to the nearest $)

5 MF Co is currently preparing its production budget for product U for the forthcoming year.

Budgeted sales of product U are 140,000 units. Opening inventory is estimated to be 11,500 units and the company wishes to reduce inventory at the end of the year by 20%.

The budgeted number of units of product U to be produced is ⌊ 127,700 ⌋ units.

6 QT Co manufactures a single product and an extract from their flexed budget for production costs is as follows.

NB Check whether there are fixed costs here!

	Activity level	
	80%	90%
	$	$
Direct material	2,400	2,700
Direct labour	2,120	2,160
Production overhead	4,060	4,080
	8,580	8,940

The total production cost allowance in a budget flexed at the 83% level of activity would be $ ⌊ 8,902 ⌋ (to the nearest $)

7 Sam Co budgets to make 4,000 units and estimates that the standard material cost per unit will be $6. In fact 4,800 units are produced at a material cost of $29,760. For the purposes of budgetary control of the expenditure on material cost, the two figures that should be compared are:

Actual $ 29,760 (to the nearest $)

Budget $ 28,800 (to the nearest $)

8 The following cost per unit details have been extracted from the selling overhead cost budget for year 8.

NB Fixed costs again!

Sales (units)	2,400	2800	3,000
Selling overhead ($ per unit)	16.25	1.25	15.00

The budget cost allowance for selling overhead for a sales level of 2,800 units is $ 43,167 (to the nearest $)

9 For a passenger coach company, 8,000 passengers were carried during October and variable costs were in line with budget. The budgeted variable cost per passenger is $0.20 and the total cost of $22,100 meant that fixed costs were $4,500 below budget.

units : 8,000
VC : 0.2 p/p = 1,6.00

The budgeted level of fixed costs for October was $ 25,000 (to the nearest $)

10 An extract from T Co's sales budget shows the following sales values.

	$
June	80,000
July	70,000
August	90,000 45,000 + 20,580 + 15,600

50% of T's sales are for cash. Of the credit sales, 60% are expected to pay in the month after sale and take a 2% discount; 39% are expected to pay in the second month after sale, and the remaining 1% are expected to be bad debts.

The value of sales receipts from credit customers to be shown in the cash budget for August is $ 36,180 (to the nearest $)

23 Budgeting IV

7/10

1 Which one of the following statements about a fixed budget is/are correct? A fixed budget is:

[ ] A budget which ignores inflation

[ ] A budget for non-current assets

[✓] A budget which is most generally used for planning purposes

[✓] A budget for a single level of activity

[ ] A budget for fixed costs

NB/ Volume Variance = Fixed - Flexed.
Expenditure variance = Flexed vs Actual.

2   Lardy Co plans to sell 1,800 units of product F next year. Opening inventory of F is budgeted to be 150 units and Lardy Co budgets to increase inventory by 10% by the end of the year. How many units of product F should be produced next year?

115

| 1815 | units

---

3   When preparing a materials purchases budget, the quantity to be purchased equals

materials usage | *minus* | opening inventory of materials | *plus* | closing inventory of materials

---

4   The quantity of material in the material purchases budget is greater than the quantity of material in the material usage budget. Which of the following statements can be inferred from this situation?

† | | Wastage of material occurs in the production process

† | | Finished goods inventories are budgeted to decrease

✓ | *✓* | Finished goods inventories are budgeted to increase

| | Raw materials inventories are budgeted to decrease

| *✓* | Raw materials inventories are budgeted to increase

---

5   A flexible budget is

| *✓* | a budget which by recognising different cost behaviour patterns is designed to change as the volume of activity changes

| | a budget for a defined period of time which includes planned revenues, expenses, assets, liabilities and cash flow

| | a budget which is prepared for a period of one year which is reviewed monthly, whereby each time actual results are reported, a further forecast period is added and the intermediate period forecasts are updated

| | a budget of semi-variable production costs only

---

6   A company is currently preparing a material usage budget for the forthcoming year for material Z that will be used in product XX. The production director has confirmed that the production budget for product XX will be 10,000 units.

Each unit of product XX requires 4 kgs of material Z. Opening inventory of material Z is budgeted to be 3,000 kgs and the company wishes to reduce inventory at the end of the year by 25%.

The usage budget for material Z for the forthcoming year is | 40,000 | kgs

---

10,000 × 4 = 40,000

– 750

Uses: 10

Opening: 4

Closing: 2

7   Which of the following would be included in the master budget?

NB/ All functional budgets not included. Just some??

- [✓] Budgeted income statement
- [✗] All functional budgets
- [✓] Budgeted cash flow
- [✓] Budgeted balance sheet

8   The following details have been extracted from the receivables collection records of X Co:

Invoices paid in the month after sale	60%
Invoices paid in the second month after sale	20%
Invoices paid in the third month after sale	15%
Bad debts	5%

Credit sales for June to August are budgeted as follows:

June	$100,000
July	$150,000
August	$130,000 *76,440 +30,000*

Customers paying in the month after sale are entitled to deduct a 2% settlement discount. Invoices are issued on the last day of the month.

The amount budgeted to be received in September from credit sales is $ ⟨*121,440*⟩ (to the nearest $)

9   Misty Co's budgetary control report for last month is as follows:

NB/ The volume variance is the increase in costs resulting from a change in the volume of activity:

Fixed - flexed

	Fixed budget $	Flexed budget $	Actual results $
Direct costs	61,100	64,155	67,130
Production overhead	55,000	56,700	54,950
Other overhead	10,000	10,000	11,500
	126,100	130,855	133,580
		Favourable	Adverse

The volume variance for last month was $ ⟨*2,475*⟩   [ ]   [✓]

10   Misty Co's budgetary control report for last month is as follows:

	Fixed budget $	Flexed budget $	Actual results $
Direct costs	61,100	64,155	67,130
Production overhead	55,000	56,700	54,950
Other overhead	10,000	10,000	11,500
	126,100	130,855	133,580
		Favourable	Adverse

The expenditure variance for last month was $ ⟨*2,725*⟩   [ ]   [✓]

24 Budgeting V

1 Leanne Co budgets to make 1,000 units next period and estimates that the standard labour cost of a unit will be $10. In fact 1,100 units are made at a labour cost of $11,500. For the purposes of budgetary control of the expenditure on labour cost which two figures should be compared?

	Actual	Budget
A	$10,000	$11,000
B	$11,500	$10,000
C	$11,500	$11,000
D	$11,000	$10,000

2 The following extract is taken from the production cost budget of S Co.

Production (units)	2,000	3,000
Production cost ($)	11,100	12,900

The budget cost allowance for an activity level of 4,000 units is

A $7,200
B $7,500
C $13,460
D $14,700

3 The following data have been extracted from the budget working papers of BL Co.

Production volume	1,000	2,000
	$/unit	$/unit
Direct materials	4.00	4.00 ✓c
Direct labour	3.50	3.50 ✓c
Production overhead – department 1	6.00	4.20 sv
Production overhead – department 2	4.00	2.00 Fc

The total fixed cost and variable cost per unit is

	Total fixed cost	Variable cost per unit
	$	$
A	3,600	9.90
B	4,000	11.70
C	7,600	7.50 ⨯
ⓓ	7,600	9.90

4 The actual output of 162,500 units and actual fixed costs of $87,000 were exactly as budgeted. However, the actual expenditure of $300,000 was $18,000 over budget.

What was the budgeted variable cost per unit?

A $1.20
B $1.31
C $1.42
D It cannot be calculated without more information

BPP
LEARNING MEDIA

5   The actual output for the period was 22,000 units and variable overhead costs were in line with budget. The budgeted variable overhead cost per unit was $3 and total overhead expenditure of $108,000 meant that fixed overheads were $8,000 under budget. What was the budgeted level of fixed overheads for the period?

A $34,000
B $50,000
C $66,000
D $116,000

6   CA Co manufactures a single product and has drawn up the following flexed budget for the year.

Ignore the %.

	60%	70%	77	80%
	$	$		$
Direct materials	120,000	140,000 154,000		160,000
Direct labour	90,000	105,000 115,500		120,000
Production overhead	54,000	58,000 60,800		62,000
Other overhead	40,000	40,000 40,000		40,000
Total cost	304,000	343,000 370,300		382,000

What would be the total cost in a budget that is flexed at the 77% level of activity?

A $330,300
B $370,300
C $373,300
D $377,300

7   The budgeted and actual figures for B Co are shown below for October. B Co uses a marginal costing system and all direct costs are wholly variable.

	Budget	Actual
Production/sales units	10,000	12,000
	$	$
Direct material	45,000	54,000
Direct labour	30,000	36,000
Variable overhead	20,000	24,000
Fixed overhead	25,000	25,000
Sales revenue	150,000	174,000

The profit shown by B Co's flexed budget for October would be:

A $11,000
B $30,000
C $36,000
D $41,000

8   The following details relate to product R.

Level of activity (units)	1,000	2,000
	$/unit	$/unit
Direct materials	4.00	4.00
Direct labour	3.00	3.00
Production overhead	3.50	2.50
Selling overhead	1.00	0.50
	11.50	10.00

The total fixed cost and variable cost per unit are:

	Total fixed cost	Variable cost per unit
	$	$
A	1,000	10.50
B	3,000	8.50
C	4,500	7.00
D	6,000	7.00

9   The following data and estimates are available for Libra Co for June, July, August and September.

	June	July	August	September
	$	$	$	$
Opening inventory	5,000	3,500	6,000	4,000
Material usage	8,000	9,000	10,000	

Purchases of direct materials are paid for in the month purchased.

The value of budgeted direct material purchases in June, July and August is:

June $ [   ]

July $ [   ]

August $ [   ]

10 Some of the steps involved in an organisation's budgetary planning process are listed below. You are required to indicate the order in which the steps would take place, indicating 1st, 2nd and so on in the boxes provided.

	Order
Prepare the master budget and submit it to the senior managers for approval	[ ]
Identify the principal budget factor (PBF) and prepare the budget for the PBF	[ ]
Establish the organisation's objectives	[ ]
Prepare all remaining functional budgets	[ ]
Form a budget committee and appoint a budget officer	[ ]
Review and co-ordinate the budgets – check their feasibility	[ ]
Adjust the functional budgets if necessary	[ ]

25 Budgeting VI

The following information relates to questions 1 and 2

Mowbray Co manufactures a single product with a single grade of labour. Its sales budget and finished goods inventory budget for period 3 of Year 6 are as follows.

Sales	700 units
Opening inventory, finished goods	50 units

Closing inventory of finished goods must be sufficient for two days' sales, based on the activity for period 3

The goods are inspected only when production work is completed, and it is budgeted that 10% of total finished work will be scrapped. The standard direct labour hour content of the product is three hours. The budgeted productivity ratio for direct labour is only 80% (which means that labour is only working at 80% efficiency). The company employs 18 direct operatives, who are expected to average 144 working hours each in period 3. The sales activity is budgeted to take place over 20 days in period 3.

1   The total production required in period 3 is ☐ units.

2   The labour hours requirement in period 3 is ☐ hours.

The following information relates to questions 3 and 4

A company manufactures a single product and has produced the following flexed budget for the year.

	Level of activity		
	70%	80%	90%
	$	$	$
Turnover	210,000	240,000	270,000
Direct materials	17,780	20,320	22,860
Direct labour	44,800	51,200	57,600
Production overhead	30,500	32,000	33,500
Administration overhead	17,000	17,000	17,000
Total cost	110,080	120,520	130,960
Profit	99,920	119,480	139,040

3   In a budget flexed at 45% level of activity, the value of:

(a)   direct materials would be $ ☐

(b)   direct labour would be $ ☐

4   In a budget flexed at 45% level of activity, the value of production overhead would be $ ☐ .

The following information relates to questions 5, 6 and 7

A&B Engineering Co produces a single product, the LSO, on an assembly line. The following production budgets represent the extremes of high and low volume of production likely to be encountered by the company over a three-month period.

	Production of 4,000 units	Production of 8,000 units
	$	$
Direct materials	80,000	160,000
Indirect materials	12,000	20,000
Direct labour	50,000	100,000
Power	18,000	24,000
Repairs	20,000	30,000
Supervision	20,000	36,000
Rent, insurance and rates	9,000	9,000

Supervision is a 'step function'. One supervisor is employed for all production levels up to and including 5,000 units. For higher levels of production an assistant supervisor ($16,000) is also required. For power, a minimum charge is payable on all production up to and including 6,000 units. For production above this level there is an additional variable charge based on the power consumed. Other variable and semi-variable costs are incurred evenly over the production range. The variable cost per unit of indirect materials is $2. The fixed cost of repairs is $10,000.

The table below will be used to prepare a set of flexible budgets for presentation to the production manager to cover levels of production over a period of three months of 4,000, 5,000, 6,000, 7,000 and 8,000 units.

	Budgets at different levels of activity				
	4,000 units	5,000 units	6,000 units	7,000 units	8,000 units
Direct materials					
Indirect materials	K	L	M	N	O
Direct labour					
Power	F	G	H	I	J
Repairs					
Supervision	A	B	C	D	E
Rent, insurance and rates					
Total					

---

5   What figures should be included at points A-E in the table above?

A   [ ]

B   [ ]

C   [ ]

D   [ ]

E   [ ]

---

6   What figures should be included at points F-J in the table above?

F   [   ]

G   [   ]

H   [   ]

I   [   ]

J   [   ]

7   What figures should be included at points K-O in the table above?

K   [   ]

L   [   ]

M   [   ]

N   [   ]

O   [   ]

8   The following extract is taken from the production cost budget for S Co:

Production (units)   4,000   6,000
Production cost ($)   11,100   12,900

The budget cost allowance for an activity level of 8,000 units is

A $7,200
B $14,700
C $17,200
D $22,200

9   F Co has recorded the following vehicle maintenance costs over the last three periods.

Miles travelled	Maintenance cost
	$
1,800	2,900
2,400	3,170
2,600	3,300

As the basis for the preparation of a flexible budget and using the high/low method, the variable maintenance cost per mile and fixed maintenance cost are

	Variable cost per mile	Fixed cost
	$	$
A	0.45	2,090
B	0.50	1,970
C	0.50	2,000
D	0.65	1,610

10   BF Co manufactures a single product and an extract from their flexed budget for production costs is as follows.

	Activity level	
	80%	90%
	$	$
Direct material	3,200	3,600
Direct labour	2,800	2,900
Production overhead	5,400	5,800
	11,400	12,300

What would be the total production cost in a budget that is flexed at the 88% level of activity?

A $12,076
B $12,120
C $12,320
D $12,540

26 Budgeting VII

1   VE Co's budgetary control report for last quarter is as follows.

	Fixed budget	Flexed budget	Actual results
	$	$	$
Direct material	18,000	20,000	19,500
Direct labour	22,000	23,000	22,800
Production overhead	25,000	27,000	26,500
Other overhead	10,000	10,000	11,000
	75,000	80,000	79,800

The expenditure and volume variances for last quarter are:

	Expenditure	Volume
	$	$
A	200 (F)	5,000 (F)
B	200 (F)	5,000 (A)
C	200 (A)	5,000 (A)
D	5,000 (A)	200 (F)

The following information relates to question 2 and 3

CV Co's budgetary control report for production costs for December is as follows.

	Fixed budget	Flexible budget	Actual results
Units produced and sold	2,000	1,850	1,850
	$	$	$
Direct material	8,000	7,400	7,800
Direct labour	1,000	925	980
Production overhead	8,000 ~150	7,850	7,950
Other overhead	3,000	3,000	2,800
	20,000	19,175	19,530

2   The standard variable cost per unit is

    Vcu ⟹ DM: $4   *FC = 6*

A $5.50   *$0.5*

B $8.50

C $10.00

D $10.36

3   The expenditure and volume variances for December are:

	Expenditure	Volume
	$	$
A	825 (F)	355 (A)
B	355 (F)	825 (F) √
C	355 (A)	825 (F) √
D	355 (A)	825 (A)

4   Which of the following statements about budgets and standards is/are correct.

(i)   Budgets can be used in situations where output cannot be measured but standards cannot be used in such situations.

(ii)   Budgets can include allowances for inefficiencies in operations but standards use performance targets which are attainable under the most favourable conditions.

(iii)   Budgets are used for planning purposes, standards are used only for control purposes.

A   All of them   *NB The use of standards is limited to*

B   (i) and (ii) only   *situations where output can be*

C   (i) only   *measured.*

D   (ii) and (iii) only

5   If a company has no production resource limitations, in which order would the following budgets be prepared?

A   Material usage budget   *3*

B   Sales budget   *1*   *NB See page 178*

C   Material purchases budget   *6*

D   Finished goods inventory budget   *2*

E   Production budget   *4*

F   Material inventory budget   *5*

67

	1st
	2nd
	3rd
	4th
	5th
	6th

6   A Local Authority is preparing a cash budget for its refuse disposal department. Which of the following items would be included in the cash budget?

Included

(i)   Capital cost of a new collection vehicle   ✓

(ii)   Depreciation of the refuse incinerator   ✗

(iii) Operatives' wages   ✓

(iv)   Fuel for the collection vehicles   ✓

7   The following extract is taken from the production cost budget of SW Co.

Production (units)	4,000	6,000	
Production cost ($)	20,600	25,600	

The budget cost allowance for an activity level of 8,000 units is $ 30,600

8   Barbados Co manufactures a single product and has drawn up the following flexed budget for the year.

Activity level	60%	70%	80%
Direct materials	240,000	280,000	320,000
Direct labour	180,000	210,000	240,000
Production overhead	108,000	116,000	124,000
Other overhead	80,000	80,000	80,000
Total cost	608,000	686,000	764,000

What would be the total budget cost allowance at the 75% level of activity?

	$645,000
	$665,000
✓	$725,000
	$735,000

BPP
LEARNING MEDIA

9 RD Co is in the process of preparing its budgets for 20X2. The company produces and sells a single product, Z.

The budgeted sales units for 20X2 are expected to be as follows:

Jan	Feb	Mar	Apr	May	Jun	July	Aug	Sep	Oct	Nov	Dec	Jan
5,000	5,500	6,000	6,000	6,250	6,500	6,250	7,000	7,500	7,750	8,000	7,500	7,000

The company expects to sell 7,000 units in January 20X3.

It is company policy to hold a closing inventory balance of finished goods equal to 20% of the following month's sales.

Changes. 1550   *Closing Ind* 1400

The production budget (in units) for Quarter 4 is ⌊ 23,100 ⌋ units

---

10 A market gardener estimates that it will take 270 active labour hours to pick this season's crop of strawberries and apples.

Unavoidable interruptions and paid rest time together make up 10 per cent of the crop pickers' paid hours.

Crop pickers are paid $8 per hour.

The budgeted labour cost for this season is:

A $1,920
B $2,160
C $2,376
Ⓓ $2,400

---

27 Budgeting VIII

1   An extract from a company's sales budget is as follows:

	$
October	224,000
November	390,000
December	402,000

Ten per cent of sales are paid for immediately in cash. Of the credit customers, 30 per cent pay in the month following the sale and are entitled to a one per cent discount. The remaining customers pay two months after the sale is made.

The value of sales receipts shown in the company's cash budget for December is:

A $285,567
B $286,620
C $290,430
D $312,830

---

2   Extracts from a company's budget are as follows:

	August	September
Production units	12,600	5,500
Fixed production overhead cost incurred	$9,440	$7,000

The standard variable production overhead cost per unit is $5. Variable production overhead is paid 70 per cent in the month incurred and 30 per cent in the following month.

Fixed production overhead cost is paid in the month following that in which it is incurred and includes depreciation of $2,280 per month.

The payment for total production overhead cost shown in the cash budget for September is:

A $32,220
B $42,870
C $45,310
D $47,590

---

3   (a)   The budgeted good production of XY Co in April 20X3 is 810 units. 10% of production is expected to be faulty.

(i)   Gross production is [   ] units

(ii)   [   ] units will be faulty.

(b)   475 units of production are required to enable AB Co's sales demand for quarter 3 of 20X3 to be met. 5% of units produced are likely to be scrapped.

The number of units that need to be produced to enable sales demand to be met is [   ].

4

	Superior model	Standard model
Forecast sales (units)	1,500	2,200
Budgeted opening finished goods inventory (units)	150	200
Budgeted closing finished goods inventory (units)	200	250
Material per unit	5 kgs	4 kgs

Budgeted opening materials inventory	800 kgs
Budgeted closing materials inventory	1,500 kgs

The materials purchase budget is [   ] kgs

---

5   Furniture Creations produces two pieces of furniture, a large chest and a wardrobe, from the same type of wood. The data below relates to period 1.

    (a)   Budgeted production   Chest   450 units

                                           Wardrobe   710 units

    (b)   Materials requirements   Chest   25 kgs

                                           Wardrobe   40 kgs

    (c)   Opening inventory of wood   40,000 kgs

    (d)   Closing inventory of wood   sufficient for 15 days' production

    (e)   Length of each period   25 days

If production levels in period 2 are expected to be 15% higher than those in period 1, the purchases budget (in whole kgs) for period 1 is ⬚ kgs.

The following information relates to questions 6 and 7.

Bertram Manufacturing Co produces a single product.

Sales of the product in the next four week period are expected to be 280 units. At the beginning of the period an inventory level of 30 units is expected, although the budgeted closing inventory level is five units.

Each unit of the product requires two hours of grade O labour and three hours of grade R labour. Grade O labour is paid $15 per hour, whereas grade R labour receive a guaranteed weekly wage of $280. Sixteen members of the workforce of twenty are paid the guaranteed weekly wage.

Just one raw material is used in production of the product. A unit of the product requires 7 kg of raw material. The expected price per kg of the raw material is $50.

6   (a)   The budget production level is ⬚ units

    (b)   The materials usage budget is ⬚ kgs, costing $ ⬚.

7   (a)   The budgeted cost for grade O labour is $ ⬚.

    (b)   The budgeted cost for grade R labour is $ ⬚.

8   Budgeted sales of product B for the forthcoming periods are as follows.

Period number	Budgeted sales units
1	3,470
2	3,280
3	3,970
4	3,770

Company policy is to hold finished goods inventory at the end of each period which is sufficient to meet 20 per cent of the sales demand for the next period.

The budgeted production of product B for period number 3 is:

A   3,930 units
B   4,010 units
C   4,068 units
D   4,724 units

9   What is meant by the term 'principal budget factor'?

A   The budget item which is forecast by the most senior manager
B   The budget item which limits the organisation's activities
C   The largest items of expenditure in the budget
D   The budget item which is subject to the most uncertainty when forecasting

10   Pearson Co manufactures two products, P and L, and is preparing its budget for Year 3. The company currently holds inventory of 800 units of P and 1,200 units of L, but 250 of these units of L have just been discovered to have deteriorated in quality, and must therefore be scrapped. Budgeted sales of P are 3,000 units and of L 4,000 units, provided that the company maintains finished goods inventory at a level equal to three months' sales.

(a) The budgeted production level of product P is ⬚ units.

(b) The budgeted production level of product L is ⬚ units.

28 Cost bookkeeping I

1   A company operates an integrated accounting system. The accounting entries for the return of unused direct material from production would be:

	Debit	Credit
A	Work in progress account	Stores control account
B	Stores control account	Work in progress account
C	Stores control account	Overhead control account
D	Finished goods inventory account	Work in progress account

2   A company operates an integrated accounting system. The accounting entries for the issue to production of indirect materials from inventory would be:

	Debit	Credit
A	Work in progress account	Stores control account
B	Stores control account	Overhead control account
C	Overhead control account	Stores control account
D	Cost of sales account	Stores control account

3   A company operates an integrated accounting system. The accounting entries for absorbed manufacturing overhead would be:

	Debit	Credit
A	Overhead control account	Work in progress control account
B	Finished goods control account	Overhead control account
C	Overhead control account	Finished goods control account
D	Work in progress control account	Overhead control account

4   A company operates an integrated accounting system. At the end of a period, the accounting entries for manufacturing overhead over absorbed would be:

	Debit	Credit
A	Overhead control account	Income statement
B	Income statement	Overhead control account
C	Work in progress account	Overhead control account
D	Overhead control account	Work in progress account

5   A company operates an integrated accounting system. The accounting entries for the factory cost of finished production would be:

	Debit	Credit
A	Cost of sales account	Finished goods control account
B	Finished goods control account	Work in progress control account
C	Costing income statement	Finished goods control account
D	Work in progress control account	Finished goods control account

6   Brixon Morter Co is a manufacturing company, which is based in a single factory location. In its cost accounts, it uses an absorption costing system. 70% of the building is taken up by the production divisions, with the remainder of the space taken up by general administration (20%) and marketing (10%). The rental cost for the premises in the year just ended was $40,000.

Which one of the following bookkeeping entries would have been recorded in the company's integrated cost/financial accounts for the period?

A	Debit	Rent account	$28,000
	Credit	Production overhead control account	$28,000
B	Debit	Cash	$40,000
	Credit	Rent account	$40,000
C	Debit	Production overhead control account	$28,000
	Credit	Rent account	$28,000
D	Debit	Production overhead control account	$40,000
	Credit	Rent account	$40,000

The following information relates to questions 7 and 8

A manufacturing company uses an integrated accounting system. The production overhead absorption rate is $3 per direct labour hour. Production overhead incurred last period was $85,000 and 27,000 direct labour hours were worked.

7 The accounting entries to record the absorption of production overhead for the period would be:

	Debit		Credit	
A	Work in progress account	$85,000	Overhead control account	$85,000
B	Finished goods account	$81,000	Overhead control account	$81,000
C	Work in progress account	$81,000	Overhead control account	$81,000
D	Overhead control account	$81,000	Work in progress account	$81,000

8 The accounting entries to record the under or over absorption of production overhead for the period would be:

	Debit		Credit	
A	Income statement	$4,000	Overhead control account	$4,000
B	Overhead control account	$4,000	Income statement	$4,000
C	Work in progress account	$4,000	Overhead control account	$4,000
D	Overhead control account	$4,000	Work in progress account	$4,000

9 The material stores control account for J Co for March looks like this:

MATERIAL STORES CONTROL ACCOUNT

	$		$
Balance b/d	12,000	Work in progress	40,000
Payable	49,000	Overhead control	12,000
Work in progress	18,000	Balance c/d	27,000
	79,000		79,000
Balance b/d	27,000		

Which of the following statements are correct?

(i) Issues of direct materials during March were $18,000
(ii) Issues of direct materials during March were $40,000
(iii) Issues of indirect materials during March were $12,000
(iv) Purchases of materials during March were $49,000

A (i) and (iv) only
B (ii) and (iv) only
C (ii), (iii) and (iv) only
D All of them

10 The production control account for R Co at the end of the period looks like this.

PRODUCTION OVERHEAD CONTROL ACCOUNT

	$		$
Stores control	22,800	Work in progress	404,800
Wages control	180,400	Income statement	8,400
Expense payable	210,000		
	413,200		413,200

Which of the following statements are correct?

(i) Indirect material issued from inventory was $22,800
(ii) Overhead absorbed during the period was $210,000
(iii) Overhead for the period was over absorbed by $8,400
(iv) Indirect wages costs incurred were $180,400

A (i), (ii) and (iii)
B (i), (iii) and (iv)
C (i) and (iv)
D All of them

29 Cost bookkeeping II

1 A company's accounting system operates so that the cost accounts are independent of the financial accounts. The two sets of accounts are reconciled on a regular basis to keep them continuously in agreement. This type of accounting system is known as

A Independent accounts
B Interlocking accounts
C Reconciled accounts
D Integrated accounts

2 Which of the following statements about integrated accounts is/are correct?

(i) Integrated systems save time and administrative effort

(ii) Integrated systems maintain two separate sets of accounts: one for financial accounts and one for cost accounts

(iii) Integrated systems avoid the need for periodic profit reconciliations

A (i) only
B (i) and (ii) only
C (i) and (iii) only
D (ii) and (iii) only

3   A firm operates an integrated cost and financial accounting system.

The accounting entries for an issue of direct materials to production would be

A   DR work in progress control account; CR stores control account
B   DR finished goods account; CR stores control account
C   DR stores control account; CR work in progress control account
D   DR cost of sales account; CR work in progress control account

---

4   The following data relate to the stores ledger control account of Duckboard Co, a manufacturing company, for the month of October.

	$
Opening inventory	18,500
Closing inventory	16,100
Deliveries from suppliers	142,000
Returns to suppliers	2,300
Cost of indirect materials issued	25,200

The issue of direct materials would have been recorded in the cost accounts as follows.

			$	$
A	Debit	Stores ledger control account	119,200	
	Credit	Work in progress control account		119,200
B	Debit	Work in progress control account	119,200	
	Credit	Stores ledger control account		119,200
C	Debit	Stores ledger control account	116,900	
	Credit	Work in progress control account		116,900
D	Debit	Work in progress control account	116,900	
	Credit	Stores ledger control account		116,900

---

5   A firm operates an integrated cost and financial accounting system. The accounting entries for direct wages incurred would be:

	Debit	Credit
A	Wages control account	Work in progress account
B	Work in progress account	Wages control account
C	Cost of sales account	Work in progress account
D	Finished goods account	Work in progress account

---

6   A firm operates an integrated cost and financial accounting system. The accounting entries for indirect wages incurred would be:

	Debit	Credit
A	Wages control account	Overhead control account
B	Work in progress account	Wages control account
C	Overhead control account	Wages control account
D	Wages control account	Work in progress account

---

7   X Co has recorded the following wages costs for direct production workers for November.

	$
Basic pay	70,800
Overtime premium	2,000
Holiday pay	500
Gross wages incurred	73,300

The overtime was not worked for any specific job.

The accounting entries for these wages costs would be:

		Debit $	Credit $
A	Work in progress account	72,800	
	Overhead control account	500	
	Wages control account		73,300
B	Work in progress account	70,800	
	Overhead control account	2,500	
	Wages control account		73,300
C	Wages control account	73,300	
	Work in progress account		70,800
	Overhead control account		2,500
D	Wages control account	73,300	
	Work in progress account		72,800
	Overhead control account		500

8   The wages control account for A Co for February is shown below.

WAGES CONTROL ACCOUNT

	$		$
Bank	128,400	Work in progress control	79,400
Balance c/d	12,000	Production overhead control	61,000
	140,400		140,400
		Balance b/d	12,000

Which of the following statements about wages for February is *not* correct?

A   Wages paid during February amounted to $128,400
B   Wages for February were prepaid by $12,000
C   Direct wages cost incurred during February amounted to $79,400
D   Indirect wages cost incurred during February amounted to $61,000

9   A firm uses standard costing and an integrated accounting system. The double entry for a favourable material usage variance is:

☐	DR	suppliers control account	CR	material usage variance account
☐	DR	material usage variance account	CR	stores control account
☐	DR	work-in-progress control account	CR	material usage variance account
☐	DR	material usage variance account	CR	work-in-progress control account

10   The bookkeeping entries in a standard cost system when the actual price for raw materials purchased is less than the standard price are:

	Debit	Credit	No entry in this account
Raw materials control account	☐	☐	☐
WIP control account	☐	☐	☐
Raw material price variance account	☐	☐	☐

30 Cost bookkeeping III

1   Q Co uses an integrated standard costing system and inventories are valued at standard price. In October, when 2,400 units of the finished product were made, the actual material cost details were as follows.

Material purchased   5,000 units @ $4.50 each
Material used   4,850 units

The standard cost details are that 2 units of the material should be used for each unit of the completed product, and the standard price of each material unit is $4.70.

The entries made in the variance accounts would be:

	Material price variance a/c		Material usage variance a/c	
A	Credit	$970	Debit	$235
B	Debit	$1,000	Credit	$235
C	Credit	$1,000	Debit	$225
D	Credit	$1,000	Debit	$235

2   When a standard cost bookkeeping system is used and the actual price paid for raw materials exceeds the standard price, the double entry to record this is:

A   debit raw material control account, credit raw material price variance account.
B   debit work-in-progress control account, credit raw material price variance account.
C   debit raw material price variance account, credit raw material control account.
D   debit raw material price variance account, credit work-in-progress control account.

3   A firm uses an integrated standard cost bookkeeping system. The double entry for a favourable labour efficiency variance is:

	Debit	Credit
A	labour efficiency variance account	wages control account
B	work in progress control account	labour efficiency variance account
C	wages control account	labour efficiency variance account
D	labour efficiency variance account	work in progress control account

4   A firm uses an integrated standard cost bookkeeping system. The double entry for a favourable labour rate variance is:

	Debit	Credit
A	labour rate variance account	wages control account
B	work in progress control account	labour rate variance account
C	labour rate variance account	work in progress control account
D	wages control account	labour rate variance account

5   A firm uses an integrated standard cost bookkeeping system. The double entry for an adverse material usage variance is:

	Debit	Credit
A	material usage variance account	work in progress control account
B	material usage variance account	stores ledger control account
C	work in progress control account	material usage variance account
D	stores ledger control account	material usage variance account

6   A company operates an integrated accounting system. The accounting entries for the factory cost of finished production would be:

	Debit	Credit
☐	Work in progress control account	Finished goods control account
☐	Costing income statement	Finished goods control account
☐	Finished goods control account	Work in progress control account
☐	Cost of sales account	Finished goods control account

7   In an integrated cost and financial accounting system, the accounting entries at the end of the period for factory overhead over-absorbed would be (tick the correct boxes):

	Debit	Credit	No entry in this account
Overhead control account	☐	☐	☐
Work in progress account	☐	☐	☐
Income statement	☐	☐	☐

8 At the end of a period, in an integrated cost and financial accounting system, the accounting entries for overheads under absorbed would be:

	DR work-in-progress control account	CR income statement
	DR income statement	CR work-in-progress control account
	DR income statement	CR overhead control account
	DR overhead control account	CR income statement

9 In a typical cost ledger, the double entry for indirect labour incurred is:

	DR	Wages control	CR	Overhead control
	DR	WIP control	CR	Wages control
	DR	Overhead control	CR	Wages control
	DR	Wages control	CR	WIP control

10 In an integrated cost and financial accounting system, the accounting entries for factory overhead absorbed would be:

	Debit	Credit	No entry in this account
Work-in-progress control account			
Overhead control account			
Cost of sales account			

31 Cost bookkeeping IV

1 XYZ Co operates an integrated accounting system. The material control account at 31 March 2001 shows the following information.

MATERIAL CONTROL ACCOUNT

	$		$
Balance b/d	50,000	Production overhead control	
Payables	100,000	account	10,000
Bank	25,000	?	125,000
		Balance c/d	40,000
	175,000		175,000

The $125,000 credit entry represents the value of the transfer to the

	Cost of sales account
	Finished goods account
	Income statement
	Work-in-progress account

BPP)))
LEARNING MEDIA

2   Cubs Co maintains a standard cost bookkeeping system. The work in progress account for the latest period is as follows.

WORK IN PROGRESS ACCOUNT

	$'000		$'000
Material stores	872	Labour efficiency variance	108
Wages control	628	Finished goods control	1,822
Production overhead control	425	Balance c/d	76
Material usage variance	81		
	2,006		2,006

Which of the following statements is/are consistent with the entries in the work in progress account?

☐ All of the material issued to production was completely processed during the period

☐ The material used in production was more than the standard allowed for the number of units produced

☐ The number of labour hours worked was greater than the standard allowed for the number of units produced

3   Browns Co maintains a standard cost bookkeeping system. The production overhead control account for the latest period is as follows.

PRODUCTION OVERHEAD CONTROL ACCOUNT

	$'000		$'000
Payables	785	Work in progress	804
Deprecation	24	Production overhead volume	
Production overhead expenditure		variance	23
variance	18		
	827		827

Which of the following statements is/are consistent with the entries in the production overhead control account?

☐ Production overhead expenditure was lower than the budget for the period

☐ Production output was higher than the budget for the period

☐ Production overhead was under absorbed during the period

4   The wages control account for June is shown below.

WAGES CONTROL ACCOUNT

	$		$
Bank	182,540	Work-in-progress control	150,940
Balance c/d	15,300	Production overhead control	46,900
	197,840		197,840
		Balance b/d	15,300

Which of the following statements about wages for June is/are correct?

☐ Direct wages cost incurred during June amounted to $150,940

☐ Indirect wages cost incurred during June amounted to $46,900

☐ Wages paid during June amounted to $197,840

☐ Wages owing at the end of June amounted to $15,300

---

5   During March, LL Co paid direct wages of $28,400. At the end of March, the total of direct wages owing was $3,200. There had been no wages owing at the end of February.

The correct accounting entries to record the direct wages incurred would be (tick the correct answer):

		Debit $		Credit $
☐	Wages control account	28,400	Bank account	28,400
☐	Wages control account	31,600	Work-in-progress account	31,600
☐	Work-in-progress account	31,600	Wages control account	31,600
☐	Work-in-progress account	28,400	Wages control account	28,400

---

6   During January, 980 units were completed at a total production cost of $11,760. The accounting entries to record this would be:

		Debit $		Credit $
☐	Cost of sales account	11,760	Finished goods control account	11,760
☐	Finished goods control account	11,760	Work-in-progress control account	11,760
☐	Work-in-progress control account	11,760	Finished goods control account	11,760
☐	Cost of sales account	11,760	Work-in-progress control account	11,760

---

7   At the end of last period, the finishing department returned to stores the excess direct material that was unused.

The correct accounting entries to record this would be:

	Debit	Credit
Stores control account	☐	☐
Work-in-progress account	☐	☐

8   When materials are purchased on credit and put into raw materials inventory, the relevant cost bookkeeping
     entries are (tick correct boxes):

	Debit $	Credit $	No entry in this a/c
Work in progress			
Materials inventory			
Cost of sales			
Cash			
Accounts payable			

9   A record of total actual expenditure incurred on indirect costs and the amount absorbed into individual units,
     jobs or processes is known as a:

     ☐ Stores control account

     ☐ Wages control account

     ☐ Work in progress control account

     ☐ Production overhead control account

10   The ledger accounts for JED Co contain the following information. The work in progress account has wages
     input of $26,200. The production overheads amount to $31,500. There was no opening inventory but the
     inventory which was completed and transferred to the finished goods account amounted to $304,660. The
     value of closing inventory was $61,520.

     The value of raw materials brought into production is

     A   296,880
     B   308,480
     C   360,880
     D   371,480

32 Process costing I

1 Changing Co manufactures a product which goes through three consecutive processes, Process 1, Process 2 then Process 3. Data for March is as follows.

	Process 1 $	Process 2 $	Process 3 $
Opening inventory of WIP	8,000	13,000	2,000
Added materials	20,000	4,000	5,000
Conversion costs	10,000	10,000	16,000
Closing inventory of WIP	6,000	9,000	4,000

What was the value of output transferred from Process 3 to the finished goods account in March?

A $22,000
B $26,000
C $69,000
D $88,000

2 What is an equivalent unit?

A A unit of output which is identical to all others manufactured in the same process
B Notional whole units used to represent uncompleted work
C A unit of product in relation to which costs are ascertained
D The amount of work achievable, at standard efficiency levels, in an hour

The following information relates to questions 3 and 4

Patacake Co produces a certain food item in a manufacturing process. On 1 November, there was no opening inventory of work in process. During November, 500 units of material were input to the process, with a cost of $9,000. Direct labour costs in November were $3,840. Production overhead is absorbed at the rate of 200% of direct labour costs. Closing inventory on 30 November consisted of 100 units which were 100% complete as to materials and 80% complete as to labour and overhead. There was no loss in process.

3 The full production cost of completed units during November was

A $10,400   500 ⁊ + 3840 + 7680
B $16,416   (9,000)
C $16,800   11520
D $20,520   976

4 The value of the closing work in progress on 30 November is

A $2,440
B $3,720
C $4,104
D $20,520

5   Process B had no opening inventory. 13,500 units of raw material were transferred in at $4.50 per unit. Additional material at $1.25 per unit was added in process. Labour and overheads were $6.25 per completed unit and $2.50 per unit incomplete.

      If 11,750 completed units were transferred out, what was the closing inventory in Process B?

      A $6,562.50

      B $12,250.00

      Ⓒ $14,437.50

      D $25,375.00

The following data relates to questions 6 and 7

A chemical is manufactured in two processes, X and Y. Data for process Y for last month is as follows.

Material transferred from process X	2,000 litres @ $4 per litre
Conversion costs incurred	$12,250
Output transferred to finished goods	1,600 litres
Closing work in progress	100 litres

Normal loss is 10% of input. All losses are fully processed and have a scrap value of $4 per litre.

Closing work in progress is fully complete for material, but is only 50 per cent processed.

6   What is the value of the completed output (to the nearest $)?

      A $15,808

      B $17,289

      C $17,244

      D $17,600

7   What is the value of the closing work in progress (to the nearest $)?

      A $674

      B $728

      C $750

      D $1,100

8   The following details relate to the main process of X Co, a chemical manufacturer.

Opening work-in-progress	2,000 litres, fully complete as to materials and 40% complete as to conversion
Material input	24,000 litres
Normal loss is 10% of input.	
Output to process 2	19,500 litres
Closing work-in-progress	3,000 litres, fully complete as to materials and 45% complete as to conversion

The numbers of equivalent units to be included in X Co's calculation of the cost per equivalent unit, using a **weighted average basis** of valuation, are

	Materials	Conversion
A	22,500	20,850
B	23,600	21,950
C	23,600	23,600
D	26,000	24,350

9   In process costing, a joint product is

    A   a product which is later divided into many parts

    (B)   a product which is produced simultaneously with other products and is of similar value to at least one of the other products

    C   a product which is produced simultaneously with other products but which is of a greater value than any of the other products

    D   a product produced jointly with another organisation

10   What is a by-product?

    A   A product produced at the same time as other products which has no value

    B   A product produced at the same time as other products which requires further processing to put it in a saleable state

    C   A product produced at the same time as other products which has a relatively low volume compared with the other products

    (D)   A product produced at the same time as other products which has a relatively low value compared with the other products

33 Process costing II

1   A food manufacturing process has a normal wastage of 10% of input. In a period, 3,000 kg of material were input and there was an abnormal loss of 75 kg. No inventories are held at the beginning or end of the process.

The quantity of good production achieved was ☐ kg.

2   In a process account, abnormal losses are valued:

☐ At their scrap value

☐ At the same rate as good production

☐ At the cost of raw materials

☐ At good production cost less scrap value

3   In process costing an equivalent unit is:

☑ A notional whole unit representing incomplete work

☐ A unit made at standard performance

☒ A unit which is identical to a competitor's product

☐ A unit being currently made which is the same as previously manufactured

☒ A unit made in more than one process cost centre

The following information relates to questions 4 and 5

PP Co makes one product, which passes though a single process. The details of the process for period 2 were as follows.

There were 400 units of opening work-in-progress, valued as follows.

Material	$49,000
Labour	$23,000
Production overheads	$3,800

No losses were expected in the process.

During the period, 900 units were added to the process, and the following costs occurred.

Material	$198,000 (900 units)
Labour	$139,500
Production overheads	$79,200

There were 500 units of closing work-in-progress, which were 100% complete for material, 90% complete for labour and 40% complete for overheads. No losses were incurred in the process.

PP Co uses weighted average costing.

4   The number of equivalent units used when calculating the cost per unit in relation to labour is ⬜ 450
     equivalent units

5   The value of completed output for the period was $ ⬜ (to the nearest $)

The following information relates to questions 6 and 7

A company makes a product, which passes through a single process.

Details of the process for the last period are as follows.

Materials	10,000 kg at 50c per kg
Labour	$1,000
Production overheads	200% of labour

Normal losses are 10% of input in the process, and without further processing any losses can be sold as scrap for 20c per kg.

The output for the period was 8,400 kg from the process.

There was no work in progress at the beginning or end of the period.

---

6 The value credited to the process account for the scrap value of the normal loss for the period will be $[   ] to the nearest $10.

---

7 The value of the abnormal loss for the period is $[   ] to the nearest $10.

---

8 A product is manufactured as a result of two processes, 1 and 2. Details of process 2 for the latest period were as follows.

Opening work in progress   Nil
Materials transferred from process 1   20,000 kg valued at $81,600
Labour and overhead costs $16,848
Output transferred to finished goods   16,000 kg
Closing work in progress   1,800 kg

Normal loss is 10% of input and losses have a scrap value of $0.30 per kg.

Closing work in progress is 100% complete for material, and 75% complete for both labour and overheads.

The value of the closing work in progress for the period was $[   ].

The following information relates to questions 9 and 10

Patacake Co produces a certain food item in a manufacturing process. On 1 November, there was no opening stock of work in process. During November, 500 units of material were input to the process, with a cost of $9,000. Direct labour costs in November were $3,840. Production overhead is absorbed at the rate of 200% of direct labour costs. Closing stock on 30 November consisted of 100 units which were 100% complete as to materials and 80% complete as to labour and overhead. There was no loss in process.

---

9 The full production cost of completed units during November was $[   ] to the nearest $.

---

10 The value of the closing work in progress on 30 November is $[   ] to the nearest $.

---

34 Process costing III

1   A company makes a product, which passes through a single process.

NB Normal losses are 10% of Materials only.

Details of the process for the last period are as follows:

Materials	5,000 kg at 50c per kg
Labour	$700
Production overheads	200% of labour

Normal losses are 10% of input in the process, and without further processing any losses can be sold as scrap for 20c per kg.

The output for the period was 4,200 kg from the process.

There was no work in progress at the beginning or end of the period.

The value credited to the process account for the scrap value of the normal loss for the period will be

$ [100]   (to the nearest $)

The following information relates to questions 2 and 3

A company makes a product, which passes through a single process.

Details of the process for the last period are as follows:

Materials	5,000 kg at 50c per kg
Labour	$700
Production overheads	200% of labour

Normal losses are 10% of input in the process, and without further processing any losses can be sold as scrap for 20c per kg.

The output for the period was 4,200 kg from the process.

There was no work in progress at the beginning or end of the period.

2   The value of the abnormal loss for the period is $ [   ] (to the nearest $)

3   The value of the output for the period is $ [   ] (to the nearest $)

The following information relates to questions 4, 5 and 6

A product is manufactured as a result of two processes, 1 and 2. Details of process 2 for the latest period were as follows:

Materials transferred from process 1	10,000 kg valued at $40,800
Labour and overhead costs	$8,424
Output transferred to finished goods	8,000 kg
Closing work in progress	900 kg

Normal loss is 10% of input and losses have a scrap value of $0.30 per kg.

Closing work in progress is 100% complete for material, and 75% complete for both labour and overheads.

4   The value of the output for the period was $ [   ] (to the nearest $)

5   The value of abnormal loss for the period was $ [   ] (to the nearest $)

6   The value of the closing work in progress for the period was $ [   ] (to the nearest $)

7   A company manufactures product Q, in a single process. At the start of the month there was no work-in-progress. During the month 300 litres of raw material were input into the process at a total cost of $6,000. Conversion costs during the month amounted to $4,500. At the end of the month 250 litres of product Q were transferred to finished goods inventory. Normal process loss is 5% of input, abnormal loss was 5 litres and the remaining work in process was 100% complete with respect to materials and 50% complete with respect to conversion costs.

The value of the normal process loss for the month is $ [525] (to the nearest $)

8   WP Co makes a product in a single process. The following data is available for the latest period.

Opening work in progress: 300 units		Closing work in progress: 150 units	
Valued as follows:	$	Degree of completion:	%
Material	3,600	Material	100
Labour	1,600	Labour	50
Overhead	400	Overhead	30

Units added and costs incurred during the period:

Material: 750 units	$11,625
Labour	$6,200
Overhead	$4,325
Losses	nil

WP Co uses the weighted average method of inventory valuation.

The value of the units transferred to finished goods was $ [   ]

9   WP Co makes a product in a single process. The following data are available for the latest period.

Opening work in progress: 300 units		Closing work in progress: 150 units	
Valued as follows:	$	Degree of completion:	%
Material	3,600	Material	100
Labour	1,600	Labour	50
Overhead	400	Overhead	30

Units added and costs incurred during the period:

Material: 750 units	$11,625
Labour	$6,200
Overhead	$4,325
Losses	nil

WP Co uses the weighted average method of inventory valuation.

The number of equivalent units to be used when calculating the cost per unit in relation to labour is

[   ] units.

---

10   A company manufactures product Q, in a single process. At the start of the month there was no work-in-progress. During the month 300 litres of raw material were input into the process at a total cost of $6,000. Conversion costs during the month amounted to $4,500. At the end of the month 250 litres of product Q were transferred to finished goods inventory. Normal process loss is 5% of input, abnormal loss was 5 litres and the remaining work in process was 100% complete with respect to materials and 50% complete with respect to conversion costs.

The equivalent units for closing work-in-progress at the end of the month would have been:

Material   [   ]   equivalent litres

Conversion costs [   ]   equivalent litres

---

35 Job, batch and contract costing I

1   A road building company has the following data concerning one of its contracts.

	$
Contract price	11,200,000
Cost of work certified to date	3,763,200
Estimated costs to completion	2,956,800

No difficulties are foreseen on the contract.

Total final profit 4,480,000
Costs to date : 6,720,000

The profit to be recognised on the contract to date is $ [2508800]

---

2   Which of the following costing methods is most likely to be used by a company involved in the construction of hotels?

[   ] Batch costing

[✓] Contract costing

[   ] Job costing

[   ] Process costing

---

3   A construction company has the following data concerning one of its contracts.

	$
Contract price	400,000
Value certified to date	18,000
Cash received to date	16,200
Costs incurred to date	10,800
Cost of work certified to date	9,900

NB/ Profit = 0
Only recognise profit later in the process, when the outcome can be assessed with reasonable accuracy.

The profit to be recognised on the contract to date is $ ☐ (to the nearest $)

4   In which of the following situation(s) will job costing normally be used?

☐   Production is continuous

☐   Production of the product can be completed in a single accounting period

☐   Production relates to a single special order

5   Contract number 145 commenced on 1 March and plant from central stores was delivered to the site. The book value of the plant delivered was $420,000. On 1 July further plant was delivered with a book value of $30,000.

Company policy is to depreciate all plant at a rate of 20% of the book value each year.

The depreciation to be charged to contract number 145 for the year ending 31 December is $ ☐

6   Which of the following item(s) are contained in a typical job cost?

☐   Actual material cost

☐   Actual manufacturing overheads

☐   Absorbed manufacturing overheads

☐   Actual labour cost

7   Which of the following is/are characteristics of job costing?

☐   Customer-driven production

☐   Complete production possible within a single accounting period

☐   Homogeneous products

8   Which of the following is/are characteristics of contract costing?

☐   Customer-driven production

☐   Work is often undertaken on the customer's premises

☐   Work is often constructional in nature

9   AL Co operates a job costing system. The company's standard net profit margin is 20 per cent of sales value.

The estimated costs for job B124 are as follows.

Direct materials   3 kg @ $5 per kg
Direct labour   4 hours @ $9 per hour

Production overheads are budgeted to be $240,000 for the period, to be recovered on the basis of a total of 30,000 labour hours.

Other overheads, related to selling, distribution and administration, are budgeted to be $150,000 for the period. They are to be recovered on the basis of the total budgeted production cost of $750,000 for the period.

The price to be quoted for job B124 is $ ☐ (to the nearest cent)

10 Which one of the following statements is incorrect?

A   Job costs are collected separately, whereas process costs are averages

B   In job costing, the direct cost of a job can be ascertained from materials requisitions notes and job tickets or time sheets

C   In process costing, information is needed about work passing through a process and work remaining in each process

D   In process costing, but not job costing, the cost of normal loss will be incorporated into normal product costs

36 Job, batch and contract costing II

1   Which of the following is a feature of job costing?

A   Production is carried out in accordance with the wishes of the customer
B   Associated with continuous production of large volumes of low-cost items
C   Establishes the cost of services rendered
D   Costs are charged over the units produced in the period

2   Which of the following statements is/are correct?

(i)   A materials requisition note is used to record the issue of direct material to a specific job

(ii)   A typical job cost will contain actual costs for material, labour and production overheads, and non-production overheads are often added as a percentage of total production cost

(iii)   The job costing method can be applied in costing batches

A   (i) only
B   (i) and (ii) only
C   (i) and (iii) only
D   (ii) and (iii) only

3   The following information relates to job 2468, which is being carried out by AB Co to meet a customer's order.

	Department A	Department B
Direct materials consumed	$5,000	$3,000 8000
Direct labour hours	400 hours	200 hours 2,600
Direct labour rate per hour	$4	$5
Production overhead per direct labour hour	$4	$4 2,400
Administration and other overhead	20% of full production cost	
Profit margin	25% of sales price	

What is the selling price to the customer for job 2468?

A $16,250
B $17,333
C $19,500
D $20,800

The following information relates to questions 4, 5 and 6

A firm makes special assemblies to customers' orders and uses job costing.

The data for a period are:

	Job number AA10	Job number BB15	Job number CC20
	$	$	$
Opening WIP	26,800	42,790	0
Material added in period	17,275	0	18,500
Labour for period	14,500	3,500	24,600
		10352	47600

The budgeted overheads for the period were $126,000.

4   What overhead should be added to job number CC20 for the period?

A $65,157
B $69,290
C $72,761
D $126,000

5   Job number BB15 was completed and delivered during the period and the firm wishes to earn $33^1/_3$% profit on sales.

What is the selling price of job number BB15?

A $69,435
B $75,521
C $84,963
D $258,435

6   What was the approximate value of closing work-in-progress at the end of the period?

   A $58,575
   B $101,675
   C $217,323
   D $227,675

Data for questions 7 and 8

A firm uses job costing and recovers overheads on direct labour.

Three jobs were worked on during a period, the details of which are as follows.

	Job 1 $	Job 2 $	Job 3 $
Opening work in progress	8,500	0	46,000
Material in period	17,150	29,025	0
Labour for period	12,500	23,000	4,500

The overheads for the period were exactly as budgeted, $140,000.

7   Jobs 1 and 2 were the only incomplete jobs.

   What was the value of closing work in progress?

   A $90,175
   B $124,250
   C $214,425
   D $230,175

8   Job 3 was completed during the period and consisted of 2,400 identical circuit boards. The firm adds 50% to total production costs to arrive at a selling price.

   What is the selling price of a circuit board?

   A   It cannot be calculated without more information
   B $31.56
   C $41.41
   D $55.21

9   A job is budgeted to require 3,300 productive hours after incurring 25% idle time. If the total labour cost budgeted for the job is $36,300, what is the labour cost per hour (to the nearest cent)?

   A $8.25
   B $8.80
   C $11.00
   D $14.67

10   P Co manufactures ring binders which are embossed with the customer's own logo. A customer has ordered a batch of 300 binders. The following data illustrate the cost for a typical batch of 100 binders.

	$
Direct materials	30
Direct wages	10
Machine set up	3
Design and artwork	15
	58

Direct employees are paid on a piecework basis.

P Co absorbs production overhead at a rate of 20 per cent of direct wages cost. Five per cent is added to the total production cost of each batch to allow for selling, distribution and administration overhead.

P Co requires a profit margin of 25 per cent of sales value.

The selling price for a batch of 300 binders (to the nearest cent) will be

A $189.00
B $193.20
C $201.60
D $252.00

37 Job, batch and contract costing III

1   A company calculates the prices of jobs by adding overheads to the prime cost and adding 30% to total costs as a profit margin. Job number Y256 was sold for $1,690 and incurred overheads of $694. What was the prime cost of the job?

A $489
B $606
C $996
D $1,300

The following information relates to questions 2 and 3

A small management consultancy has prepared the following information.

Overhead absorption rate per consulting hour	$12.50
Salary cost per consulting hour (senior)	$20.00
Salary cost per consulting hour (junior)	$15.00

The firm adds 40% to total cost to arrive at a selling price

2   Assignment number 652 took 86 hours of a senior consultant's time and 220 hours of junior time.

    What price should be charged for assignment number 652?

    A $7,028
    B $8,845
    C $12,383
    D $14,742

3   During a period 3,000 consulting hours were charged out in the ratio of 1 senior to 3 junior hours.
Overheads were exactly as budgeted.

    What was the total gross margin for the period?

    A $34,500
    B $57,500
    C $86,250
    D $120,750

4   Job 198 requires 380 active labour hours to complete. It is expected that there will be five per cent idle time.
The wage rate is $6 per hour. The labour cost of Job 198 is:

    A $2,166
    B $2,280
    C $2,394
    D $2,400

5   Ali Pali Co is a small jobbing company. Budgeted direct labour hours for the current year were 45,000 hours and budgeted direct wages costs were $180,000.

    Job number 34679, a rush job for which overtime had to be worked by skilled employees, had the following production costs.

	$	$
Direct materials		2,000
Direct wages		
Normal rate (400 hrs)	2,000	
Overtime premium	500	
		2,500
Production overhead		4,000
		8,500

    Production overhead is based on a direct labour hour rate

    If production overhead had been based on a percentage of direct wages costs instead, the production cost of job number 34679 would have been:

    A $5,500
    B $9,000
    C $10,250
    D $10,750

6   Which of the following statements about contract costing are correct?

    (i)   Work is undertaken to customers' special requirements

    (ii)   Work is usually undertaken on the contractor's premises

    (iii)   Work is usually of a relatively long duration

    A   (i) and (ii) only

    B   (i) and (iii) only

    C   (ii) and (iii) only

    D   All of them

7   Contract number 789 obtained some plant and loose tools from central stores on 1 January year 3. The book values of the plant and tools at that date were $380,000 and $4,000 respectively. On 30 June year 3 some plant was removed from the contract site. The written down value of this plant at that date was $120,000. On 31 December year 3 the plant and tools remaining on site had written down values of $180,000 and $2,500 respectively.

The depreciation cost of the equipment to be charged to contract 789 for year 3 is:

    A $81,500

    B $182,500

    C $201,500

    D $264,000

8   A construction company has the following data concerning one of its contracts.

	$
Contract price	2,000,000
Value certified	1,300,000
Cash received	1,200,000
Costs incurred	1,050,000
Cost of work certified	1,000,000

The notional profit is:

    A $150,000

    B $200,000

    C $300,000

    D $700,000

9   Another contract has the following data.

	$
Contract price	800,000
Value certified	40,000
Cash received	30,000
Costs incurred	20,000
Cost of work certified	15,000

The profit to be attributed to the contract is:

    A $0

    B $18,750

    C $25,000

    D $20,000

10   The following data relates to contract A520.

	$
Contract price	86,250
Value certified	57,900
Cash received	54,000
Cost of work certified	65,625
Cost to be incurred to complete contract	29,375

The turnover and cost of sales to be shown in the income statement for the year in respect of contract A520 are:

	Turnover	Cost of sales
A	$57,900	$65,625
B	$57,900	$66,650
C	$86,250	$65,625
D	$86,250	$95,000

38 Service costing

1   State which of the following are characteristics of service costing.

(i)   High levels of indirect costs as a proportion of total costs
(ii)   Use of composite cost units
(iii)   Use of equivalent units

A   (i) only
B   (i) and (ii) only
C   (ii) only
D   (ii) and (iii) only

2   Which of the following would be appropriate cost units for a transport business?

(i)   Cost per tonne-kilometre
(ii)   Fixed cost per kilometre
(iii)   Maintenance cost of each vehicle per kilometre

A   (i) only
B   (i) and (ii) only
C   (i) and (iii) only
D   All of them

3   Which of the following organisations should *not* be advised to use service costing.

A   Distribution service
B   Hospital
C   Maintenance division of a manufacturing company
D   A light engineering company

4   Calculate the most appropriate unit cost for a distribution division of a multinational company using the following information.

Miles travelled	636,500
Tonnes carried	2,479
Number of drivers	20
Hours worked by drivers	35,520
Tonne-miles carried	375,200
Costs incurred	$562,800

A $0.88
Ⓑ $1.50
C $15.84
D $28,140

5   Which of the following are characteristics of service costing?

☐ High levels of indirect costs as a proportion of total cost

☐ Cost units are often intangible

☐ Use of composite cost units

☐ Use of equivalent units

6   Which of the following would be appropriate cost units for a private taxi company?

☐ Vehicle cost per passenger-kilometre

☐ Maintenance cost per vehicle per kilometre

☐ Fixed cost per passenger

☐ Fuel cost per kilometre

7   Which of the following would be suitable cost units for a hospital?

☐ Patient/day

☐ Operating theatre hour

☐ Ward

☐ X-ray department

☐ Outpatient visit

8   The formula used to calculate the cost per service unit is:

Cost per service unit = $\dfrac{A}{B}$

✓

A   [Costs]

B   [No of service units.]

---

9   Match up the following services with their typical cost units.

Service	Cost unit
Hotels	D
Education	C
Hospitals	B
Catering organisations	A

✓

A = Meal served
B = Patient day
C = Full-time student
D = Occupied bed-night

---

10   Service costing has four specific characteristics. They are:

[ ]

[ ]

[ ]

[ ]

---

39 Mixed bank I

1   *Machine operating costs compared with level of activity*

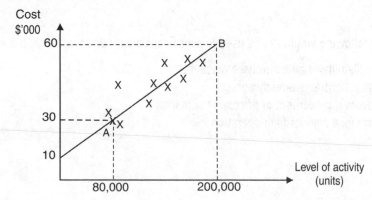

BE Co has established the above line of best fit on a graph of its machine operating costs for a range of levels of activity. When forecasting machine operating costs for next period, the best estimate of the variable machine operating cost per unit is:

A $0.05
B $0.25
C $0.30
D $0.375

---

2 Which of the following statements is/are correct?

(i) An advantage of the high/low method of cost estimation is that it takes into account the full range of available data

(ii) The result of a cost estimate using the scattergraph technique is a subjective approximation

(iii) A cost estimate produced using the high/low method can be used to accurately predict costs outside the relevant range

A All of them
B (i) and (ii) only
C (ii) only
D (ii) and (iii) only

---

3 LG Co is in the process of setting standard costs for next period. Product F uses two types of material, M and N. 6 kg of material M and 5 kg of material N are to be used, at a standard price of $2 per kg and $3 per kg respectively.

Three hours of skilled labour and one hour of semi-skilled labour will be required for each unit of F. Wage rates will be $8 per hour and $6 per hour respectively.

Production overhead is to be absorbed at a rate of $4 per labour hour. Ten per cent is to be added to total production cost to absorb administration, selling and distribution costs.

The standard cost of production for one unit of F will be:

A $57.00
B $69.00
C $73.00
D $80.30

---

4 Which of the following would *not* be used to estimate standard direct material prices?

A The availability of bulk purchase discounts
B Purchase contracts already agreed
C The forecast movement of prices in the market
D Performance standards in operation

BPP
LEARNING MEDIA

5   What is an attainable standard?

A   A standard which includes no allowance for losses, waste and inefficiencies. It represents the level of performance which is attainable under perfect operating conditions

B   A standard which includes some allowance for losses, waste and inefficiencies. It represents the level of performance which is attainable under efficient operating conditions

C   A standard which is based on currently attainable operating conditions

D   A standard which is kept unchanged, to show the trend in costs

---

6   In a standard cost bookkeeping system, the correct double entry to record a favourable labour efficiency variance is:

	Debit	Credit	No entry in this account
Labour efficiency variance account	☐	☐	☐
Wages control account	☐	☐	☐
Work-in-progress account	☐	☐	☐

---

7   In a standard cost bookkeeping system, when the actual hourly rate paid to labour is less than the standard hourly rate, the correct entries to record the variance are:

☐ Debit labour rate variance account

☐ Debit wages control account

☐ Debit work-in-progress account

☐ Credit wages control account

☐ Credit labour rate variance account

☐ Credit work-in-progress account

---

8   In a period, 12,000 litres were input to a mixing process. The normal process loss is 5% of input and in the period there was an abnormal loss of 100 litres while the completed production was 9,500 litres.

There was no opening work-in-progress (WIP).

The volume of closing WIP is ☐ litres.

---

9   Sometimes materials are lost during processing and the materials may be scrapped; sometimes scrap may have a value. If this is the case, the accounting treatment for the scrap value of normal loss is:

Debit ☐ account

Credit ☐ account

---

10   A team of five employees is rewarded by means of a group incentive scheme. The team receives a basic hourly rate for output up to and including 200 units per day.

The basic rate of pay for members of the team is:

	Number of employees	Hourly rate
		$
Team leader	1	14
Operatives	3	10
Junior operative	1	6

For outputs exceeding 200 units per day the hourly rate for all members of the team is increased, for all hours worked that day. The increases in hourly rates, above the basic hourly rate, are as follows.

Output per day Units	Increase in hourly rate %
201 to 250	10
251 to 280	12
281 to 300	15

Due to a limitation on machine capacity it is not possible to exceed an output of 300 units per day. Complete the following remuneration table.

Output per day Units	Hourly group remuneration $
Up to 200	
201 to 250	
251 to 280	
281 to 300	

40 Mixed bank II

1   In a period, there was an adverse labour efficiency variance of $27,000. The standard wages rate per hour was $6 and 30 hours were allowed for each unit as standard. Actual labour hours worked were 52,500.

The number of units produced in the period was ☐

2   In a period 4,920 units were made with a standard labour allowance of 6.5 hours per unit at $5 per hour. Actual wages were $6 per hour and there was a favourable efficiency variance of $36,000.

The number of labour hours actually worked was ☐

3   Freezit Co uses standard costing. It makes a component for which the following standard data are available.

Standard labour hours per component	12
Standard labour cost per hour	$8

During a period 850 components were made, there was a nil rate variance and a favourable efficiency variance of $4,400.

Labour hours actually worked were ☐ hours

4   Which of the following statements about a standard hour is/are correct? A standard hour is:

☐ Always equivalent to a clock hour

☐ Useful for monitoring output in a standard costing system

☐ Any hour during which no idle time occurs

☐ The quantity of work achievable at standard performance in an hour

☐ A basis for measuring output when dissimilar products are manufactured

☐ An hour throughout which units of the same type are made

---

5   The variable overhead production cost of product X is as follows.

2 hours at $1.50 = $3 per unit

During the month, 400 units of product X were made. The labour force worked 820 hours, of which 60 hours were recorded as idle time. The variable overhead cost was $1,230.

		Favourable	Adverse
The variable overhead expenditure variance is $ ☐		☐	☐
The variable overhead efficiency variance is $ ☐		☐	☐

---

6   The standard price of material K is $3 per kg.

Inventories of material K are recorded at standard price. During June, 30,000 kg of K were purchased for $105,000 on 12 June, of which 20,000 kg were issued to production on 28 June. The correct entries to record the issue to production are:

		$
☐	Debit work-in progress account	60,000
☐	Debit material price variance account	15,000
☐	Debit work-in-progress account	70,000
☐	Debit material price variance account	10,000
☐	Credit material stores account	70,000
☐	Credit payables control account	15,000
☐	Credit material stores account	15,000
☐	Credit material stores account	60,000

---

7   The following standard data is available.

	Rate per hour	Product	
		Able	Baker
Direct materials per unit		$10	$30
Direct labour			
Grinding	$5.00	7 hours	5 hours
Finishing	$7.50	15 hours	9 hours
Selling price per unit		$206.50	$168
Budgeted production		1,200 units	600 units
Maximum sales for the period		1,500 units	800 units

The labour used for the grinding processes is highly specialised and in short supply, although there is just sufficient to meet the budgeted production. However, it will not be possible to increase the supply for the budget period.

In order to maximise profits for the period the ranking of the two products is:

1st [   ]

2nd [   ]

---

8   ABC Co makes three products, all of which use the same machine which is available for 50,000 hours per period.

The standard costs of the products per unit are as follows.

	Product A	Product B	Product C
	$	$	$
Direct materials	70	40	80
Direct labour:			
Machinists ($8 per hour)	48	32	56
Assemblers ($6 per hour)	36	40	42
Total variable cost	154	112	178
Selling price per unit	$200	$158	$224
Maximum demand (units)	3,000	2,500	5,000

Fixed costs are $300,000 per period.

The deficiency in machine hours for the next period is [   ] hours.

---

9   A company produces a single product from one of its manufacturing processes. The following information of process inputs, outputs and work in process relates to the most recently completed period.

	Kg
Opening work in process	21,700
Materials input	105,600
Output completed	87,100
Closing work in process	28,200

The closing work in process is complete as to materials and 50% complete as to conversion costs.

The opening work in process included raw material costs of $56,420 and conversion costs of $30,405. Costs incurred during the period were as follows.

Materials input	$291,572
Conversion costs	$226,195

Normal loss is 10 per cent of input. All losses are completely processed and have a scrap value of $2 per kg.

The cost per equivalent kg for the period was:

Materials $ [   ] per equivalent kg

Conversion costs $ [   ] per equivalent kg

---

10   Which of these graphs represents a step fixed cost – when the vertical axis represents total cost incurred?

[   ] Graph 1

[   ] Graph 2

[   ] Graph 3

[   ] Graph 4

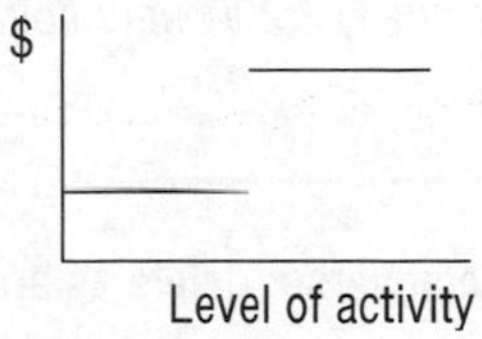

Graph 1

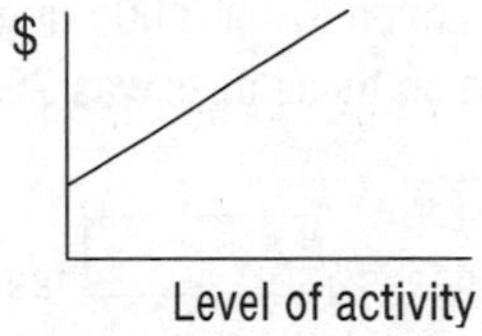

Graph 2

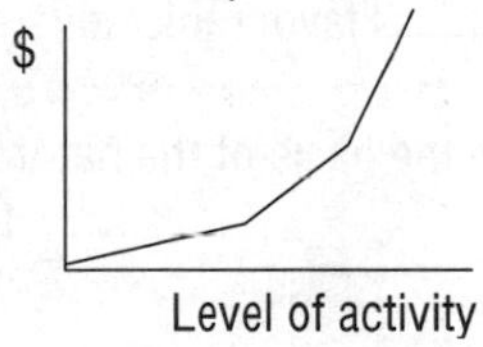

Graph 3

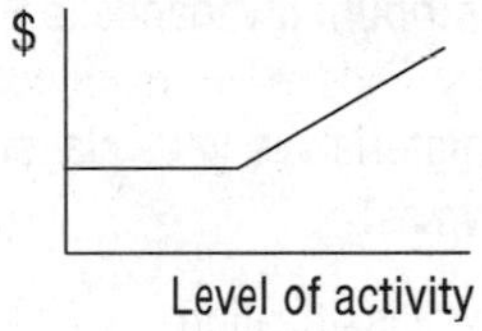

Graph 4

---

41 Mixed bank III

1   A product has the following costs.

	$
Direct materials	5
Direct labour	3
Variable overheads	7

Fixed overheads are $10,000 per month. Budgeted sales per month are 400 units.

The mark-up which needs to be added to marginal cost to allow the product to break even is [   ] %.

2   Which of the following is/are cost objects? Tick all those that apply.

☐   A pint of milk produced by a dairy

☐   A call taken at a call centre

☐   One of a bank's business customers

☐   The home delivery service of a department store

The following information relates to questions 3 and 4

M Co manufactures product D. The standard marginal cost of product D is $56, and the standard selling price is $140. During 20X5 the company planned to sell 3,000 units but actually 3,200 were sold at a price of $120. The actual contribution margin achieved on these units was $55.

3   The sales price variance is $ ☐ favourable/adverse (delete as applicable).

4   The sales volume contribution variance is $ ☐ favourable/adverse (delete as applicable).

5   Expenditure on raw materials is to be classified on the basis of the nature of the expenditure. This type of classification is known as:

A   Responsibility classification
B   Subjective classification
C   Objective classification
D   Cost classification

6   Objective classification of cost incurred on labour using a cost code could indicate:

A   That the assembly department cost centre should be charged
B   That the expenditure was incurred on skilled labour grade 4
C   That the expenditure was the responsibility of the production manager
D   That the cost was a production overhead

7   If a more expensive material than the standard material is used in the production of product A, there will be an adverse material price variance. Which of the following might be an interrelated variance? Put a tick in all boxes that apply.

☐   A favourable sales volume variance

☐   A favourable labour efficiency variance

☐   A favourable material usage variance

☐   A favourable sales price variance

8 B Company has been approached by two customers to provide 2,000 units of product X by a certain date. B Company can only fulfil one of these orders. Customer X is a long-standing customer and the contribution on customer X's order would be $50,000. B Company has not dealt with customer Y before and so they do not receive the discount given to customer X. The contribution on customer Y's order will be $60,000. B Company decides to fulfil customer X's order. The marginal cost of the 2,000 units is $25,000. What is the economic cost of customer X's order?

  A $50,000
  B $60,000
  C $25,000
  D $35,000

9 Revenues and costs of L Company in February were as follows.

	$'000	$'000
Direct materials		60
Direct labour		10
Variable overhead: materials	1	
labour	4	
		5
Total variable costs		75
Fixed overhead: materials	5	
labour	5	
depreciation	5	
		15
Total costs		90
Sales		100
Profit		10

The value added by L Company during February was $ [   ].

10 FOB Co compares its year 1 results with year 0 results as follows.

	Year 1 $	Year 0 $
Sales	160,000	20,000
Cost of sales		
Direct materials	40,000	20,000
Direct labour	40,000	30,000
Production overhead	22,000	20,000
Marketing overhead	42,000	35,000
	144,000	105,000
Profit	16,000	15,000

The gross margin (to two decimal places) of FOB Co is [   ]% in year 1 and [   ]% in year 0.

42 Mixed bank IV

1   What type of cost is supervisor salary costs, where one supervisor is needed for every ten employees added to the staff?

[   ] A fixed cost

[   ] A variable cost

[   ] A mixed cost

[   ] A step cost

2   Which of the following statements about overhead absorption rates are *not* true?

		Not true
(i)	They are predetermined in advance for each period	[ ]
(ii)	They are used to charge overheads to products	[ ]
(iii)	They are based on actual data for each period	[ ]
(iv)	They are used to control overhead costs	[ ]

3   The following data are available for unit X128.

	Labour hours worked on unit	*Machine hours worked on unit*
Extrusion department	1	5
Machining department	2	7
Finishing department	6	1

Overhead absorption rates

Extrusion department = $13.31 per machine hour
Machining department = $10.50 per machine hour
Finishing department = $5.22 per labour hour

The total production overhead cost of unit X128 is $ [   ].

4   The Utopian Hotel is developing a cost accounting system. Initially it has been decided to create four cost centres: Residential and Catering deal directly with customers while Housekeeping and Maintenance are internal service cost centres.

The management accountant has completed the initial overhead allocation and apportionment exercise and has derived the following total cost centre overheads.

	Residential $	*Catering* $	*Housekeeping* $	*Maintenance* $	*Total* $
Total	85,333	68,287	50,370	23,010	227,000

Housekeeping works 70% for Residential and 30% for Catering, and Maintenance works 20% for Housekeeping, 30% for Catering and 50% for Residential.

BPP)))
LEARNING MEDIA

After the apportionment of the service cost centres the total overhead for the Residential cost centre will be $ ☐ .

5   QRS Co has three main departments – Casting, Dressing and Assembly – and for period 3 has prepared the following production overhead budgets.

Department	Casting	Dressing	Assembly
Production overheads	$225,000	$175,000	$93,000
Expected production hours	7,500	7,000	6,200

During period 3, actual results were as follows.

Department	Casting	Dressing	Assembly
Production overheads	$229,317	$182,875	$94,395
Production hours	7,950	7,280	6,696

(a)   The overhead absorption rate for the Casting department was $ ☐ per production hour.

(b)   The overhead in the Dressing department in period 3 was ☐ absorbed by $ ☐ .

6   Duo Co makes and sells two products, Alpha and Beta. The following information is available for period 1.

	Production Units	Sales Units
Alpha	2,500	2,300
Beta	1,750	1,600

	Product	
	Alpha	Beta
	$	$
Unit selling price	90	75
Unit variable costs		
Direct materials	15	12
Direct labour ($6/hr)	18	12
Variable production overheads	12	8

Fixed costs for the company in total were $110,000 in period 1 and are recovered on the basis of direct labour hours.

The profit reported for period 1 using marginal costing principles is $ ☐ .

7   The following data relate to the Super.

Material cost per unit	$15.00
Labour cost per unit	$52.05
Production overhead cost per machine hour	$9.44
Machine hours per unit	7
General overhead absorption rate	8% of total production cost

The capital invested in manufacturing and distributing 9,530 units of the Super per annum is estimated to be $36,200.

If the required annual rate of return on capital invested in each product is 14%, the selling price per unit of the Super is, to the nearest $0.01:

A $133.66
B $144.31
C $152.61
D $163.91

---

8 The following data relate to product L.

Material cost per unit	$57.50
Labour cost per unit	$17.90
Production overhead cost per machine hour	$14.10
Machine hours per unit	11
General overhead absorption rate	20% of total production cost

The total cost per unit of product L, to the nearest $0.01 is $ _____

---

9 Product X is produced in two production cost centres. Budgeted data for product X are as follows.

	Cost centre A	Cost centre B
Direct material cost per unit	$60.00	$30.30
Direct labour hours per unit	3	1
Direct labour rate per hour	$20.00	$15.20
Production overhead absorption rate per direct labour hour	$12.24	$14.94

General overhead costs are absorbed into product costs at a rate of ten per cent of production cost.

If a 20 per cent return on sales is required from product X, its selling price per unit should be, to the nearest $0.01:

A $260.59
B $271.45
C $286.66
D $298.60

---

10 The Mega is produced in two production cost centres. Budgeted data for the Mega are as follows.

	Cost centre 1	Cost centre 2
Direct material cost per unit	$171.00	$67.50
Direct labour hours per unit	5	11
Direct labour rate per hour	$15.00	$34.00
Production overhead absorption rate per direct labour hour	$19.50	$4.10

General overhead costs are absorbed into product costs at a rate of 40% of production cost.

The total **production cost** per unit of the Mega, to the nearest $0.01, is $ _____

---

43 Mixed bank V

1   A technical writer is to set up her own business. She anticipates working a 40-hour week and taking four weeks' holiday per year. General expenses of the business are expected to be $10,000 per year, and she has set herself a target of $40,000 a year salary.

Assuming that only 90% of her time worked will be chargeable to customers, her charge for each hour of writing (to the nearest cent) should be $ ☐

2   The following information relates to a management consultancy organisation.

Overhead absorption rate per consulting hour	$25.00
Salary cost per consulting hour (senior)	$40.00
Salary cost per consulting hour (junior)	$30.00

The organisation adds 35% to total cost to arrive at the selling price.

Assignment number 3036 took 172 hours of a senior consultant's time and 440 hours of junior time.

The price that should be charged for assignment number 3036 is $ ☐

3   Contract number 3830 obtained some plant and loose tools from central stores on 1 January 20X1. The book values of the plant and tools at that date were $760,000 and $8,000 respectively. On 30 June 20X1 some plant was removed from the contract site. The written down value of this plant at that date was $240,000. On 31 December 20X1 the plant and tools remaining on site had written down values of $360,000 and $5,000 respectively.

The depreciation cost of the equipment to be charged to contract 3830 for 20X1 is $ ☐

4   Which of the following would be inappropriate cost units for a transport business?

(i)   Cost per tonne-kilometre
(ii)   Fixed cost per kilometre
(iii) Maintenance cost of each vehicle per kilometre

A   (i) only
B   (ii) only
C   (iii) only
D   (ii) and (iii) only

5   Which of the following statements about process losses are correct?

(i)   Units of normal loss should be valued at full cost per unit.

(ii)   Units of abnormal loss should be valued at their scrap value.

(iii) When there is closing WIP and losses, abnormal gain units are an addition to the total equivalent units produced, abnormal loss units are subtracted in arriving at the total number of equivalent units produced.

A   (i) and (ii) only
B   (ii) and (iii) only
C   None of them
D   All of them

6   Which of the following statements in connection with process costing are correct?

(i)   A loss expected during the normal course of operations, for unavoidable reasons, is abnormal loss.
(ii)   An unexpected loss is an abnormal loss.
(iii) An abnormal loss arises if the actual loss is greater than the expected loss.
(iv)   A normal loss is never less than actual loss.

A   (i) and (ii)
B   (ii) and (iii)
C   (i) and (iv)
D   (ii) and (iv)

7   In a process account, abnormal gains are valued at:

A   the same unit rate as good production
B   the cost of raw material
C   their scrap value
D   the cost of good production less scrap value

8   In a particular process, the input for the period was 2,000 units. There were no inventories at the beginning or end of the process. Normal loss is 5 per cent of input. In which of the following circumstances is there an abnormal gain?

(i)   Actual output = 1,800 units
(ii)   Actual output = 1,950 units
(iii) Actual output = 2,000 units

A   (i) only
B   (ii) only
C   (i) and (ii) only
D   (ii) and (iii) only

9   In process costing, if an abnormal loss arises, the process account is generally

A   debited with the scrap value of the abnormal loss units
B   debited with the full production cost of the abnormal loss units
C   credited with the scrap value of the abnormal loss units
D   credited with the full production cost of the abnormal loss units

10   In process costing, where losses have a positive scrap value, when an abnormal gain arises the abnormal gain account is

A   debited with the normal production cost of the abnormal gain units and debited with the scrap value of the abnormal gain units

B   debited with the normal production cost of the abnormal gain units and credited with the scrap value of the abnormal gain units

C   credited with the normal production cost of the abnormal gain units and debited with the scrap value of the abnormal gain units

D   credited with the normal production cost of the abnormal gain units and credited with the scrap value of the abnormal gain units

Answers to objective test questions

1 Introduction to management accounting and

1   C   This is CIMA's definition of a cost unit.

In options A and B, the hour of operation and the unit of electricity are b
for which costs have been ascertained.

Option D is an example of a particular cost unit which may be used for c
definition of the term 'cost unit'.

2   C   This is the correct definition of a cost centre.

Option A is the definition of a cost unit.

Option B describes the *cost* of an activity or cost centre.

Option D describes a budget centre. Although a budget centre may also be a cost centre at times, this is not always the case.

3   D   It would be appropriate to use the cost per invoice processed and the cost per supplier account for control purposes. Therefore items (ii) and (iii) are suitable cost units and the correct answer is D.

Postage cost, item (i), is an expense of the department, therefore option A is not a suitable cost unit.

If you selected option B or option C you were probably rushing ahead and not taking care to read all the options. Items (ii) and (iii) *are* suitable cost units, but neither of them are the *only* suitable suggestions.

4   B   Prime cost is the total of direct material, direct labour and direct expenses. Therefore the correct answer is B.

Option A describes total production cost, including absorbed production overhead. Option C is only a part of prime cost. Option D is an overhead or indirect cost.

5   A   Option A is a part of the cost of direct materials.

Options B and D are production overheads. Option C is a selling and distribution expense.

6   A   Special designs, and the hire of tools etc for a particular job can be traced to a specific cost unit. Therefore they are direct expenses and the correct answer is A.

Item (iii) is a selling and distribution overhead and item (iv) describes production overheads.

7   A   Depreciation is an indirect cost because it does not relate directly to the number of units produced.

Items (ii) and (iii) can be traced directly to specific cost units therefore they are direct expenses.

8   D   The deliveries occur after a sale is made, therefore drivers' wages are a selling and distribution overhead.

Options A, B and C are all a part of total production cost, incurred before an item is sold.

9   D   The first two digits in the code refer to the cost centre and the last three digits are the type of expense. Thus for (14) maintenance and (460) depreciation of non-production equipment the code is 14460. The correct answer is D.

ption A has an incorrect cost centre code.

Options B and C have the wrong type of expense.

A   For (10) machining department use of (410) indirect materials the code is 10410.

Option B has an incorrect expense type.

Options C and D have the incorrect cost centre code. The code indicates the cost centre *incurring* the cost, ie receiving the materials.

---

2 Introduction to management accounting and costing II

1   B   The only direct costs are the wages paid to direct workers for ordinary time, plus the basic pay for overtime.
$25,185 + $5,440 = $30,625.

If you selected option A you forgot to include the basic pay for overtime of direct workers, which is always classified as a direct labour cost.

If you selected option C you have included overtime premium and shift allowances, which are usually treated as indirect costs. However, if overtime and shiftwork are incurred specifically for a particular cost unit, then they are classified as direct costs of that cost unit. There is no mention of such a situation here.

Option D includes sick pay, which is classified as an indirect labour cost.

2   C   The maintenance assistant is not working directly on the organisation's output but is performing an indirect task. All the other three options describe tasks that involve working directly on the output.

3   ☑ Cheque received and processed
     ☑ Customer account

Telephone expense is a cost for the department, not a potential cost unit.

4   ☑ A stores assistant in a factory store

The stores assistant's wages cannot be charged directly to a product, therefore the stores assistant is part of the indirect labour force.

5   ☑ Direct expense

The royalty cost can be traced in full to the company's product, therefore it is a direct expense.

6   ☑ Constant in total when activity changes

CIMA *Official Terminology* defines a fixed cost as 'a cost incurred for an accounting period, that, within certain output or turnover limits, tends to be unaffected by fluctuations in the levels of activity (output or turnover).'

7   ☑ A function or location for which costs are ascertained

A cost centre acts as a 'collecting place' for costs before they are analysed further.

BPP)))
LEARNING MEDIA

8   ☑ Not a cash cost

☑ Part of production overheads

The depreciation on production equipment is an indirect expense incurred in the factory and is therefore included in production overheads.

9   ☑ Production overheads

Overtime premium is always classed as production overheads unless it is: worked at the specific request of a customer to get his/her order completed; or worked regularly by a production department in the normal course of operations, in which case it is usually incorporated into the direct labour hourly rate.

10

	$
Variable costs 8,000 × $8	64,000
Fixed costs	12,000
	76,000

3 Cost behaviour

1   A   Variable costs are conventionally deemed to increase or decrease in direct proportion to changes in output. Therefore the correct answer is A. Descriptions B and D imply a changing unit rate, which does not comply with this convention. Description C relates to a fixed cost.

2   A   The depicted cost has a basic fixed element which is payable even at zero activity. A variable element is then added at a constant rate as activity increases. Therefore the correct answer is A.

Graphs for the other options would look like this.

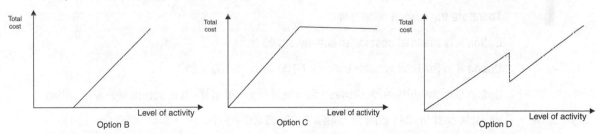

3   B   The cost described consists of a fixed amount up to a certain level of activity. This will be represented by a straight horizontal line. At a certain point a variable element is added and the cost line will slope upwards at a constant rate. Graph 2 demonstrates this pattern therefore the correct answer is B.

If you selected option D, graph 4, you had the right idea for the second part of the graph. However, graph 4 depicts zero cost up to a certain level, which is not correct.

4   A   The cost described will increase in steps, remaining fixed at each step until another supervisor is required. Graph 1 depicts a step cost therefore the correct answer is A.

5   C   The cost described begins as a linear variable cost, increasing at a constant rate in line with activity. At a certain point the cost becomes fixed regardless of the level of activity. Graph 3 demonstrates this behaviour pattern. Therefore the correct answer is C.

6   D   The salary is part fixed ($650 per month) and part variable (5 cents per unit). Therefore it is a semi-variable cost and answer D is correct.

If you chose options A or B you were considering only part of the cost.

Option C, a step cost, involves a cost which remains constant up to a certain level and then increases to a new, higher, constant fixed cost.

7   B   A variable cost will result in a constant cost per unit at each activity level. A semi-variable cost will result in a different cost per unit at each activity level, because of the spreading of fixed costs. A fixed cost is the same absolute amount of total cost for each activity level.

Cost type	Cost per unit for 100 units $	Cost per unit for 140 units $	Cost behaviour
W	80.00	75.43	Semi-variable
X	Constant cost for both activity levels		Fixed
Y	65.00	65.00	Variable
Z	67.00	61.29	Semi-variable

8   C

	Units	$
High output	1,100	18,300
Low output	700	13,500
Variable cost of	400	4,800

Variable cost per unit $4,800/$400 = $12 per unit

Fixed costs = $18,300 − ($12 × 1,100) = $5,100

Therefore the correct answer is C.

Option A is the total cost for an activity of 700 units

Option B is the total variable cost for 1,100 units (1,100 × $12)

Option D is the difference between the costs incurred at the two activity levels recorded.

9   A   Variable cost for 340 guest-nights = $570 − $400 = $170

Variable cost per guest-night = $170/340 = $0.50

Therefore the correct answer is A

If you selected option B you have calculated the fixed cost per guest-night for the stated activity level ($400 ÷ 340).

If you selected option C you have calculated the average total cost per guest-night ($570 ÷ 340).

10   D

	Deliveries	$
High activity	930	9,860
Low activity	840	9,680
Variable cost of	90	180

Variable cost per delivery $180/90 = $2 per delivery

Fixed costs = $9,860 − ($2 × 930) = $8,000

Total costs = fixed costs + (variable cost per delivery × number of deliveries)
         = $8,000 + ($2 × number of deliveries)

Therefore the correct answer is D.

If you selected options A or B you simply calculated the average cost at either of the two activity levels – but the fixed cost remains constant for each activity level.

If you selected option C you did the calculations correctly but forgot that variable costs must be **added** to fixed costs to derive the total cost.

4 Overhead costs – absorption costing I

1   B   Overhead absorption (option A) is the final process of absorbing the total cost centre overheads into product costs. Overhead allocation (option C) is the allotment of whole items of overhead costs to a particular cost centre or cost unit. Overhead analysis (option D) is the general term used to describe all of the tasks of processing overhead cost data.

2   D   Costs are controlled using budgets and other management information, therefore option A is not correct. Option B describes overhead cost absorption and option C describes cost allocation.

3   A   Overhead absorption rates are determined in advance for each period, usually based on budgeted data. Therefore statement (i) is correct and statement (iii) is incorrect. Overhead absorption rates are used in the final stage of overhead analysis, to absorb overheads into product costs. Therefore statement (ii) is correct. Statement (iv) is not correct because overheads are controlled using budgets and other management information. Therefore the correct answer is A.

4   D   Number of employees in packing department = 2 direct + 1 indirect = 3

Number of employees in all production departments = 15 direct + 6 indirect = 21

Packing department overhead

Canteen cost apportioned to packing department	=	$\dfrac{\$8,400}{21} \times 3$
	=	$1,200
Original overhead allocated and apportioned	=	$8,960
Total overhead after apportionment of canteen costs	=	$10,160

ANSWERS

If you selected option A you forgot to include the original overhead allocated and apportioned to the packing department. If you selected option B you included the four canteen employees in your calculation, but the question states that the basis for apportionment is the number of employees in each **production** cost centre.

If you selected option C you based your calculations on the direct employees only.

5   D   Department 1 appears to undertake primarily machine-based work, therefore a machine-hour rate would be most appropriate.

$$\frac{\$27,000}{45,000} = \$0.60 \text{ per machine hour}$$

Therefore the correct answer is D.

Option A is not the most appropriate because it is not time-based, and most items of overhead expenditure tend to increase with time.

Options B and C are not the most appropriate because labour activity is relatively insignificant in department 1, compared with machine activity.

6   C   Department 2 appears to be labour-intensive therefore a direct labour-hour rate would be most appropriate.

$$\frac{\$18,000}{25,000} = \$0.72 \text{ per direct labour hour}$$

Option B is based on labour therefore it could be suitable. However differential wage rates exist and this could lead to inequitable overhead absorption. Option D is not suitable because machine activity is not significant in department 2.

7   B   Using the high-low method, we can calculate the variable overheads per prescription as follows.

$$\frac{\$(109,000-97,000)}{16,000-13,000} = \frac{\$12,000}{3,000} = \$4.00 \text{ per prescription}$$

$$\therefore \text{ Fixed overhead } = \$109,000 - (16,000 \times 4)$$
$$= \$45,000$$

If you selected option A or C you calculated the correct $4 per prescription for variable overhead, but then deducted this from the total rate of $7 to determine a unit rate for fixed overhead of $3 per unit. You then applied this rate to one of the given activity levels. This is not valid because the unit rate of $3 for fixed overhead applies only to the budgeted level of activity.

If you selected option D you simply multiplied the given rate of $7 per unit by the activity level of 13,000 prescriptions.

124   BPP
LEARNING MEDIA

8 B Variable overhead per prescription + fixed overhead per prescription = total overhead per prescription

∴ Fixed overhead per prescription = $7 – $4 = $3

Total fixed overheads = $45,000

∴ Budgeted activity level = $\dfrac{\$45,000}{\$3}$ = 15,000 prescriptions

If you selected options A, C or D you based your calculations on your incorrect answer from question 7.

9 B From the four options available, a basis relating to space occupied would seem to be most appropriate. This eliminates options C and D. Since heating is required to warm the whole of the space occupied, from floor to ceiling, the volume of space is most appropriate. Therefore the correct answer is B.

10 C Option C correctly describes reciprocal servicing, for example where a maintenance department does work for the stores and canteen, stores issues are made to the maintenance department, and staff from all cost centres use the canteen.

5 Overhead costs – absorption costing II

1 A Statement (i) is correct because a constant unit absorption rate is used throughout the period. Statement (ii) is correct because 'actual' overhead costs, based on actual overhead expenditure and actual activity for the period, cannot be determined until after the end of the period. Statement (iii) is incorrect because under/over absorption of overheads is caused by the use of predetermined overhead absorption rates.

2 A Description B could lead to under-absorbed overheads if actual overheads far exceeded both budgeted overheads and the overhead absorbed. Description C could lead to under-absorbed overheads if overhead absorbed does not increase in line with actual overhead incurred. Description D could also lead to under absorption if actual overhead does not decrease in line with absorbed overheads.

3 A Budgeted overhead absorption rate = $\dfrac{\$258,750}{11,250}$ = $23 per machine hour

	$
Overhead absorbed = $23 × 10,980 hours	252,540
Overhead incurred	254,692
Under-absorbed overhead	2,152

If you selected option B or C you calculated the difference between the budgeted and actual overheads and interpreted the result as an under or over absorption.

If you selected option D your calculations were correct but you misinterpreted the result as over absorbed.

4   B   Overhead absorption rate $= \dfrac{\text{budgeted overheads}}{\text{budgeted labour hours}} = \dfrac{\$148{,}750}{8{,}500} = \$17.50$ per hr

If you selected option A you divided the actual overheads by the budgeted labour hours. Option C is based on the actual overheads and actual labour hours. If you selected option D you divided the budgeted overheads by the actual hours.

5   D

		$
Overhead absorbed = $17.50 × 7,928 =		138,740
Overhead incurred =		146,200
Under-absorbed overhead =		7,460

If you selected options A or B you calculated the difference between the budgeted and actual overheads and interpreted it as an under or over absorption. If you selected option C you performed the calculations correctly but misinterpreted the result as an over absorption.

6   D

	$
	14,625

Overhead absorbed $= \dfrac{\$15{,}000}{20{,}000} \times 19{,}500$

Overhead incurred	14,000
Over-absorbed overhead	625

Statement A is untrue because lower expenditure is more likely to lead to over absorption, unless there is a corresponding reduction in the actual labour hours.

Statement B is incorrect because the decrease in labour hours in isolation would have resulted in an under absorption of $375 (500 hours × $0.75 per hour).

If you selected statement C you performed the calculations correctly but misinterpreted the result as an under absorption.

7   C   When expenditures are as budgeted, but actual and budgeted production activity levels are different, only the fixed overhead can be under or over absorbed. Variable overhead absorbed would be (1,000 × $2.50) $2,500 less than originally budgeted but variable overhead incurred would be $2,500 less as well, leaving neither under- or over- absorbed variable overheads.

∴ Under-absorbed overheads $=$ 1,000 hours × $4 = $4,000

Option A is incorrect because the shortfall in hours would have caused an under absorption, unless the fixed overhead expenditure also reduced accordingly.

Option B is incorrect because the variable overhead would not be under absorbed as discussed above.

Option D is incorrect because it includes the reduced variable overhead of $2,500.

BPP
LEARNING MEDIA

8   B

	$
Actual overheads	295,000
Under-absorbed overheads	9,400
Overheads absorbed for 70,000 hours at budgeted absorption rate (x)	285,600

$$70,000x = \$285,600$$
$$x = \$285,600/70,000$$
$$= \$4.08$$

Option A is incorrect because it is based on the budgeted overhead and the actual machine hours. Option C is incorrect because it is the actual overhead rate per machine hour.

If you selected option D you added the under-absorbed overhead by mistake, at the beginning of the calculation.

9   C   Budgeted absorption rate for fixed overhead = $360,000/8,000
                                        = $45 per unit

	$
Fixed overhead absorbed (9,000 × $45)	405,000
Variable overhead absorbed (9,000 × $3)	27,000
	432,000

If you selected option A you based your absorption calculations on sales units instead of production units.

If you selected option B you calculated the correct figure for fixed overhead absorbed but forgot to add on the variable overheads.

Option D is the figure for actual total overhead incurred.

10   A   Actual overhead incurred:

	$
Variable (9,000 units × $3)	27,000
Fixed	432,000
	459,000
Overhead absorbed (from question 9)	432,000
Overhead under absorbed	27,000

If you selected option B you simply calculated the difference between the budgeted and actual fixed overhead. If you selected option C you based your absorption calculations on sales units instead of production units. If you selected option D you performed the calculations correctly but misinterpreted the result as an over absorption.

6 Overhead costs – absorption costing III

1. [✓] Spread common costs over cost centres

   Overhead apportionment involves sharing overhead costs as fairly as possible over a number of cost centres. Apportionment is used when it is not possible to allocate the whole cost to a single cost centre.

2. The budgeted overhead absorption rate was $ [25] per machine hour (to the nearest $).

	$
Actual overheads incurred	496,500
Over-absorbed overhead	64,375
Actual overheads absorbed	560,875

   $$\frac{\text{Actual overheads absorbed}}{\text{Actual machine hours}} = \text{Amount absorbed per machine hour}$$

   $$\frac{\$560,875}{22,435} = \$25 \text{ per machine hour}$$

3. The fixed overhead full rate per unit (to the nearest cent) was $ [3.20]

   Change in inventory = 33,480 units – 25,920 units = 7,560 units
   Difference in profit = $228,123 – $203,931 = $24,192

   $$\therefore \text{Fixed overhead full rate} = \frac{\text{Difference in profit}}{\text{Change in inventory}}$$

   $$= \frac{\$24,192}{7,560 \text{ units}}$$

   $$= \$3.20 \text{ per unit}$$

4. The machine hour full rate (to the nearest $) $ [45] per machine hour.

   $$\text{Machine hour full rate} = \frac{\text{Budgeted overheads}}{\text{Budgeted machine hours}}$$

   $$= \frac{\$690,480}{15,344}$$

   $$= \$45 \text{ per machine hour}$$

5. Overhead for the period was [under] absorbed by $ [43,790]

   $$\text{Overhead full rate} = \frac{\$690,480}{15,344} = \$45 \text{ per machine hour}$$

	$
Overhead absorbed = $45 × 14,128 hrs =	635,760
Overhead incurred	679,550
Overhead under absorbed	43,790

6 | 13,000 | hours

	$
Actual overheads	344,000
Under-absorbed overheads	17,440
Overhead recovery for 12,560 hrs	326,560

$\therefore$ Overhead full rate $= \dfrac{\$326,560}{12,560} = \$26$ per hour

Budgeted labour hours $= \dfrac{\text{Budgeted overheads}}{\text{Overhead absorption rate}}$

$= \dfrac{\$338,000}{\$26} = 13,000$ hrs

7   The fixed overhead full rate per unit (to the nearest $) is $ | 10 |

	Units
Opening inventory	825
Closing inventory	1,800
Increase in inventory level	975

	$
Full costing profit	60,150
Marginal costing profit	50,400
Difference in profit	9,750

$\therefore$ Overhead full rate $= \dfrac{\$9,750}{975} = \$10$ per unit

8   Overheads were | under | absorbed by $ | 28,200 |

Overhead full rate $= \dfrac{\text{Budgeted overheads}}{\text{Budgeted machine hours}}$

$= \dfrac{\$316,800}{14,400}$

$= \$22$ per machine hour

	$
Overhead absorbed = $22 × 14,100	310,200
Overhead incurred	338,400
Under full	28,200

9 The estimate of the overheads if 13,800 square metres are to be painted is \$ $\boxed{78,255}$

$$\text{Variable overhead} \;=\; \frac{\$83,585 - \$73,950}{15,100 - 12,750} = \frac{\$9,635}{2,350}$$

$$= \$4.10 \text{ per square metre}$$

Fixed overhead $= \$73,950 - (\$4.10 \times 12,750)$
$$= \$73,950 - \$52,275 = \$21,675$$

Overheads on 13,800 square metres

therefore $= \$21,675 + (\$4.10 \times 13,800)$
$$= \$21,675 + \$56,580$$
$$= \$78,255$$

10 The overhead full rate per hour was \$ $\boxed{15}$ (to the nearest \$)

Overheads absorbed = Actual overheads + over-absorbed overheads
$$= \; 109,000 + 14,000$$
$$= \; \$123,000$$

$$\text{Overhead full rate} \;=\; \frac{\text{Overheads absorbed}}{\text{Hours worked}}$$

$$= \frac{\$123,000}{8,200}$$

$$= \; \$15 \text{ per hour}$$

7 Overhead costs – absorption costing IV

1 The budgeted overhead absorption rate per hour was \$ $\boxed{14}$ (to the nearest \$)

	\$
Actual overheads	640,150
Over-recovered overheads	35,000
Overheads recovered for 48,225 hours at budgeted overhead full rate (x)	675,150

$$48,225 \, x \;=\; 675,150$$

$$x \;=\; \frac{675,150}{48,225}$$

$$x \;=\; \$14$$

2   The profit using absorption costing would be $ [23,900]

	Litres
Opening inventory	(8,500)
Closing inventory	6,750
Change in inventory	(1,750)
× overhead full rate	$2
Profit difference	$3,500

Since inventories reduced during the period the full costing profit would be lower than the marginal costing profit. Full costing profit = $27,400 – $3,500 = $23,900.

3   The number of machine hours (to the nearest hour) budgeted to be worked was [14,850] hours.

$$\text{Budgeted hours} = \frac{\text{Budgeted overheads}}{\text{Budgeted overhead absorption rate}}$$

$$= \frac{\$475,200}{\$32}$$

$$= 14,850$$

4   The overhead for the period was [over] absorbed by $ [33,132]

	$
Overheads absorbed (16,566 × $32)	530,112
Actual overheads	496,980
Over-absorbed overheads	33,132

5   The machine hour absorption rate is $ [5] per hour.

$$\text{Overhead full rate} = \frac{\text{Budgeted overheads}}{\text{Budgeted machine hours}}$$

$$= \frac{\$85,000}{17,000}$$

$$= \$5$$

6   The overhead for the period was [under] absorbed by $ [4,250]

Overhead over-/(under)-absorbed = overhead absorbed – overhead incurred
                                 = (21,250 × $5) – $110,500
                                 = $(4,250)

7   [✓]   Charge overheads to products

8   [✓]   No under or over absorption occurred

Overhead absorption rate   = $165,000/55,000
                           = $3 per standard labour hour

	$
Overhead incurred	180,000
Overhead absorbed ($3 × 60,000 hrs)	180,000
Under/over absorption	nil

9   A   [$225,000]

     B   [Employees]

     C   [$36,000]

     D   [$150,000]

Workings

A   Total area occupied = 20,000 square metres

Apportionment to assembly department $= \dfrac{6,000}{20,000} \times \$750,000$

$= \$225,000$

C   Total number of employees = 350

Apportionment to assembly department $= \dfrac{210}{350} \times \$60,000$

$= \$36,000$

D   Total cost of equipment = $1,600,000

Apportionment of depreciation to machining department $= \dfrac{1,200,000}{1,600,000} \times \$200,000$

$= \$150,000$

10   At the end of the year, the overheads absorbed in the Assembly department were [under] absorbed by $ [100,000]

Workings

Assuming that the units are homogenous, we will use a rate per unit for overhead absorption.

Overhead absorption rate per unit   = $2,400,000/30,000

                                    = $80 per unit

Overheads absorbed = $80 × 35,000	$2,800,000
Overheads incurred	$2,900.000
Under-absorbed overhead	$100,000

8 Overhead costs – absorption costing V

1   B   Production overhead absorption rate   = $165,000/60,000
                                                           = $2.75 per machine hour

           Production overhead absorbed   = $2.75 × 55,000 hours
                                                           = $151,250

           Production overhead incurred   = $165,000

           Production overhead under absorbed   = $13,750

2   C

	$
Actual overhead incurred	23,592
Overhead under absorbed	(937)
Overhead absorbed during period	22,655

Overhead absorption rate per direct labour hour = $22,655/4,925
                                                     = $4.60

Number of direct labour hours budgeted = $25,760/$4.60
                                               = 5,600

3   B   Situation A is more likely to lead to over absorption, depending on the difference between the budgeted and actual production volume.

           Under absorption will not necessarily arise if production is lower than budgeted (C) because actual overhead incurred might also be lower than budgeted.

           Neither will under absorption definitely arise if actual overheads are higher than budgeted (D) because actual production might also be higher than budgeted.

4   The overhead absorption rate per call made was $ 1.50

	$
Actual overhead incurred	107,415
Overhead under recovered	(5,115)
Total overhead recovered by 68,200 calls made	102,300

Overhead absorption rate per call made   = $102,300/68,200
                                              = $1.50

5 The actual production overhead incurred during the period was $ | 36,792 |

	$
Production overhead absorbed (11,970 hours × $2.60)	31,122
Production overhead under absorbed	5,670
Production overhead incurred	36,792

6 D

	$
Overhead absorbed during period (101,235 hrs × $12.15)	1,230,005
Overhead incurred	807,033
Overhead over absorbed	422,972

7 D Production overhead absorption rate = $190,960/51,150

              = $3.73 per machine hour

	$
Production overhead absorbed (58,305 hrs × $3.73)	217,478
Production overhead incurred	194,350
Production overhead over absorbed	23,128

8 The production overhead absorption rate is $ | 73 |

Production overhead absorption rates are always based on the budgeted figures.

Absorption rate = $347,115/4,755

     = $73 per labour hour

9 D Production overhead absorption rate = $95,480/17,050

              = $5.60 per machine hour

	$
Production overhead absorbed (19,500 hrs × $5.60)	109,200
Production overhead incurred	99,820
Production overhead over absorbed	9,380

10 C Production overhead absorption rates are always based on the budgeted figures.

Absorption rate = $53,480/1,910

     = $28 per labour hour

9 Inventory valuation I

1 B Use of the LIFO inventory valuation method results in closing inventories being valued at the oldest prices. Since prices are rising, the oldest prices will be the lowest prices. Therefore the correct answer is B.

   If you chose option C (NIFO) you selected the method which would result in the highest inventory valuation of all, since NIFO uses the next price to be paid.

2 A With LIFO, if newer inventories cost more to buy from suppliers than older inventories, the costs of material issued and used will be higher. It follows that the cost of sales will be higher and the profit lower.

Closing inventories with LIFO will be priced at the purchase price of earlier items that were received into inventory. In a period of rising prices, this means that closing inventories will be valued at old, out-of-date and lower prices. Therefore the correct answer is A.

If you chose option B you were correct about the profits but your reasoning concerning the inventory values was wrong.

3 A FIFO uses the oldest prices in inventory to charge issues. If product costs were overstated then issue costs were unrepresentatively high compared with current prices. Current prices must therefore be lower than the older prices in inventory. The correct answer is therefore A.

If you chose option C or D your reasoning was the 'wrong way round'. Option B cannot be correct because if prices were unchanged there would be no problem with under or overstating costs and profits.

4 A Under FIFO, the items in inventory will be valued at the most recent purchase prices. Since inventory turnover is high the inventory prices are presumably close to current prices. Therefore the correct answer is A.

Option C applies if inventory is very old or LIFO is used. Option B relates to LIFO, and option D relates to the average price method.

Workings for both questions 5 and 6.

| | | FIFO | | | LIFO | | |
		Units	$/unit	Value $	Units	$/unit	Value $
Purchase	1/1	4,000	2.50	10,000	4,000	2.50	10,000
	31/1	1,000	2.00	2,000	1,000	2.00	2,000
		5,000		12,000	5,000		12,000
Sales	15/2	(3,000)	2.50	(7,500)	(1,000)	2.00	(2,000)
					(2,000)	2.50	(5,000)
		2,000		4,500	2,000		5,000
Purchase	28/2	1,500	2.50	3,750	1,500	2.50	3,750
		3,500		8,250	3,500		8,750
Sales	14/3	(500)	2.50	(1,250)	(500)	2.50	(1,250)
		3,000		7,000	3,000		7,500

5 C *See workings above.* If you selected the wrong option then check your workings carefully against the above table.

6 C *See workings above.* If you selected the wrong option then check your workings carefully against the above table.

7 D Each time a purchase is made at a different price, this changes the average price of the items held in inventory. If it is required to keep prices up to date, the average price must be re-calculated each time a purchase is made at a different price to the average price. Therefore the correct answer is D.

Option A is incorrect because the average price of remaining inventory items is not altered when an issue is made at the average price.

Re-calculating the average price at the end of each accounting period would not keep prices up to date. Therefore option B is incorrect.

If you selected option C you probably rushed in and did not read all the options before making your selection. If purchases are made at the same price as the average price of the items already held in inventory then there is no need to recalculate the average.

8   B

Date	Received	Issued	Balance	Total inventory value $	Unit cost $
1 June			100	500	5.00
3 June	300			1,440	4.80
			400	1,940	4.85 *
5 June		220	180	(1,067)	4.85
				873	4.85
12 June	170			884	5.20
			350	1,757	5.02 *
24 June		300		(1,506)	5.02
Closing inventory			50	251	5.02

* A new weighted average price is calculated every time there are receipts into inventory.

From the above records, it can be seen that the cost of material issued on 5 June was $1,067. Therefore the correct answer is B.

If you selected option A you used a unit rate of $4.80, ie the price of the latest goods received, rather than the average price of $4.85.

If you selected option C you used a simple average price of $4.90, rather than a weighted average price.

If you selected option D you used a unit rate of $5, ie the price of the oldest items in inventory.

9   C   From the table in solution 8, the closing inventory value is $251.

If you selected option A you took a periodic weighted average of all inventory at the month end, instead of recalculating the average every time there are receipts into inventory.

If you selected option B you calculated a simple average of all three available prices.

Option D would be the correct solution if the FIFO method of inventory valuation was used.

10   C

	FIFO		LIFO	
	$	$	$	$
Sales value $3 × 800		2,400		2,400
Less cost of sales:				
400 × $1.80	720			
400 × $2.10	840			
		1,560		
600 × $2.10			1,260	
200 × $1.80			360	
				1,620
Gross profit		840		780

If you selected option A you have interchanged the LIFO and FIFO calculations.

If you selected option B you priced all units at the first price of $1.80 for FIFO and all units at the latest price of $2.10 for LIFO. However, you must deal with the separate batches of units, taking account of how many were received at each price.

Option D shows the correct figures for cost of sales, but the question asked for the gross profit for each method.

10 Inventory valuation II

1   B $4,492

		Units	$
Opening inventory	300 × $25	300	7,500
Issue on 2 Jan	256 × $25	(250)	(6,250)
		50	1,250
Receipt on 12 Jan		400	10,300
		450	11,550
Issues on 21 Jan and 29 Jan			
(11,550/450) × (200 + 75)		(275)	(7,058)
		175	4,492

2   A   Profits would increase by $4,080.

Under the LIFO method the value of the issues would be:

(180 × $40) + (40 × $40) + (60 × $25) + (60 × $48) = $13,180

Date (June)	Receipts Units		Issues Units	Cost/unit $
1	300 240			25
8	220 40	0		40
15			180	
16			100	
21	120 60			48
25			60	
28	180			55

Under the FIFO method the value of the issues would be:

$(180 \times \$25) + (100 \times \$25) + (20 \times \$25) + (40 \times \$40) = \$9,100$

Date (June)	Receipts Units				Issues Units	Cost/unit $
1	~~300~~	~~120~~	~~20~~	0		25
8	~~220~~	180				40
15					180	
16					100	
21	~~120~~	60				48
25					60	
28	180					55

The difference between the values of issues = $\$13,180 - \$9,100$
                                            = $\$4,080$

Since the issues are valued at a lower cost, this increases the profit.

3   ☐ ✓ ☐   Product costs are understated and profits overstated

FIFO uses the price of the oldest items in inventory. When prices are rising this will be the items with the lowest prices. Consequently costs are lower and profits are higher.

4

Date of issue	Quantity issued Units	Valuation	$
25 May	1,700	$700 \times \$18.10$	12,670
		$800 \times \$17.20$	13,760
		$200 \times \$15.50$	3,100
			29,530

5   Using the FIFO method, the total value of the issues on 30 April is $ ⟦ 2,765 ⟧

Date	Receipts Units	Issues Units	Balance		$
1 April			275 @ $3.20		880
8 April	600		600 @ $3.00		1,800
15 April	400		400 @ $3.40		1,360
					4,040
30 April		900			$
		275 @ $3.20	=		880
		600 @ $3.00	=		1,800
		25 @ $3.40	=		85
					2,765

6 ☑ Falling

FIFO uses the oldest prices in inventory to charge issues. If product costs were overstated, then issue costs were unrepresentatively high compared with current prices. Current prices must therefore be lower than the older prices in inventory. Therefore prices were falling during the period.

7 Using the weighted average price method of inventory valuation, the total value of the components remaining in inventory on 23 March was $ 20,790

Average price of inventory on 23 March:

Units			$
2,400	×	$6	14,400
4,000	×	$6.20	24,800
2,000	×	$6.86	13,720
8,400			52,920

Average price per component = $52,920/8,400 = $6.30

Value of inventory on 23 March = (8,400 – 5,100) × $6.30
= $20,790

8 Using the FIFO method of inventory valuation, the total value of the components issued on 23 March was $ 31,140 (to the nearest $)

The FIFO method uses the price of the oldest batches first:

			$
2,400	×	$6	14,400
2,700	×	$6.20	16,740
5,100			31,140

9 Using the LIFO method of inventory valuation, the total value of the components issued on 23 March was $ 32,940

The LIFO method uses the price of the latest batches first:

			$
2,000	×	$6.86	13,720
3,100	×	$6.20	19,220
5,100			32,940

10 Using the LIFO method, the total value of the issues on 29 April was $ 14,880 (to the nearest $)

The prices of the latest units received are used first.

	Units	Price per unit $	Value of issues $
Units from 23 April	600	9.00	5,400
Units from 10 April	1,000	8.60	8,600
Units from opening inventory	100	8.80	880
	1,700		14,880

11 Breakeven analysis and limiting factor analysis I

1   D   Statement (i) can be correct when there are **bulk discounts** on larger quantities. For example, suppose there is a bulk purchase discount of 10% on items costing $10 each, for orders above 100,000 units.

	$
Cost of 100,000 = 100,000 × $10	1,000,000
Cost of, say, 110,000 = 110,000 × $10 × 90%	990,000
Incremental cost of 10,000 units	(10,000)

Statement (ii) is correct for **sales revenue** but **not for profit**.

Statement (iii) is correct. A direct cost is a cost that can be identified separately in a product cost, service cost or department cost. Direct costs can often be fixed costs, for example the salary of the manager of department A is a fixed, direct cost of that department.

Therefore the correct answer is D.

2   B   Breakeven point = $\dfrac{\text{Fixed costs}}{\text{Contribution per unit}}$ = $\dfrac{\$30,000}{\$(15-5)}$ = 3,000 units

If you selected option A you divided the fixed cost by the selling price, but remember that the selling price also has to cover the variable cost. Option C is the margin of safety, and if you selected option D you seem to have divided the fixed cost by the variable cost per unit.

3   A   Breakeven point = $\dfrac{\text{Fixed costs}}{\text{Contribution per unit}}$ = $\dfrac{\$96,000}{\$(12-8)}$ = 24,000 units

Budgeted sales	30,000 units
Margin of safety	6,000 units

Expressed as a % of budget = $\dfrac{6,000}{30,000}$ × 100% = 20%

If you selected option B you calculated the correct margin of safety in units, but you then expressed this as a percentage of the breakeven point. If you selected option C you divided the fixed cost by the selling price to determine the breakeven point, but the selling price also has to cover the variable cost. You should have been able to eliminate option D; the margin of safety expressed as a percentage must always be less than 100 per cent.

4   D   Breakeven point = $\dfrac{\text{Fixed costs}}{\text{Contribution per unit}}$

= $\dfrac{10,000 \times (\$4.00 + 0.80)}{(\$6.00 - (\$1.20 + \$0.40))}$ = $\dfrac{\$48,000}{\$4.40}$ = 10,909 units

If you selected option A you divided the fixed cost by the selling price, but the **selling price also has to cover the variable cost.** Option B ignores the selling costs, but these are costs that **must be covered before the breakeven point is reached**. Option C is the budgeted sales volume, which happens to be below the breakeven point.

5   D   Contribution required for target profit = fixed costs + profit
                                                 = \$48,000 + \$11,000
                                                 = \$59,000

÷ Contribution per unit (from qu 4) = \$4.40

∴ Sales units required = 13,409 units

If you selected option A you divided the required profit by the contribution per unit, but the fixed costs must be covered before any profit can be earned. If you selected option B you identified correctly the contribution required for the target profit, but you then divided by the selling price per unit instead of the contribution per unit. Option C ignores the selling costs, which must be covered before a profit can be earned.

6   C

	\$ per unit
New selling price (\$6 × 1.1)	6.60
New variable cost (\$1.20 × 1.1) + \$0.40	1.72
Revised contribution per unit	4.88
New fixed costs (\$40,000 × 1.25) + \$8,000	\$58,000

Revised breakeven point = $\dfrac{\$58,000}{\$4.88}$ = 11,885 units

If you selected option A you divided the fixed cost by the selling price, but the **selling price also has to cover the variable cost**. Option B fails to allow for the increase in variable production cost and option D increases all of the costs by the percentages given, rather than the production costs only.

7   A   Breakeven point = $\dfrac{\$48,000}{0.4}$ = \$120,000 sales value

Margin of safety (in \$) = \$140,000 – \$120,000 = \$20,000 sales value
Margin of safety (in units) = \$20,000 ÷ \$10 = 2,000 units

Option B is the breakeven point and option C is the actual sales in units. If you selected option D you calculated the margin of safety correctly as 20,000 but you misinterpreted the result as the sales **volume** instead of the sales **value**.

8   D   Breakeven quantity = $\dfrac{\text{Fixed costs}}{\text{Contribution per unit}}$

Since we do not know the contribution per unit, and we cannot determine it from the information available, it is not possible to calculate the breakeven point in terms of units. Therefore the correct answer is D.

We can determine the **value** of breakeven sales as \$90,000/0.4 = \$225,000, but this does not tell us the number of units required to break even. If you selected option C you probably performed this calculation.

9   A   Breakeven point $= \dfrac{\text{Fixed costs}}{\text{C/S ratio}} = \dfrac{\$76,800}{0.40} = \$192,000$

Actual sales	= $224,000
Margin of safety in terms of sales value	$32,000
÷ selling price per unit	÷ $16
Margin of safety in units	2,000

If you selected option B you calculated the breakeven point in units, but forgot to take the next step to calculate the margin of safety. Option C is the actual sales in units and D is the margin of safety in terms of sales value.

10   C   Contribution per unit = $90 – $40 = $50. The sale of 6,000 units just covers the annual fixed costs, therefore the fixed costs must be $50 × 6,000 = $300,000.

If you selected option A you calculated the correct contribution of $50 per unit, but you then divided the 6,000 by $50 instead of multiplying. Option B is the total annual variable cost and option D is the annual revenue.

---

12 Breakeven analysis and limiting factor analysis II

1   B   The profit/volume ratio (P/V ratio) is another term used to describe the contribution/sales ratio (C/S ratio)

$$\text{P/V ratio} = \dfrac{\text{Contribution per unit}}{\text{Selling price per unit}}$$

$$= \dfrac{\$(20 - 4 - 3 - 2 - 1)}{\$20} \times 100\% = 50\%$$

If you selected option A you calculated profit per unit as a percentage of the selling price per unit. Option C excludes the variable selling costs from the calculation of contribution per unit and option D excludes the variable production overhead cost, but **all variable costs must be deducted from the selling price to determine the contribution.**

2   C

	$
Target profit	6,000
Fixed costs (5,000 × $2)	10,000
Target contribution	16,000
Contribution per unit ($10 – $6)	$4
Units required to achieve target profit	4,000

If you selected option A you divided $6,000 target profit by the $4 contribution per unit, but **the fixed costs must be covered before any profit can be earned**. If you selected option B you divided by the selling price, but the variable costs must also be taken into account. If you selected option D you divided by the profit per unit instead of the contribution per unit, but the fixed costs are taken into account in the calculation of the target contribution.

3   B

Fixed costs ($10,000 × 120%)	$12,000
Units required now to break even (÷ $4 contribution)	3,000
Budgeted units of sales	5,000
Margin of safety (units) (5,000 − 3,000)	2,000

In percentage terms, margin of safety = $\dfrac{2,000}{5,000} \times 100\% = 40\%$

Option A increases the **variable** cost by 20% and option C increases the **activity** by 20%. If you selected option D you calculated the margin of safety as a percentage of the breakeven volume, but it is **usually expressed as a percentage of budgeted sales.**

4   A

Original budgeted profit:	$
Contribution (5,000 × $4)	20,000
Fixed costs	10,000
Profit	10,000

	$ per unit
New sales price ($10 × 1.20)	12.00
New variable cost ($6 × 1.12)	6.72
New contribution	5.28

Contribution required (as above)	$20,000
Sales volume now needed (÷ $5.28)	3,788 units

This is 1,212 units or 24.24% less than the original budgeted level of 5,000 units of sales.

If you selected option B you identified the correct percentage change but you misinterpreted it as a required increase. If you selected options C or D you took $6,000 as your figure for the original budgeted profit. However, the budgeted profit would be based on the budgeted level of activity of 5,000 units for the period.

5   B

	$
Total cost of 150,000 units (× $41.50)	6,225,000
Total cost of 100,000 units (× $47.50)	4,750,000
Variable cost of 50,000 units	1,475,000
Variable cost per unit	$29.50

Substituting:	$
Total cost of 100,000 units	4,750,000
Variable cost of 100,000 units (× $29.50)	2,950,000
Fixed costs	1,800,000

∴ Breakeven point = $\dfrac{\$1,800,000}{\$(49.50 - 29.50)}$ = 90,000 units

If you selected option A you divided the fixed cost by the unit selling price, but the variable costs must also be taken into account. If you selected option C you assumed that the production overheads and the marketing and administration costs were wholly fixed. In fact the marketing costs are the only wholly fixed costs. You can test this by multiplying the unit rate by the output volume at each level of activity. If you selected option D you divided the fixed cost by the profit per unit instead of the contribution per unit.

6 A Currently weekly contribution = 12% × $280,000 = $33,600

	$
Extra contribution from 5% increase in sales = 5% × $33,600	1,680
Loss on product Z each week 3,000 × $(1.90 – 2.20 – 0.15)	(1,350)
Weekly increase in profit	330

If you selected option B you forgot to allow for the variable cost of distributing the 3,000 units of Z. Option C is based on a five per cent increase in **revenue** from the other products; however extra variable costs will be incurred, therefore the gain will be a five per cent increase in **contribution**. If you selected option D you made no allowance for the variable costs of either product Z or the extra sales of other products.

7 C Contribution at level of activity x = sales value less variable costs, which is indicated by distance C. Distance A indicates the profit at activity x, B indicates the fixed costs and D indicates the margin of safety in terms of sales value.

8 B Statement (i) is incorrect. The starting point of the profit-volume line is the point on the y axis representing the loss at zero activity, which is the fixed cost incurred.

Statement (ii) is correct. The point where the profit-volume line crosses the x-axis is the point of zero profit and zero loss, ie the breakeven point.

Statement (iii) is correct. The profit can be read from the y axis at any point beyond the breakeven point.

9 C Above the breakeven point, contribution = fixed costs + profit, therefore distance C indicates the contribution at level of activity L.

Distance A indicates the profit at level of activity L, B indicates the fixed costs and D indicates the margin of safety.

10 B Statement (i) is correct. The line which passes through the origin indicates the sales revenue at various levels of activity. The sales revenue is for 10,000 units therefore the selling price is $10 per unit.

Statement (ii) is incorrect. The sloping line which intercepts the vertical axis at $30,000 shows the total cost at various levels of activity. The **total cost** for 10,000 units is $80,000. The fixed costs of $30,000 (the cost at zero activity) must be subtracted from this to derive the variable cost of 10,000 units, which is $50,000. Therefore the variable cost per unit is $5.

Statement (iii) is correct. The fixed cost is the cost incurred at zero activity and is shown as a horizontal line at $30,000.

Statement (iv) is incorrect. The profit for 10,000 units is the difference between the sales value ($100,000) and the total cost ($80,000) which amounts to $20,000.

Therefore the correct answer is B.

13 Breakeven analysis and limiting factor analysis III

1   [✓] Fixed cost

The profit line on a profit/volume chart cuts the y-axis at the point representing **the loss incurred at zero activity.** This is the fixed cost which must be paid **even if no units are sold.**

2   [✓] Profit volume chart

The chart shows a single line depicting **the profit for a range of levels of activity.** Therefore it is a profit volume chart.

All of the other options would depict cost lines rather than profit lines, and the first two options would also include a sales revenue line.

3   The direct wages cost for the period was $ [64,224]

Contribution earned for the period   = $48,000 + $5,520
                                                         = $53,520
∴ Sales value = $53,520/0.2   = $267,600
Variable cost = $(267,600 − 53,520)   = $214,080
Direct wages cost = $214,080 × 0.3   = $64,224

4   First: product [K]

     Second: product [L]

     Third: product [J]

	Product J $ per unit	Product K $ per unit	Product L $ per unit
Selling price	140	122	134
Variable cost	106	86	77
Contribution	34	36	57
Kg of material	11	7	13
Contribution per kg	$3.09	$5.14	$4.39
Ranking	3	1	2

5   The profit/volume ratio for product Q is [25] % (to the nearest percent)

The profit/volume ratio (P/V ratio) is another term used to describe the contribution/sales ratio (C/S ratio).

$$P/V\ ratio = \frac{Contribution\ per\ unit}{Selling\ price\ per\ unit}$$

$$= \frac{\$(60 - 14 - 12 - 19)}{\$60} \times 100\%$$

$$= 25\%$$

6   ☑ An increase in the direct material cost per unit

      ☑ An increase in the trade discount per unit sold

      ☑ An increase in the royalty payable per unit

All of these situations would **reduce the contribution per unit,** thus reducing the slope of the line and increasing the breakeven point.

An increase in the fixed cost would not affect the slope of the line, but it would **lower the point at which the line cuts the vertical axis.**

7   ☑ The product incurs fixed costs of $60,000 per period

      ☑ The product earns a contribution of $12 per unit

The fixed costs are depicted by the point where the profit line cuts the vertical axis, ie the loss at zero activity, $60,000.

The unit contribution can be deduced as follows.

$$\text{Breakeven point} = \frac{\text{fixed costs}}{\text{contribution per unit}}$$

$$\therefore 5,000 = \frac{\$60,000}{\text{contribution per unit}}$$

Contribution per unit = $60,000/5,000 = $12

In order to deduce the selling price we would need to know the variable cost per unit.

8   ☑ The sales revenue line passes through the origin

      ☑ The total cost line cuts the vertical axis at the point which is equal to the period fixed costs.

The first statement is incorrect because the fixed costs are depicted by a straight line parallel to the **horizontal** axis.

The last statement is incorrect because the breakeven point is the point where the sales revenue line crosses the **total cost line.**

9   If the selling price and variable cost per unit increase by 10% and 7% respectively, the sales volume will need to ⟨decrease⟩ to ⟨16,515⟩ units in order to achieve the original budgeted profit for the period.

Current contribution per unit = $(108 − 73) = $35

$$\text{Current sales volume} = \frac{\$(196,000 + 476,000)}{\$35}$$

$$= 19,200 \text{ units}$$

Revised contribution per unit:

	$ per unit
Selling price $108 × 1.10	118.80
Variable cost $73 × 1.07	(78.11)
Contribution	40.69

$$\text{Required sales volume} = \frac{\$(196,000 + 476,000)}{\$40.69}$$

$$= 16,515 \text{ units}$$

10   The limiting factor(s) next period will be:

✓ Material

	Quantity per unit	Quantity required	Quantity available
Material ($72 ÷ $8)	9 litres (× 2,000)	18,000 litres	16,000 litres
Labour ($49 ÷ $7)	7 hours (× 2,000)	14,000 hours	15,000 hours

14 Standard costing and variance analysis I

1   D   Required liquid input = 2 litres × $\dfrac{100}{70}$ = 2.86 litres

Standard cost of liquid input = 2.86 × $1.20 = $3.43 (to the nearest cent)

If you selected option A you made no allowance for spillage and evaporation. Option B is the figure for the quantity of material input, not its cost. If you selected option C you simply added an extra 30 per cent to the finished volume. However, the wastage is 30 per cent of the liquid **input**, not 30 per cent of output.

2   D   Hours of labour required per unit = 9 active hours × $\dfrac{100}{90}$ = 10 labour hours

Labour cost per unit = 10 hours × $4 = $40

Option A is the figure for the number of labour hours required, not their cost. Option B is the basic labour cost, with no allowance for idle time. Option C simply adds an extra ten per cent to the active labour hours, but idle time is ten per cent of the **total** hours worked.

3   C   A standard hour is the quantity of output achievable, at standard performance, in an hour. It is often used to measure total output when **dissimilar units** are made.

The situation described in option A is **ideal operating conditions,** and option B describes a typical situation for many organisations that are involved in mass production.

4   C

	Units produced		Standard hours per unit		Standard hours produced
Sheds	270	×	1.2	=	324
Tables	80	×	0.7	=	56
Workbenches	140	×	1.0	=	140
					520

Option A is the total number of units produced, but there is very little meaning in adding together such **dissimilar units**. Option B is the actual hours worked, which is **not a measure of output**. If you selected option D you multiplied the total units by the combined time for one unit of each product. This would only be applicable if the products were manufactured in **batches**, and then we would have to express the output in terms of batches, rather than in terms of total units produced.

5   A   Standard material cost per unit = $42,000 ÷ $7,000 units = $6 per unit

	$
Standard direct material cost = 7,200 units × $6 per unit	43,200
Actual direct material cost	42,912
Total direct material cost variance	288 (F)

If you selected option B you calculated the variance correctly but misinterpreted it as adverse. Actual cost was less than the standard cost, therefore the variance is favourable. Option C is the difference between the standard cost for 7,000 units and the actual cost for 7,200 units. This is not a valid comparison of cost **for control purposes** because of the **difference in output volumes**. Option D suffers from a similar problem; it compares the standard cost for 7,200 units with the standard cost for 7,000 units.

6   B

	$
Material price variance	
5,000 litres did cost	16,000
But should have cost (× $3)	15,000
	1,000 (A)
Material usage variance	
1,270 units did use	5,000 litres
But should have used (× 4 litres)	5,080 litres
Usage variance in litres	80 (F)
× standard cost per litre	×$3
	240 (F)

If you selected options A or C you calculated the money values of the variances correctly but misinterpreted their direction.

If you selected option D you valued the usage variance in litres at the actual cost per litre instead of the standard cost per litre.

7　C　**Material price variance**

	$
8,200 kg did cost	6,888
but should have cost (× $0.80)	6,560
	328 (A)

If you selected option A or B you based your calculations on the materials issued to production. However, the material inventory account is **maintained at standard cost**, therefore the material price variance is **calculated when the materials are purchased**. If you selected option D you calculated the size of the variance correctly but you misinterpreted it as favourable.

8　B　**Material usage variance**

870 units did use	7,150 kg
but should have used (× 8kg)	6,960 kg
Usage variance in kg	190(A)
× standard cost per kg	× $0.80
	152 (A)

If you selected option A you calculated the size of the variance correctly but you misinterpreted it as favourable. If you selected option C you evaluated the usage variance in kg at the actual price per kg, instead of the standard price per kg. Option D bases the calculation of standard usage on the budgeted production of 850 units. This is not comparing like with like.

9　C　Purchase price variance per unit purchased = $\dfrac{\$544}{6,800}$ = 8c/unit (A)

∴ Actual purchase price per unit = 8c + 85c = 93c/unit

If you selected option A or D you calculated the purchase price variance per unit based on the standard allowance, rather than the actual purchase quantity.

If you selected option B you subtracted the price variance per unit from the standard price, but an adverse variance means that the actual price is higher than the standard.

10　B　Total standard cost of 11,280 kgs = $46,248
∴ Standard cost per kg = $46,248/11,280 = $4.10 per kg
Usage variance in kgs = 492/4.10 = 120 kgs
11,280 kgs were used. There was an adverse usage variance of 120 kgs and so (11,280 − 120) kgs = 11,160 kgs should have been used.

If you selected optn A you deducted the money value of the usage variance from the actual quantity used. You were correct to deduct the variance, but you should first have **converted it to a quantity of material**.

Option C is the actual material used, which cannot be the same as standard because there is a usage variance. If you selected option D you added the usage variance to the actual usage, instead of subtracting it. The variance is adverse, therefore standard usage must be lower than actual usage.

15 Standard costing and variance analysis II

1   D   Standard labour cost per unit = $39,360 ÷ 9,840 units = $4 per unit

	$
Standard direct labour cost for 9,600 units (× $4)	38,400
Actual direct labour cost	43,200
Total direct labour cost variance	4,800 (A)

If you selected option A you compared the standard cost for 9,600 units with the standard cost for 9,840 units. This shows the **volume effect** of the change in output but it is not the total direct labour cost variance. Option B is the difference between the standard cost for 9,840 units and the actual cost for 9,600 units. This is not a valid comparison for **control purposes** because of the **different output volumes**. If you selected option C you calculated the variance correctly but misinterpreted it as favourable.

2   B

	$
11,700 hrs should cost (× $6.40)	74,880
but did cost	64,150
Labour rate variance	10,730 (F)

2,300 units should take (× 4.5 hrs)	10,350 hrs
but did take	11,700 hrs
Variance in hrs	1,350 hrs (A)
× standard rate per hr	× $6.40
Labour efficiency variance	$8,640 (A)

If you selected options A or C you calculated the money values of the variances correctly but misinterpreted their direction.

If you selected option D you valued the efficiency variance in hours at the actual rate per hour instead of the standard rate per hour.

3   B

	$
13,450 hours should have cost (× $6)	80,700
but did cost	79,893
Direct labour rate variance	807 (F)

3,350 units should have taken (× 4 hrs)	13,400 hrs
but did take	13,450 hrs
Variance in hrs	50 hrs (A)
× standard rate per hour	× $6
Direct labour efficiency variance	$300 (A)

If you selected option A you valued the efficiency variance in hours at the actual rate per hour instead of the standard rate per hour.

If you selected option C you based your calculation of the efficiency variance on the budgeted output instead of the actual output.

If you selected option D you calculated the correct money values of the variances but you misinterpreted their direction.

4   C

	$
2,300 hours should have cost (× $7)	16,100
but did cost	18,600
Rate variance	2,500 (A)

Option A is the total direct labour cost variance. If you selected option B you calculated the correct money value of the variance but you misinterpreted its direction. If you selected option D you based your calculation on the 2,200 hours worked, but **2,300 hours were paid for** and these hours should be the basis for the calculation of the rate variance.

5   D

260 units should have taken (× 10 hrs)	2,600 hrs
but took (active hours)	2,200 hrs
Efficiency variance in hours	400 hrs (F)
× standard rate per hour	× $7
Efficiency variance in $	$2,800 (F)

Option A is the total direct labour cost variance. If you selected option B you based your calculations on the 2,300 hours paid for; but efficiency measures should be based on the **active hours only**, ie 2,200 hours.

If you selected option C you calculated the correct money value of the variance but you misinterpreted its direction.

6   B   Idle time hours (2,300 – 2,200) × standard rate per hour = 100 hrs × $7
                                                 = $700 (A)

If you selected option A you calculated the correct money value of the variance but you misinterpreted its direction. The **idle time variance is always adverse**.

If you selected option C or D you evaluated the idle time at the actual hourly rate instead of the standard hourly rate.

7   B   Budgeted direct labour cost for September = $117,600
        Budgeted direct labour hours = (3,350 + 150 units) × 4 = 14,000 hours
        Standard direct labour rate = $8.40 per hour

	$
13,450 hours should have cost (× $8.40)	112,980
But did cost	111,850
Direct labour rate variance	1,130 (F)

Option A is the total direct labour cost variance.

If you selected option C you calculated the correct money value of the variance but you misinterpreted its direction.

Option D is a fixed budget comparison of the budgeted direct labour cost of 3,500 units with the actual direct labour cost of 3,350 units.

8   B

3,350 units should have taken (× 4)	13,400 hrs
But did take	13,450 hrs
Direct labour efficiency variance in hrs	50 (A)
× standard rate per hour	× 8.40
Direct labour efficiency variance (in $)	420 (A)

If you selected option A you valued the labour efficiency in hours at the actual rate instead of the standard rate.

If you selected option C you calculated the correct money value of the variance but you misinterpreted its direction.

Option D is the total direct labour cost variance.

9   D

Production should have taken	X hours
but did take	17,500 hours
Variance in hours	X – 17,500 hours(F)
× standard rate per hour	× $6.50
Variance in $	$7,800 (F)

$\therefore 6.5(X - 17,500) = 7,800$

$X - 17,500 = 1,200$
$X = 18,700$

Option A is the efficiency variance in terms of hours, and option C is the actual hours worked.

If you selected option B you treated the efficiency variance as adverse instead of favourable.

10   C   Let x = the number of hours 12,250 units should have taken

12,250 units should have taken	X hrs
but did take	41,000 hrs
Labour efficiency variance (in hrs)	X – 41,000 hrs

Labour efficiency variance (in $) = $11,250 (F)

$\therefore$ Labour efficiency variance (in hrs) = $\dfrac{\$11{,}250\ (F)}{\$6}$

= 1,875 (F)

$\therefore$ 1,875 hrs = (x – 41,000) hrs

$\therefore$ standard hours for 12,250 units =   41,000 + 1,875

=   42,875 hrs

$\therefore$ Standard hours per unit = $\dfrac{42{,}875\ \text{hrs}}{12{,}250\ \text{units}}$

=   3.50 hrs

If you selected option A you treated the efficiency variance as adverse. Option B is the actual hours taken per unit and option D is the figure for the standard wage rate per hour.

16 Standard costing and variance analysis III

1 B Standard variable overhead cost per unit = $3,120 ÷ 520 units
                                                = $6 per unit

	$
Standard variable overhead cost for 560 units (× $6)	3,360
Actual variable overhead cost	4,032
	672 (A)

If you selected option A you compared the standard cost for 560 units with the standard cost for 520 units. This indicates the **volume effect** of the change in output but it is not the total variable production overhead cost variance.

If you selected option C you calculated the correct money value of the variance but you misinterpreted its direction.

Option D is the difference between the standard cost for 520 units and the actual cost for 560 units. This is not a valid comparison for **control purposes** because of the **different output volumes**.

2 A Standard variable production overhead cost per hour = $3,120/1,560
                                                          = $2

	$
2,240 hours of variable production overhead should cost (× $2)	4,480
But did cost	4,032
	448 (F)

If you selected option B you calculated the correct money value of the variance but you misinterpreted its direction. Option C is the variable production overhead total variance. If you selected option D you made the same error as for option D in question 1.

3 B Standard time allowed for one unit = 1,560 hours ÷ 520 units
                                          = 3 hours

560 units should take (× 3 hours)	1,680 hours
But did take	2,240 hours
Efficiency variance in hours	560 hours (A)
× standard variable production overhead per hr	× $2 (from answer 2)
	$1,120 (A)

If you selected option A you valued the efficiency variance in hours at the actual variable production overhead rate per hour.

If you selected option C you calculated the correct money value of the variance but you misinterpreted its direction.

If you selected option D you based your calculation on the difference between the original budgeted hours for 520 units and the actual hours worked for 560 units. This is **not comparing like with like.**

4   B

		$
1,660 hours of variable production overhead should cost (× $1.70)		2,822
But did cost		2,950
		128 (A)

If you selected option A you based your expenditure allowance on all of the labour hours worked. However, it is usually assumed that **variable overheads are incurred during active working hours**, but are not incurred during idle time.

If you selected option C you calculated the correct money value of the variance but you misinterpreted its direction.

Option D is the variable production overhead total variance.

5   B

400 units of Product B should take (× 4 hours)	1,600 hours
But did take (active hours)	1,660 hours
Efficiency variance in hours	60 hours (A)
× standard rate per hour	× $1.70
	102 (A)

If you selected option A you calculated the correct money value of the variance but you misinterpreted its direction.

If you selected option C you valued the efficiency variance in hours at the actual variable production overhead rate per hour. Option D bases the calculation on all of the hours worked, instead of only the **active hours**.

6   B   The correct labour efficiency variance is calculated as follows, comparing budgeted hours with actual hours spent for the production achieved.

((11,000 units × 0.75 hrs) – 8,000 hrs) × $20 per hr = $5,000 favourable

7   C   The correct variable overhead variance is calculated by comparing the budgeted variable overheads per labour hour worked with the actual variable overheads incurred during the month.

(8000 hours × $15 per labour hour – $132,000) = $12,000 Adverse

8   D   The direct labour rate variance for April is calculated as:

The actual direct labour rate paid is calculated as:

$$\frac{\text{Direct labour cost}}{\text{Direct labour hours}} = \frac{\$336,000}{24,000 \text{ hours}} = \$14 \text{ per hour}$$

The direct labour rate variance is calculated as:

Actual hours worked × [standard rate per hour – actual rate per hour] = 24,000 hours × [$15 – $14] = $24,000 favourable.

The correct answer is D

9   A   The variable overhead efficiency variance for April is:

[Standard labour hours for production achieved – Actual labour hours] × standard variable overhead rate = [(11,000 units × 2 hours per unit) – 24,000 hours] × $6 = $12,000 adverse.

10 A **Statement 1** is consistent with the variances because a fairly large favourable price variance arose at the same time as an adverse usage variance, which could have been caused by the higher wastage.

Statement 2 is consistent with the variances because the trend is towards higher percentage variances. Even if these variances are still within any control limits set by management, the persistent trend is probably worthy of investigation.

Statement 3 is not consistent with the variances, because more effective use of material should produce a favourable usage variance.

17 Standard costing and variance analysis IV

1 B Statement (i) is consistent with an adverse material price variance. Higher quality material is likely to cost more. Statement (ii) is consistent with an adverse material price variance. Removal of bulk discounts would result in a higher material price.

Statement (iii) is not consistent with an adverse material price variance. **Favourable** variances would result if the standard was set too high.

Therefore the correct answer is B.

2 C Statement (i) is not consistent with a favourable labour efficiency variance. Employees of a lower skill level are likely to work less efficiently, resulting in an **adverse efficiency variance**.

Statement (ii) is consistent with a favourable labour efficiency variance. **Time would be saved in processing** if the material was easier to process.

Statement (iii) is consistent with a favourable labour efficiency variance. **Time would be saved in processing** if working methods were improved.

Therefore the correct answer is C.

3 A A wage rate increase could result in an **adverse direct labour rate variance**, it is not necessarily a cause of an idle time variance. Therefore reason A is not consistent with the variance and the correct answer is A.

Options B, C and D could all result in a loss of active production time.

4 B Statement (i) is consistent with a favourable direct material usage variance, because higher quality material may lead to **lower wastage.**

Statement (ii) is consistent with a favourable direct material usage variance, because lower losses would **reduce material usage**.

Statement (iii) is not consistent with a favourable direct material usage variance. If activity levels were lower than budget this would not affect the materials used **per unit** of production. The usage variance would be calculated based on the **standard usage for the actual output.**

5 A All of the statements are consistent with a favourable labour rate variance. Therefore the correct answer is A.

Employees of a lower grade (statement (i)) are likely to be paid a **lower hourly rate**.
An unrealistically high standard (statement (ii)) would result in **favourable rate variances**.
If a pay increase did not occur (statement (iii)) this would lead to **savings in labour rates**.

6

Variance	Favourable	Adverse
(a) Material price	Unforeseen discounts received	
(b) Material usage		Defective material
(c) Labour rate		Wage rate increase

7

Variance	Favourable	Adverse
(a) Labour efficiency		Lack of training of production workers
(b) Variable overhead expenditure	More economical use of non-material resources	
(c) Idle time		Machine breakdown

8   B   Statement (i) is consistent with a favourable materials price variance. In a period of inflation, and with a **mid-year standard price**, reported variances early in the year would probably be favourable.

Statement (ii) is consistent with a favourable materials price variance. Bulk purchase discounts may **reduce the unit price paid for materials.**

Statement (iii) is not consistent with a favourable materials price variance. Early settlement discounts are a **financial matter** and **do not affect the actual purchase price of materials.**

9   C   The direct material price variance is $2,000 adverse ($800 adverse – $1,200 favourable).

Both statements are consistent with the variances, because both situations would lead to a **higher price** for materials (adverse material price variance) and **lower usage** (favourable material usage variance). Therefore the correct answer is C.

10   D   The interpretation of a variable production overhead efficiency variance is **the same as that for a direct labour efficiency variance**. Statements (i) and (iii) would both result in a slower output rate and therefore adverse efficiency variances.

Statement (ii) is not consistent with an adverse variable overhead efficiency variance. It is usually assumed that **variable overheads are incurred during active working hours only**. Therefore idle time would not cause overspending on variable production overhead.

Therefore the correct answer is D.

BPP
LEARNING MEDIA

18 Standard costing and variance analysis V

1   Standard hours per unit = ☐ 7 ☐

Actual hours worked $= \dfrac{\$294{,}800}{\$8}$

$= 36{,}850$ hours

Adverse efficiency variance, in hours $= \dfrac{\$26{,}000}{\$8}$

$= 3{,}250$ hours

∴ Standard hours for 4,800 units $= 36{,}850 - 3{,}250$

$= 33{,}600$ hours

Standard hours per unit $= \dfrac{33{,}600}{4{,}800}$

$= 7$ hours

2   The standard price per kg was $ ☐ 4.50 ☐ (to the nearest cent)

Standard cost of material purchased − Actual cost of material purchased = Price variance

Standard cost $= \$32{,}195 - \$1{,}370$

$= \$30{,}825$

Standard price per kg $= \dfrac{\$30{,}825}{6{,}850}$

$= \$4.50$

3

	Favourable	Adverse
Material price $ ☐ 4,860 ☐ (to the nearest $)	✓	
Material usage $ ☐ 1,040 ☐ (to the nearest $)		✓

Direct materials price variance

	$
9,720 kg should have cost (× $13)	126,360
but did cost	121,500
	4,860 (F)

Direct materials usage variance

	$
4,820 units should have used (× 2 kg)	9,640 kg
but did use	9,720 kg
Materials usage variance in kg	80 kg (A)
× standard usage per kg	$13
Materials usage variance (in $)	$1,040 (A)

4

		Favourable	Adverse
Labour rate $	3,160		✓
Labour efficiency $	424	✓	

Direct labour rate variance

	$
15,800 hrs of labour should have cost (× $4)	63,200
but did cost	66,360
	3,160 (A)

Direct labour efficiency variance

	$
4,820 units should have taken (× 3.3 hrs)	15,906 hrs
but did take	15,800 hrs
Labour efficiency variance in hrs	106 hrs (F)
× standard rate per hour	× $4
Labour efficiency variance in $	424 (F)

5   Idle time variance was $ 1,400 adverse/~~favourable~~

Idle time variance   = 200 idle hours × $7 standard labour rate per hour
                     = $1,400 (A)

6

		Favourable	Adverse
The direct labour rate variance for June was $	1,200	✓	

	$
2,400 hours should have cost (× $9)	21,600
but did cost	20,400
Direct labour rate variance	1,200 (F)

7

		Favourable	Adverse
The direct labour efficiency variance for June was $	1,800		✓

Standard hours per unit of production = $18/$9 = 2 hours

1,100 units should have taken (× 2 hours)	2,200 hours
but did take	2,400 hours
Efficiency variance in hours	200 hours (A)
× standard rate per hour	× $9
Efficiency variance in $	$1,800 (A)

8   ✓ Variable overhead efficiency variance

✓ Variable overhead expenditure variance

✓ Fixed overhead expenditure variance

The only fixed overhead variance in a standard marginal costing system is the fixed overhead expenditure variance. A fixed overhead volume variance cannot arise in a standard marginal costing system. It represents the under or over full of fixed overheads caused by a change in the production volume. Since fixed overhead is not absorbed into production costs in a marginal costing system, this situation cannot arise.

9

	Favourable	Adverse
The ingredients usage variance for May was $ 756		✓

Standard ingredient usage per unit = $14/$7 = 2 litres

856 units produced should have used (× 2 litres)	1,712 litres
but did use	1,820 litres
Usage variance in litres	108 litres (A)
× standard price per litre	× $7
Ingredient usage variance in $	$756 (A)

10

	Favourable	Adverse
The ingredients usage variance for May was $ 364	✓	

	$
1,820 litres should cost (× $7)	12,740
but did cost	12,376
Ingredients price variance	364 (F)

19 Standard costing and variance analysis VI

1

	$
Actual sales at actual prices	204,120
Actual sales at standard prices (× $^{100}/_{108}$)	189,000
Standard sales	180,000
Increase in sales at standard prices	9,000

Percentage increase in sales = $9,000/$180,000 = 5 % increase

2 Sales volume variance in a marginal costing system = increase in standard contribution resulting from the higher level of sales.

Increase in sales volume = 5% (see answer to (1) for working)

∴ Increase in standard contribution = 5% × $60,000 = $3,000

	Favourable	Adverse
∴ Variance = $ 3,000	✓	

3

	Favourable	Adverse
The variable production overhead expenditure variance for last period is $ 2,990		✓

Standard variable production overhead cost per hour = $\frac{\$13,475}{3,850}$ = $3.50

	$
2,990 hours of variable production overhead should cost (× $3.50)	10,465
but did cost	13,455
Variable production overhead expenditure variance	2,990 (A)

	Favourable	Adverse
4 The ingredient price variance for June was $ [72]	[ ]	[✓]

	$
350 litres should have cost (× $14)	4,900
but did cost	4,972
Ingredient price variance	72 (A)

5   The sales price variance was $ [1,200] favourable/~~adverse.~~

The sales volume variance was $ [900] ~~favourable~~/adverse.

	$
200 units should sell for (× $70)	14,000
but did sell for	15,200
Sales price variance	1,200 (F)

The budgeted contribution per unit = $\dfrac{\text{budgeted monthly contribution}}{\text{budgeted monthly sales volume}}$

$$= \frac{\$6,900}{230} = \$30 \text{ per unit}$$

Budgeted sales volume	230 units
Actual sales volume	200 units
Sales volume variance in units	30 units (A)
× standard contribution per unit	× $30
Sales volume contribution variance	$900 (A)

6   A

	$
Sales revenue should have been (521 × $300)	156,300
but was (521 × $287)	149,527
Sales price variance	6,773 (A)

7   A   Budgeted C/S ratio = 30%

∴ Budgeted contribution = 30% × budgeted selling price

= 30% × $300

= $90

Sales volume should have been	500 units
but was	521 units
Sales volume variance in units	21 units (F)
× standard contribution per unit	× $90
Sales volume contribution variance	$1,890 (F)

8   ☑ A personnel manager

A personnel manager would usually keep information concerning the expected rates of pay for employees with a given level of experience and skill.

9   His gross pay for the day will be $ 54 (to the nearest $)

	Hours
Standard time for 50 units (× 12/60)	10
Actual time taken	8
Time saved	2
	$
Bonus = 50% × 2 hours saved × $6 =	6
Basic daily pay = 8 hours × $6 =	48
Total gross pay	54

10   In a week when he produces 28 units, his gross wage will be $ 484.70 (to the nearest cent)

	$
Piecework earnings:	
1-25 units = 25 × $2.30	57.50
26-28 units = 3 × $2.40	7.20
Total piecework earnings	64.70
Guaranteed weekly wage	420.00
Gross wage	484.70

20 Budgeting I

1   B   **Coordination** (i) is an objective of budgeting. Budgets help to ensure that the **activities of all parts of the organisation are coordinated towards a single plan.**

Communication (ii) is an objective of budgeting. The budgetary planning process **communicates targets** to the managers responsible for achieving them, and it should also provide a **mechanism for junior managers to communicate to more senior staff** their estimates of what may be achievable in their part of the business.

Expansion (iii) is not in itself an objective of budgeting. Although a budget may be set **within a framework of expansion plans**, it is perfectly possible for an organisation to **plan for a reduction in activity.**

Resource allocation (iv) is an objective of budgeting. Most organisations face a situation of **limited resources** and an objective of the budgeting process is to ensure that these resources are allocated among budget centres in the most efficient way.

2   B   The production cost budget would not be contained in a budget manual. The budget manual provides **guidelines and information about the budget process**; the production cost budget is part of the result of the budgetary planning process.

A timetable (option A), an organisation chart (option C) and specimen budgetary control reports (option D) are all useful information about the budget process and would therefore usually be contained in the budget manual.

3   B   The **master budget** is the summary budget into which all subsidiary budgets are consolidated. It usually comprises the **budgeted income statement**, **budgeted balance sheet** and **budgeted cash flow statement**.

The master budget is used **in conjunction with the supporting subsidiary budgets**, to plan and control activities. The subsidiary budgets are not in themselves a part of the master budget. Therefore option D is not correct.

4   D   The **principal budget factor** is the factor which limits the activities of an organisation.

Although cash and profit are affected by the level of sales (options B and C), sales is not the only factor which determines the level of cash and profit.

5   D   A functional budget is a budget prepared for a particular function or department. A cash budget is **the cash result of the planning decisions included in all the functional budgets**. It is not a functional budget itself. Therefore the correct answer is D.

The production budget (option A), the distribution cost budget (option B) and the selling cost budget (option C) are all prepared for specific functions, therefore they are functional budgets.

6   D   The annual budget is set **within the framework of the long-term plan.** It acts as the first step towards the **achievement of the organisation's long-term objectives.** Therefore the long term objectives must be established before any of the other budget tasks can be undertaken and the correct answer is D.

The principal budget factor (option A) may be affected by the organisation's long-term objectives. Although it must be identified before the other budgets can be prepared, it is not the first task in the list provided.

Since sales are often the limiting factor the sales demand (option B) must be established early in the planning process. However, the establishment of the long-term objectives must come first because, for example, the objectives may affect the decision about which markets to enter.

The predetermined overhead absorption rate (option C) cannot be calculated until the level of activity is known, which in turn will be affected by the principal budget factor and the long-term objectives.

7   B   Since there are no production resource limitations, sales would be the principal budget factor and the sales budget (2) would be prepared first. Budgeted inventory changes included in the finished goods inventory budget (4) would then indicate the required production for the production budget (5). This would lead to the calculation of the material usage (1) which would then be adjusted for the budgeted change in material inventory (6) to determine the required level of budgeted material purchases (3).Therefore the correct answer is B.

If you selected option A you began with production as the principal budget factor. However, there are no production resource limitations so production output is not a limiting factor. If you selected option C or D you correctly identified sales as the principal budget factor, but you did not identify the correct flow through the inventory adjustments to determine the required production and material purchases.

8   C   Since there are no production resource limitations, sales would be the principal budget factor therefore the sales budget must be prepared before the production budget (i). The budgeted change in finished goods inventory (iii) would then indicate the required volume for the production budget. Therefore the correct answer is C.

Item (ii), the material purchases, would be information derived **from** the production budget after adjusting for material inventory changes, and item (iv), the standard direct labour cost per unit, would be required for the **production cost budget**, but not for the production budget, which is **expressed in volume terms.**

9   B   Any opening inventory available at the beginning of a period will **reduce** the additional quantity required from production in order to satisfy a given sales volume. Any closing inventory required at the end of a period will **increase** the quantity required from production in order to satisfy sales and leave a sufficient volume in inventory. Therefore we need to **deduct** the opening inventory and **add** the required closing inventory.

10   C   Once the material usage budget has been prepared, based on the budgeted production volume, the usage is adjusted for the budgeted change in materials inventories in order to determine the required budgeted purchases. If purchases exceed production requirements this means that raw material inventories are being increased, and the correct answer is C.

Option A is incorrect because wastage would have been allowed for in determining the material usage budget. Option B is incorrect because a budgeted increase in finished goods inventory would have been allowed for in determining the production budget and hence the material usage budget.

21 Budgeting II

1   C

	Units
Required for sales	24,000
Required to increase inventory (2,000 × 0.25)	500
	24,500

If you selected option A you subtracted the change in inventory from the budgeted sales. However, if inventories are to be increased then **extra units must be made for inventory**.

Option B is the budgeted sales volume, which would only be equal to budgeted production if there were no planned changes to inventory volume.

If you selected option D you increased the sales volume by 25 per cent, instead of adjusting inventory by this percentage.

2   B

	Units
Required increase in finished goods inventory	1,000
Budgeted sales of Alpha	60,000
Required production	61,000

	kg
Raw materials usage budget (× 3 kg)	183,000
Budgeted decrease in raw materials inventory	(8,000)
Raw materials purchase budget	175,000

If you selected option A you made no allowance for the increase in finished goods inventory. If you selected option C you did not adjust for the budgeted decrease in raw materials inventory, and option D adjusts for an increase in raw materials inventory, rather than a decrease.

3   D

	Units
Budgeted sales	18,000
Budgeted reduction in finished goods	(3,600)
Budgeted production of completed units	14,400
Allowance for defective units (10% of output = 1/9 of input)	1,600
Production budget	16,000

If you selected option A you deducted a ten per cent allowance for defective units, instead of adding it, and option B makes no allowance for defective units at all. If you selected option C you added ten per cent to the required completed units to allow for the defective units, but the ten per cent **should be based on the total number of units output**, ie ten per cent of 16,000 = 1,600 units.

4   D

	Hours
Active hours required for production = 200 × 6 hours =	1,200
Allowance for idle time (20% of total time = 25% of active time)	300
Total hours to be paid for	1,500
× $7 per hour	
Direct labour cost budget	$10,500

If you selected option A you deducted 20% from the active hours for idle time, instead of **adding an allowance of 20% of total time paid for**. Option B makes no allowance for idle time, while option C calculates the allowance based on the active hours rather than on the hours paid for.

5   D

	Units
Planned increase in inventories of finished goods	4,600
Budgeted sales	36,800
Budgeted production (to pass quality control check)	41,400

This is 92% of total production, allowing for an 8% rejection rate.

$$\text{Budgeted production} = \frac{100}{92} \times 41,400 = 45,000 \text{ units}$$

Budgeted direct labour hours = (× 5 hours per unit) 225,000 hours

If you selected option A you deducted eight per cent from the budgeted production, instead of **adding a rejection allowance of eight per cent of the final output**. Option B makes no allowance for rejects while option C calculates the number of rejects based on the budgeted good production rather than on the total output.

6   B   Depreciation is not a cash item and would be excluded from the cash budget.

All of the other options are cash items which would be included in the cash budget.

7   B

		Received in September
		$
August sales	$60,000 × 60% × 98%*	35,280
July sales	$40,000 × 25%	10,000
June sales	$35,000 × 12%	4,200
		49,480

*This reduction allows for the 2% settlement discount.

If you selected option A you misinterpreted 'month **after** sale' to be the month the sale was made. The invoices are issued on the last day of each month, therefore cash receipts in respect of each month's sales will begin in the following month.

Option C makes no allowance for the settlement discount and option D includes the receipt of bad debts; those amounts will never be received cash.

8   A

	$
40% of May sales for cash (40% × $55,000)	22,000
70% of April credit sales less 2% discount (70% × 60% × $70,000 × 98%)	28,812
27% of March credit sales (27% × 60% × $60,000)	9,720
	60,532

If you selected option B you forgot to allow for the two per cent discount. Option C works on the assumption that receipts from cash sales occur in the month after sale; by definition, **cash sales receipts occur as soon as the sale is made**. If you selected option D you calculated the credit receipts on the basis that all sales were made on credit; **only 60 per cent of sales were on a credit basis.**

9   C   Payments in June will be in respect of May purchases.

	May
Production requirements (8,400 units × 3kg)	25,200 kg
Closing inventory	4,100 kg
	29,300 kg
Less opening inventory	4,200 kg
Purchase budget	25,100 kg
× $2 per kg = payment for purchases in June	$50,200

Option A is the figure for the quantity of material to be paid for, not its value. Option B is the value of June purchases, which will be paid for in July. If you selected option D your adjustments for opening and closing material inventories were the wrong way round.

10   B

	$
75% × May wages cost = 75% × 8,400 × $7 × 4 hours	176,400
25% × April wages cost = 25% × 7,800 × $7 × 4 hours	54,600
Wage payments for May	231,000

If you selected option A you calculated the payment the wrong way round as 25% of May wages cost and 75% of April wages cost. If you selected option C you calculated the payment as 75% to be paid in the month and 25% in advance for the following month. Option D is the labour cost for May, which makes no allowance for the timing of cash payments.

22 Budgeting III

1 ☑ A factor which limits the activities of an undertaking.

The principal budget factor is also known as the key budget factor or the limiting budget factor.

2 ☑ Depreciation of computer terminals

Depreciation is not a cash flow, so it would not be included in a cash budget.

3 The budgeted labour cost is $ 30,800 (to the nearest $)

Hours to be paid for × 80% = 3,520

∴ Hours to be paid for = 3,520 ÷ 0.8 = 4,400

Budgeted labour cost = $7 × 4,400 hr = $30,800

4 The budgeted labour cost for the job is $ 40,800 (to the nearest $)

Hours to be paid for × 90% = 4,590

∴ Hours to be paid for = 4,590 ÷ 0.9 = 5,100

Budgeted labour cost = $8 × 5,100 hr = $40,800

5 The budgeted number of units of product U to be produced is 137,700 units.

	Units
Budgeted sales	140,000
Less inventory reduction (11,500 units × 20%)	2,300
Budgeted production	137,700

6 The total production cost allowance in a budget flexed at the 83% level of activity would be $ 8,688 (to the nearest $)

Direct material cost per 1% = $30

Direct labour and production overhead:

			$
At	90%	activity	6,240
At	80%	activity	6,180
Change	10%		60

Variable cost per 1% activity = $60/10% = $6

Substituting in 80% activity:

Fixed cost of labour and production overhead = $6,180 − (80 × $6)
= $5,700

Flexed budget cost allowance:

Direct material $30 × 83

Direct labour and production overhead:

variable $6 × 83

fixed

7   Actual $ 29,760 (to the nearest $)

Budget $ 28,800 (to the nearest $)

The actual material cost ($29,760) should be compared with the budget cost allowance for the actual production (4,800 units × $6 = $28,800).

8   The budget cost allowance for selling overhead for a sales level of 2,800 units is $ 43,000 (to the nearest $)

			$
Total cost for	3,000	units (× $15.00)	45,000
Total cost for	2,400	units (× $16.25)	39,000
Variable cost of	600	units	6,000

∴ Variable cost per unit = $6,000/600 = $10

∴ Fixed cost = $45,000 − (3,000 × $10) = $15,000

∴ Total cost allowance for 2,800 units:

	$
variable cost (2,800 × $10)	28,000
fixed cost	15,000
	43,000

9   The budgeted level of fixed cost for October was $ 25,000 (to the nearest $)

	$
Actual total cost	22,100
Fixed costs below budget	4,500
Budgeted total cost	26,600
Less budgeted variable cost (8,000 passengers × $0.20)	1,600
Budgeted fixed cost	25,000

10   The value of sales receipts from credit customers to be shown in the cash budget for August is $ 36,180 (to the nearest $)

	$
60% of July credit sales less 2% discount	
($70,000 × 50% × 60% × 98%)	20,580
39% of June credit sales ($80,000 × 50% × 39%)	15,600
	36,180

☑ A budget which is most generally used for planning purposes

☑ A budget for a single level of activity

Fixed budgets are prepared for a single level of activity and do not include any provision for the event that actual volumes may differ from the budget. They are generally used for planning purposes because they use a single level of activity for coordination and resource allocation.

2 │ 1,815 │ units

	Units
Required for sales	1,800
Plus increase in inventory (150 × 10%)	15
Budgeted production	1,815

3 Materials usage │ – │ opening inventory of materials │ + │ closing inventory of materials

Any opening inventory available at the beginning of the period will **reduce** the quantity to be purchased for a given volume of usage. Any closing inventory required at the end of a period will **increase** the quantity to be purchased in order to satisfy production and leave a sufficient quantity in inventory.

4 ☑ Raw materials inventories are budgeted to increase

Once the material usage budget has been prepared, based on the budgeted production volume, the usage is adjusted for the budgeted change in materials inventories in order to determine the required budgeted purchases. If purchases are greater than production requirements this means that raw material inventories are being increased.

5 ☑ A budget which by recognising different cost behaviour patterns is designed to change as the volume of activity changes.

A flexible budget shows the budgeted costs and revenues at different levels of activity. The budgeted variable costs and revenues are **increased or decreased in line with changes in activity,** and the budgeted fixed cost remains **unaltered**.

6 The usage budget for material Z for the forthcoming year is │ 40,000 │ kgs

Material usage budget = production units × material usage per unit
= 10,000 × 4 kgs
= 40,000 kgs

7 ☑ Budgeted income statement

☑ Budgeted cash flow

☑ Budgeted balance sheet

8   The amount budgeted to be received in September from credit sales is $ **121,440** (to the nearest $)

Amount receivable from

		$
August sales	$130,000 × 60% × 98%	76,440
July sales	$150,000 × 20%	30,000
June sales	$100,000 × 15%	15,000
		121,440

9   *Favourable*   *Adverse*

The volume variance for last month was $ **4,755**   ☐   ✓

The volume variance is the increase in cost resulting from a change in the volume of activity, ie the difference between the original budget and the flexed budget.

Volume variance   = $126,100 − $130,855
                       = $4,755 (A)

10   *Favourable*   *Adverse*

The expenditure variance for last month was $ **2,725**   ☐   ✓

The expenditure variance is the difference between the flexed budget and the actual results.

Expenditure variance   = $130,855 − $133,580
                                = $2,725 (A)

24 Budgeting V

1   C   The actual labour cost ($11,500) should be compared with the **budget cost allowance for the actual production** (1,100 × $10 = $11,000).

Option A includes the figures for output volume. Option B is incorrect because it compares the actual expenditure with the original budget. This would not be useful for the control of expenditure because **it is not possible to identify how much of the extra expenditure is due to the change in activity**.

2   D

	Units	$
High activity	3,000	12,900
Low activity	2,000	11,100
Increase	1,000	1,800

Variable cost per unit $= \dfrac{\$1,800}{1,000} = \$1.80$ per unit

Fixed cost, substituting in high activity   = $12,900 − (3,000 × $1.80)
                                                  = $7,500

Budget cost allowance for 4,000 units:	$
Variable cost (4,000 × $1.80)	7,200
Fixed cost	7,500
	14,700

Option A is the variable cost allowance only and option B is the fixed cost allowance only. If you selected option C your variable cost per unit calculation was upside down ($1,000/1,800 instead of $1,800/1,000).

3   D   Department 1

	Units		$
Total production overhead cost for	1,000	= 1,000 × $6 =	6,000
Total production overhead cost for	2,000	= 2,000 × $4.20 =	8,400
Increase	1,000		2,400

Variable overhead cost per unit	=	$2.40
Fixed overhead cost	=	$6,000 − (1,000 × $2.40)
	=	$3,600

Department 2

	Units		$
Total production overhead cost for	1,000	= 1,000 × $4 =	4,000
Total production overhead cost for	2,000	= 2,000 × $2 =	4,000

The production overhead cost in department 2 is wholly fixed.

Summary

	Total fixed cost	Variable cost per unit
	$	$
Direct materials		4.00
Direct labour		3.50
Production overhead – 1	3,600	2.40
Production overhead – 2	4,000	
	7,600	9.90

If you selected option A you omitted the fixed cost for department 2. Option B treats the unit rate for 2,000 units in department 1 as wholly variable, but it is a semi-variable cost. If you selected option C you forgot to include the variable cost per unit for department 1.

4   A

	$
Budgeted expenditure $(300,000 − 18,000)	282,000
Budgeted fixed costs	87,000
Budgeted variable costs	195,000

Budgeted variable cost per unit = $\dfrac{\$195,000}{162,500}$ = $1.20 per unit.

If you selected option B you forgot to adjust for the $18,000 overspending, and if you selected option C you did adjust for it, but in the wrong direction.

5   B

	$
Actual expenditure on overheads	108,000
Fixed overheads under budget	8,000
Budgeted expenditure on overheads	116,000
Less budgeted variable overhead expenditure	
= actual expenditure ($3 × 22,000)	66,000
Budgeted fixed overhead expenditure	50,000

If you selected option A you adjusted for the fixed overheads under budget by subtracting them instead of adding them to the actual expenditure. Option C is the budgeted variable overhead expenditure for the actual production and option D is the total budgeted overhead for the period.

6   B   Direct material cost per 1% activity = $2,000
Direct labour cost per 1% activity = $1,500

Production overhead		$
At	60% activity	54,000
At	80% activity	62,000
Change	20%	8,000

Variable cost per 1% change in activity = $\dfrac{\$8,000}{20}$ = $400

Substituting in 80% activity:

	$
Variable cost = 80 × $400	32,000
Total cost	62,000
∴ Fixed cost	30,000

Other overhead is a wholly fixed cost

Budget flexed at 77% level of activity

	$'000
Direct material 77 × $2,000	154.0
Direct labour 77 × $1,500	115.5
Production overhead:	
Variable 77 × $400	30.8
Fixed	30.0
Other overhead	40.0
	370.3

If you selected option A you did not include a fixed cost allowance for the other overhead. Option C ignores the fact that production overhead is a semi-variable cost and option D simply multiplies the total cost for 70% activity by a factor of 1.1. This makes no allowance for the fact that there is an element of fixed costs within production overhead, and other overhead is wholly fixed.

7   D   Contribution for 10,000 units

	$'000
Sales revenue	150
Direct material	(45)
Direct labour	(30)
Variable overhead	(20)
	55

	$
∴ contribution for 12,000 units = 55 × 1.2 =	66,000
Less fixed costs	25,000
Flexed budget profit for 12,000 units	41,000

If you selected option A you flexed the allowance for variable costs correctly but you did not flex the budgeted sales revenue. Option B is the original budgeted profit for 10,000 units. If you selected option C you flexed the fixed overhead cost, which is not correct; fixed overheads are not affected by changes in volume.

8   B   Production overhead

		$
Production overhead for	1,000 units =	3,500
Production overhead for	2,000 units =	5,000
Variable cost of	1,000 units =	1,500

Selling overhead

Selling overhead for 1,000 units = $1,000
Selling overhead for 2,000 units = $1,000

The selling overhead is therefore wholly fixed.

Variable cost per unit

	$
Direct materials	4.00
Direct labour	3.00
Production overhead	1.50
	8.50

Total fixed cost = $(2,000 + 1,000) = $3,000

If you selected option A you assumed that production overhead was a variable cost; it is a semi-variable cost therefore you need to use the high-low method to determine the fixed and variable cost elements. If you selected options C or D you assumed that production overhead was a fixed cost.

9	June	$	6,500
	July	$	11,500
	August	$	8,000

Workings

	June $	July $	August $
Material usage	8,000	9,000	10,000
Closing inventory (= next month's opening inventory)	3,500	6,000	4,000
Total requirements for month	11,500	15,000	14,000
Less opening inventory	(5,000)	(3,500)	(6,000)
Direct material purchases for month	6,500	11,500	8,000

10

	Order
Prepare the master budget and submit it to the senior managers for approval	7th
Identify the principal budget factor (PBF) and prepare the budget for the PBF	3rd
Establish the organisation's objectives	1st
Prepare all remaining functional budgets	4th
Form a budget committee and appoint a budget officer	2nd
Review and co-ordinate the budgets - check their feasibility	5th
Adjust the functional budgets if necessary	6th

25 Budgeting VI

1   The total production required is [800] units.

Production budget

Remember production = sales + closing inventory – opening inventory.

		Units
Sales		700
Closing inventory (700 units/20 days × 2 days' inventory)	70	
Opening inventory	50	
Increase in inventory		20
Production required of 'good' output		720

Total production required (ie gross production) = 100/90 × 720 = 800 units

2   The labour hours requirement is [3,000] hours.

Standard hours per unit	3
Total standard hours required = 800 units × 3 hours	2,400 hours
Productivity ratio	80%

Gross hours required = 100/80 × productive hours = 100/80 × 2,400 = 3,000 hours

3 (a) Direct materials would be $ | 11,430 |

Direct materials is a variable cost.

Check: **Cost per %**

70%: $17,780/70 = $254
80%: $20,320/80 = $254
90%: $22,860/90 = $254

∴ Direct materials at 45% level of activity = $254 × 45 = $11,430

(b) Direct labour would be $ | 28,800 |

Direct labour is a variable cost.

Check: **Cost per %**

70%: $44,800/70 = $640
80%: $51,200/80 = $640
90%: $57,600/90 = $640

∴ Direct materials at 45% level of activity = $640 × 45 = $28,800

4 Production overhead would be $ | 26,750 |

Production overhead is a semi-variable cost.

Check: **Cost per %**

70%: $30,500/70 = $436
80%: $32,000/80 = $400
90%: $33,500/90 = $372

Variable cost of (90% − 70%) activity = $(33,500 − 30,500)

∴ Variable cost of 20% = $3,000

∴ Variable cost of 1% change in activity = $3,000/20 = $150

∴ Fixed cost = $33,500 − (90 × $150) = $20,000

∴ Total cost at 45% level of activity = $20,000 + (45 × $150) = $26,750

5 A | $20,000 |
B | $20,000 |
C | $36,000 |
D | $36,000 |
E | $36,000 |

We are told supervision is a step cost. For 4,000 and 5,000 units the budget will be $20,000. Over 5,000 units the budget will be $20,000 + $16,000 = $36,000. Example: budget for 6,000 units = $36,000.

BPP)))
LEARNING MEDIA

6   F $18,000

     G $18,000

     H $18,000

     I $21,000

     J $24,000

If the minimum charge is payable on all production up to and including 6,000 units then it is paid on production of 4,000 units and is $18,000. This represents a fixed cost at all levels of production. On production over 6,000 units there is a variable charge based on power consumed.

Production of 8,000 units will have incurred the variable charge on 2,000 units. This variable charge for 2,000 units = $(24,000 − 18,000) = $6,000. The charge per unit = $6,000/2,000 = $3.

For production up to 6,000 units, the budget is $18,000. For production over 6,000 units, the budget is $18,000 plus $3 per unit over 6,000 units.

Example: budget for 7,000 units = $18,000 + ((7,000 − 6,000) × $3) = $21,000

7   K $12,000

     L $14,000

     M $16,000

     N $18,000

     O $20,000

A doubling of production does not result in a doubling of cost. Indirect materials is therefore a mixed cost.

Consider the total cost of 4,000 units.

	$
Variable cost (4,000 × $2)	8,000
Total cost	12,000
Fixed cost	4,000

The total cost of indirect materials is therefore based on a fixed cost of $4,000 plus a variable cost of $2 per unit. Example: budget for 6,000 units = $4,000 + $(6,000 × 2) = $16,000.

8   B   Variable cost per unit $= \dfrac{\$12,900 - \$11,100}{(6,000 - 4,000)\,\text{units}}$

$$= \dfrac{\$1,800}{2,000\,\text{units}} = \$0.90 \text{ per unit}$$

Fixed costs $= \$11,100 - (4,000 \times \$0.90)$
$= \$11,100 - \$3,600 = \$7,500$

∴ Budgeted cost allowance for an activity level of 8,000 units is

	$
Fixed cost	7,500
Variable cost ($0.90 × 8,000)	7,200
	14,700

If you selected option A you did not include an allowance for fixed cost, and if you selected C or D you calculated the allowance on a pro rata basis from the data given. This does not take account of the fixed element of the production cost.

9   C

	Miles	$
High	2,600	3,300
Low	1,800	2,900
Change	800	400

Variable cost per mile = $400/800 = $0.50

Fixed cost = $3,300 – (2,600 × $0.50) = $2,000

If you selected Options A, B or D you included the middle level of activity in your calculations; by definition, the **high-low method must be applied to the data for the highest and lowest activity.**

10   B   Direct material cost per 1% activity = $40

Direct labour cost per 1% activity is not a constant amount at both activity levels, so this must be a semi-variable cost. Since production overhead is also a semi-variable cost the two costs can be analysed together, to save time (since the question asks only for a total cost in the answer).

Direct labour and production overhead

		$
At	80% activity	8,200
At	90% activity	8,700
Change	10%	500

Variable cost per 1% change in activity = $500/10% = $50

Substituting in 80% activity:

	$
Variable cost = 80 × $50	4,000
Total cost	8,200
∴ Fixed cost	4,200

Flexed budget cost at 88% level of activity

	$
Direct material 88 × $40	3,520
Direct labour and production overhead	
Variable 88 × $50	4,400
Fixed	4,200
	12,120

If you selected options A or C you assumed that direct labour was a variable cost. Although this is often the case, you should always **test the cost behaviour patterns** to be sure. If you selected option

D you simply multiplied the total cost for 80% activity by a factor of 1.1. This makes no allowance the fact that there is an element of fixed costs within production overhead.

26 Budgeting VII

1   B   The expenditure variance is the difference between the flexed budget and the actual results.

Expenditure variance = $80,000 – $79,800 = $200 (F)

The variance is favourable because actual expenditure was lower than the flexible budget cost allowance.

The volume variance is the increase or decrease in cost resulting from a change in volume of activity, ie the difference between the original budget and the flexed budget.

Volume variance = $75,000 – $80,000 = $5,000 (A)

The variance is adverse because extra expenditure was budgeted to be incurred as a result of the increase in volume.

If you selected option A or C you calculated the correct variances but misinterpreted their direction. If you selected option D you interchanged the expenditure and volume variances.

2   A   The variable costs are indicated by the change in budgeted expenditure when the budget is flexed.

$$\text{Variable cost per unit} = \frac{\$20,000 - \$19,175}{2,000 - 1,850}$$

$$= \$5.50$$

If you selected option B you calculated the total standard production cost per unit for 2,000 units. However, this includes the production overhead cost which contains a fixed element.

Options C and D are the total standard cost per unit for a level of activity of 2,000 units and 1,850 units respectively.

3   C   The expenditure variance is the difference between the flexed budget and the actual results.

Expenditure variance = $19,175 – $19,530 = $355 adverse

The variance is adverse because actual expenditure was higher than the flexible budget cost allowance.

The volume variance is the reduction in cost resulting from the change in volume of activity.

Volume variance = $20,000 –$19,175 = $825 favourable.

The variance is favourable because budgeted expenditure was reduced as a result of the reduction in volume.

If you selected option A you interchanged the expenditure and volume variances. If you selected option B or D you calculated the correct variances but misinterpreted their direction.

4   C   Statement (i) is correct. **The use of standards is limited to situations where output can be measured.**

ement (ii) is not correct. Standards can include allowances for inefficiencies in operations, ugh the use of **attainable standards**.

ement (iii) is not correct. Standards and budgets are both used for **planning and control** poses.

5

1st	B
2nd	D
3rd	E
4th	A
5th	F
6th	C

Since there are no production resource limitations, sales would be the principal budget factor and the sales budget (B) would be prepared first. Budgeted inventory changes included in the finished goods inventory budget (D) would then indicate the required production for the production budget (E). This would lead to the calculation of the material usage (A) which would then be adjusted for the budgeted change in material inventory (F) to determine the required level of budgeted material purchases (C).

6
Included

(i)   Capital cost of a new collection vehicle   ✓

(iii)   Operatives' wages   ✓

(iv)   Fuel for the collection vehicles   ✓

Depreciation is not a cash item and would not be included in the cash budget. Items (i), (iii) and (iv) however, would be included in the cash budget.

7   The budget cost allowance for an activity level of 8,000 units is $ 30,600

	Units	$
High activity	6,000	25,600
Low activity	4,000	20,600
	2,000	5,000

Variable cost per unit = $\dfrac{\$5,000}{2,000}$ = $2.50 per unit

Fixed cost, substituting in high activity   = $25,600 − (6,000 × $2.50)
                                            = $10,600

Budget cost allowance for 8,000 units:

	$
Variable cost (8,000 × $2.50)	20,000
Fixed cost	10,600
	30,600

8   ✓ $725,000

Direct material cost per 1% activity   = $4,000
Direct labour cost per 1% activity   = $3,000

Production overhead

			$
At	60% activity		108,000
At	80% activity		124,000
Change	20%		16,000

Variable cost per 1% change in activity $= \dfrac{\$16,000}{20} = \$800$

	$
Substituting in 80% activity	
Variable cost = 80 × $800	64,000
Total	124,000
∴ Fixed cost	60,000

Other overhead is a wholly fixed cost.

Budget flexed at 75% level of activity

	$ '000
Direct material 75 × $4,000	300
Direct labour 75 × $3,000	225
Production overhead	
Variable 75 × $800	60
Fixed	60
Other overhead	80
	725

9   The production budget (in units) for Quarter 4 is ⌈ 23,100 ⌉ units.

Workings

	Quarter 4 Units
Total sales volume (7,750 + 8,000 + 7,500)	23,250
Required closing inventory (20% × 7,000)	1,400
	24,650
Less opening inventory (20% × 7,750)	1,550
	23,100

10   D

	Hours
Active hours required	270
Plus interruptions and rest time (270 × 10/90)	30
Total paid hours required	300
× budgeted hourly rate	× $8
Budgeted labour cost	$2,400

27 Budgeting VIII

1   A

		$
Cash sales in December ($402,000 × 10%)		40,200
Receipts from November credit sales ($390,000 × 90%× 30% × 99%)		104,247
Receipts from October credit sales ($224,000 × 90% × 70%)		141,120
Total sales receipts in December		285,567

2   C

	$
Variable production overhead payment:	
for August production (12,600 × $5 × 30%)	18,900
for September production (5,500 × $5 × 70%)	19,250
Total variable production overhead payment	38,150
Fixed overhead cash payment ($9,440 – $2,280)	7,160
Total cash payment	45,310

3   (a)   (i)   Gross production is ⌐ 900 ⌐ units.

Good production = (100 – 10)% = 90%
Gross production = 100/90 × 810 units = 900 units

(ii)   ⌐ 90 ⌐ units will be faulty.

Faulty units = 10/90 × 810 units = 90 units (or 900 units – 810 units)

(b)   Units produced is ⌐ 500 ⌐

Gross production = 100/95 × 475 units = 500 units

4   Materials purchase budget is ⌐ 17,450 ⌐ kgs

To determine materials purchases we first need to draw up a production budget.

Sales + closing inventory – opening inventory = production

Production budget

	Superior model		Standard model	
	Units	Units	Units	Units
Sales volume		1,500		2,200
Closing inventory	200		250	
Opening inventory	(150)		(200)	
Increase in inventory		50		50
Production		1,550		2,250

Material used in production + closing inventory – opening inventory = purchases

Materials purchases budget

	Kgs	Kgs
Material required for superior model (1,550 × 5 kgs)		7,750
Material required for standard model (2,250 × 4 kgs)		9,000
Total material required for production		16,750
Closing inventory	1,500	
Opening inventory	(800)	
Increase in inventory		700
Material purchases		17,450

5   Purchases budget is ⸤ 27,009 ⸥ kgs

	kgs	kgs
Wood issued to production (chest: 450 × 25 kgs)		11,250
(wardrobe: 710 × 40 kgs)		28,400
		39,650
Closing inventory (39,650 × 115% × 15 days/25 days)*	27,359	
Opening inventory	(40,000)	
Decrease in inventory		(12,641)
Purchases		27,009

*Production in period 2 will be 15% higher than that in period 1 and so closing inventory must take this into account.

6   (a)   The budgeted production level is ⸤ 255 ⸥ units.

Production budget

Production = sales + closing inventory – opening inventory

	Units	Units
Budgeted sales		280
Closing inventory	5	
Opening inventory	(30)	
Decrease in inventory		(25)
Budgeted production		255

(b)   The budgeted materials usage is ⸤ 1,785 ⸥ kgs, costing $ ⸤ 89,250 ⸥.

Materials usage budget

Production	255 units
× usage per unit	× 7 kgs
Total budgeted usage in kgs	1,785 kgs
× budgeted cost per kg	× $50
Total budgeted usage in $	$89,250

7   (a)   The budgeted cost for grade O labour is $ ☐ 7,650 ☐.

Labour utilisation budget – grade O

Budgeted production	255 units
× hrs per unit	× 2 hrs
Total budgeted labour hrs	510 hrs
× budgeted cost per hr	× $15
Budgeted labour cost	$7,650

   (b)   The budgeted cost for grade R labour $ ☐ 17,920 ☐.

Note that the budgeted labour cost is not dependent on the hours worked.

Budgeted labour cost = 16 × $280 × 4 weeks = $17,920

8   A

	Units
Units required for sales	3,970
Plus required closing inventory (3,770 × 20%)	754
	4,724
Less required opening inventory (3,970 × 20%)	(794)
Budgeted production	3,930

9   B   The principal budget factor is sometimes called the key budget factor or limiting budget factor. The organisation cannot extend its activities beyond the limits of the principal budget factor.

The principal budget factor is often sales demand but it can also be other factors such as office space, the availability of key personnel or of cash.

10   (a)   The budgeted production level of product P is ☐ 2,950 ☐ units.

   (b)   The budgeted production level of product L is ☐ 4,050 ☐ units.

Production = sales + closing inventory – opening inventory.

	Product P		Product L	
	Units	Units	Units	Units
Budgeted sales		3,000		4,000
Closing inventory (3/12 of 3,000/4,000)	750		1,000	
Opening inventory (minus inventory scrapped)	800		950	
(Decrease)/increase in inventory		(50)		50
Production		2,950		4,050

The layout of this answer shows that inventories of product P have decreased, while those of product L have increased. A reasonableness check on an answer would therefore require production of P to be less than sales, but production of L to be greater than sales.

28 Cost bookkeeping I

1   B   The entries for the return of direct material to stores are the **reverse** of those made when the material is first issued to production. The **work in progress account is credited** to 'remove' the cost of the material from the production costs. The **stores account is debited** to increase the value of inventory. Therefore the correct answer is B.

If you selected option A you identified the correct accounts but your entries were reversed.

Option C represents the entries for the return of indirect materials to stores. Option D represents the entries for the transfer of the cost of completed production to finished goods inventory.

2   C   The cost of indirect materials issued is **credited to the stores account** and 'collected' in the overhead control account **pending its absorption into work in progress**. Therefore the correct answer is C.

Option A represents the entries for the issue to production of **direct materials**.

If you selected option B you identified the correct accounts but **your entries were reversed**.

Option D is not correct. The issue of materials should not be charged direct to cost of sales. The cost of materials issued should first be analysed as direct or indirect and charged to work in progress or the overhead control account accordingly.

3   D   Overhead is absorbed into the cost of production by **debiting the work in progress account** with the appropriate amount of overhead based on the predetermined overhead absorption rate. The credit entry is made in the **overhead control account**, where the overhead has been 'collected' in the debit side. Therefore the correct answer is D.

If you selected option A you identified the correct accounts but your **entries were reversed**. Option B is incorrect because the cost of production must first be 'collected' in the **work in progress account** before the final transfer of the cost of completed production to the finished goods account. If you selected option C you made the same mistake and your entries were reversed.

4   A   Over-absorbed overhead means that the overhead charged to production was too high therefore there must be a **credit to income statement**. The debit entry is made in the **overhead control account.** Therefore the correct answer is A.

If you selected option B you identified the correct accounts but your **entries were reversed**. These entries represent those that would be made for **under-absorbed** overhead.

Options C and D are incorrect because the only overhead charge made to work in progress (WIP) is the overhead **absorbed into production based on the predetermined rate**. Under or over absorption does not affect WIP.

5   B   The factory cost of finished production is transferred as a **debit to the finished goods account** and **credited from the work in progress account**.

Option A describes the double entry for the production cost of goods **sold**. Option C describes the same thing, where a **cost of sales account is not in use**. Option D uses the correct accounts but **the entries are reversed**.

6   C   The rent account for the period would look like this.

RENT ACCOUNT

	$		$
Cash	40,000	Production overhead	28,000
		Admin overhead	8,000
		Marketing overhead	4,000
	40,000		40,000

The debit balance in the rent account is analysed between the various functional classifications of overhead. Therefore the correct answer is C.

Option A uses the correct accounts but the entries are reversed. Option B is the reverse of the entries that would be used to record the original rent payment. Option D uses the correct accounts but only 70% of overhead should be charged to production.

7   C   Overhead absorbed = 27,000 hours × $3 = $81,000. This amount is **debited in the work in progress account** as part of the cost of production for the period. The credit entry is made in the **overhead control account.**

If you selected option A you identified the correct accounts but you used the figure for **actual overheads incurred**. Option B is incorrect because the cost of production must first be 'collected' in the **work in progress account** before the final transfer of the cost of completed production to the finished goods account. Option D uses the correct values and accounts, but the **entries are reversed**.

8   A

	$
Overhead absorbed	81,000
Overhead incurred	85,000
Under-absorbed overhead	4,000

This means that the overhead charged to production was too low therefore there must be a **debit to income statement**. The credit entry is made in the **overhead control account**.

Option B demonstrates the entries for **over-absorbed overhead**.

Options C and D are incorrect because under or over absorption of overhead does not affect work in progress (WIP). The only overhead charge made to WIP is the **overhead absorbed based on the predetermined rate.**

9   C   Statement (i) is not correct. A debit to stores with a corresponding credit to work in progress (WIP) indicates that **direct materials returned** from production were $18,000.

Statement (ii) is correct. **Direct costs of production** are 'collected' in the WIP account.

Statement (iii) is correct. **Indirect costs of production or overhead** are 'collected' in the overhead control account.

Statement (iv) is correct. The purchases of materials on credit are credited to the suppliers account and debited to the material stores control account.

Therefore the correct answer is C.

10   C   Statement (i) is correct. The cost of indirect material issued is 'collected' in the overhead control account **pending absorption into work in progress**.

Statement (ii) is incorrect. The overhead cost **incurred** was $210,000. The overhead **absorbed into work in progress** during the period was $404,800.

Statement (iii) is incorrect. The $8,400 is **debited to income statement**, indicating an extra charge to compensate for the overhead **under absorbed.**

Statement (iv) is correct. The indirect wage cost is 'collected' in the overhead control account **pending absorption into work in progress**.

Therefore the correct answer is C.

29 Cost bookkeeping II

1   B   The question describes interlocking accounts, where the cost accounts are distinct from the financial accounts.

With integrated accounts, option D, a single set of accounting records provides both financial and cost accounts.

2   C   Statement (i) is correct because **only one set of accounts is kept in an integrated system.** Statement (ii) is incorrect because in a system of integrated accounts the financial and cost accounts are **combined** in one set of accounts. Statement (iii) is correct because **profit differences do not arise with an integrated system.**

3   A   Direct costs of production are **debited to the work in progress account**. Direct materials are taken from stores and therefore the credit will be in the **stores control account**.

Option B is incorrect because **all production costs must be collected in the work in progress account** before the transfer of the cost of completed output to the finished goods account.

Option C has the correct entries, but they are reversed.

Option D is incorrect because a **transfer to cost of sales cannot be made until the cost of production has been determined.**

4   D   The easiest way to solve this question is to draw up a stores ledger control account.

STORES LEDGER CONTROL ACCOUNT

	$		$
Opening inventory b/f	18,500	Suppliers (returns)	2,300
Suppliers/cash (deliveries)	142,000	Overhead account (indirect	
		materials)	25,200
		WIP (balancing figure)	116,900
		Closing inventory c/f	16,100
	160,500		160,500

If you selected option C you determined the correct value of the direct materials issued but you **reversed the entries.**

If you selected options A or B you placed the figure for returns on the **wrong side of your account**, and in option A you **reversed the entries** for the issue of direct materials from stores.

5   B   The **direct costs of production**, of which direct wages are a part, are **debited to the work in progress account**. The credit entry is made in the **wages control account**, where the wages cost has been 'collected' **prior to its analysis** between direct and indirect wages.

If you selected option A you identified the correct accounts but **your entries were reversed.**

Option C is incorrect because the transfer to cost of sales is made from the finished goods account. Option D represents the entries that are made to transfer the absorption cost of completed production from work in progress to the finished goods inventory.

6   C   Indirect costs of production, of which indirect wages are a part, are '**collected' as debits in the overhead control account**, from where they will eventually be **absorbed into work in progress**. The credit entry is made in the wages control account, where the wages cost has been 'collected' **prior to its analysis** between direct and indirect wages.

If you selected option A you identified the correct accounts but your entries were reversed.

Option B represents the accounting entries for direct wages incurred, and option D is the reverse of these entries.

7   B   The overtime was not worked for any specific job and is therefore an **indirect wages cost** to be 'collected' in the overhead control account. Similarly, the holiday pay is an **indirect cost**, therefore the total **debit to the overhead control account** is $2,500. The **direct wages** of $70,800 is **debited to the work in progress account** and the total wages cost is **credited to the wages control account**.

If you selected option C you identified the correct accounts but your entries were reversed.

If you selected option A you treated the overtime premium as a direct cost, and if you selected option D you made the same mistake and your entries were reversed.

8   B   The credit balance on the wages control account indicates that the amount of wages incurred and analysed between direct wages and indirect wages was **higher** than the wages paid through the bank. Therefore there was a $12,000 balance of **wages owing** at the end of February and statement B is not correct. Therefore the correct option is B.

Statement A is correct. $128,400 of wages was paid from the bank account.

Statement C is correct. $79,400 of direct wages was transferred to the work in progress control account.

Statement D is correct. $61,000 of indirect wages was transferred to the production overhead control account.

9   ☑   DR   work-in-progress control account   CR   material usage variance account

A favourable variance is credited in the relevant variance account. The usage variance is eliminated where it arises, therefore the debit entry is made in the work-in-progress account.

10

	Debit	Credit	No entry in this account
Raw materials control account	✓		
WIP control account			✓
Raw material price variance account		✓	

When materials are purchased for more or less than their standard price, the variance is debited or credited respectively to the material price variance account.

30 Cost bookkeeping III

1   D   Since materials inventory is valued at standard price, materials price variances are extracted when the material is purchased.

	$
5,000 units should cost (× $4.70)	23,500
but did cost	22,500
Materials price variance	1,000 (F)

Favourable variances are credited to the relevant variance account.

2,400 units should use (× 2)	4,800 units
but did use	4,850 units
Variance in units	50 units (A)
× standard cost per unit	× $4.70
Materials usage variance	$235 (A)

Adverse variances are debited to the relevant variance account.

If you selected option A you based the calculation of the materials price variance on the materials used; **since inventory is valued at standard the price variance should be based on the materials purchased**.

If you selected option B you calculated the correct values for the variances, but your entries were the 'wrong way round'.

If you selected option C you valued the usage variance at the actual cost per unit of material instead of at the standard cost.

2   C   The situation described results in an **adverse** raw material price variance and therefore a **debit** to the raw material price variance account. This eliminates options A and B. The price variance is **eliminated where it arises**, ie on receipt into materials inventory, therefore the credit entry is made in the raw material control account, and the correct answer is C.

3   B   A **favourable** labour efficiency variance is **credited** to the labour efficiency variance account. This eliminates options A and D.

The efficiency variance is **eliminated where it arises** therefore the debit entry is made in the work in progress account, and the correct answer is B.

4   D   A **favourable** labour rate variance is **credited** to the labour rate variance account. This eliminates options A and C.

The rate variance is **eliminated where it arises**, ie on payment of the wages, therefore the debit entry is made in the wages control account, and the correct answer is D.

5   A   An **adverse** material usage variance is **debited** to the material usage variance account. This eliminates options C and D.

The usage variance is **eliminated where it arises**, therefore the credit entry is made in the work in progress account, and the correct answer is A.

6

Debit	**Credit**
✓ Finished goods control account	Work in progress control account

The factory cost of finished production is transferred as a debit to the **finished goods account** and **credited from the work in progress account**.

7

	Debit	*Credit*	*No entry in this account*
Overhead control account	✓		
Work in progress account			✓
Income statement		✓	

Over-absorbed overhead means that the overhead charged to production was too high therefore there must be a credit to income statement.

8   ✓   DR income statement; CR overhead control account

Under-absorbed overhead means that the overhead charged to production was too low therefore there must be a debit to income statement. The credit entry is made in the overhead control account.

9   ✓   DR   Overhead control   CR   Wages control

Indirect wages are 'collected' in the overhead control account, for subsequent full into work in progress.

10

	Debit	*Credit*	*No entry in this account*
Work-in-progress control account	✓		
Overhead control account		✓	
Cost of sales account			✓

A key feature of full costs is that overheads are absorbed into units of work-in-progress rather than being posted straight to cost of sales.

31 Cost bookkeeping IV

1 ☑ Work-in-progress account

Material may be issued from stores to be used either as direct material or as indirect material. The indirect material is debited to the production overhead control account and in this case is shown as $10,000. The amount of $125,000 must therefore be the issue of direct material, which is debited to the work-in-progress account.

2 ☑ The number of labour hours worked was greater than the standard allowed for the number of units produced.

The first statement is incorrect because there is some closing work in progress to be carried forward to the next period.

The second statement is incorrect because the material usage variance will be transferred as a credit in the variance account. This means that the material usage variance is favourable and that less material than standard was used in production.

The third statement is correct because the labour efficiency variance will be transferred as a debit in the variance account. This means that the labour efficiency variance is adverse and that the number of labour hours worked was greater than the standard allowed.

3 ☑ Production overhead expenditure was lower than the budget for the period
   ☑ Production overhead was under absorbed during the period

The first statement is correct because the production overhead expenditure variance will be transferred as a credit in the variance account. This means that the production overhead expenditure variance is favourable and that expenditure was lower than the budget for the period.

The second statement is incorrect because if production output is higher than budget this results in a favourable production overhead volume variance. However, the variance will be transferred as a debit in the variance account, therefore it is an adverse variance and production volume was lower than budgeted.

The third statement is correct because the total production overhead variance is adverse, indicating that the overhead was under absorbed.

Volume variance $23,000 adverse + expenditure variance $8,000 favourable = Total variance $5,000 adverse

4 ☑ Direct wages cost incurred during June amounted to $150,940
   ☑ Indirect wages cost incurred during June amounted to $46,900
   ☑ Wages owing at the end of June amounted to $15,300

The wages **paid** are indicated by the amount transferred from the bank account, ie $182,540. The total of $197,840 is the amount of wages **incurred** during June.

5

		Debit		Credit
		$		$
☑	Work-in-progress account	31,600	Wages control account	31,600

The direct wages incurred are $(28,400 + 3,200) = $31,600. The direct costs of production, of which direct wages are a part, are debited to the work-in-progress account. The credit entry is made in the wages control account, where the wages cost has been 'collected' prior to its analysis between direct and indirect wages.

6		Debit $		Credit $
✓	Finished goods control account	11,760	Work-in-progress control account	11,760

The factory cost of finished production is transferred as a debit to the finished goods account and credited from the work-in-progress account.

7

	Debit	Credit
Stores control account	✓	
Work-in-progress account		✓

The entries for the return of direct material to stores are the reverse of those made when the material is first issued to production. The work-in-progress account is credited to 'remove' the cost of the unused material from the production costs for the period. The stores account is debited to increase the value of inventory.

8

	Debit $	Credit $	No entry in this a/c
Work in progress			✓
Materials inventory	✓		
Cost of sales			✓
Cash			✓
Payables		✓	

9 ✓ Production overhead control account

10 B

WIP control account

	$		$
Wages	26,200	Transferred to finished goods	304,660
Overheads	31,500	Closing inventory	61,520
Raw materials (balancing figure)	308,480		
	366,180		366,180

32 Process costing I

1   C

	Process 1 $'000	Process 2 $'000	Process 3 $'000
Opening inventory	8	13	2
Value of goods transferred	–	32	50
Added materials	20	4	5
Conversion costs	10	10	16
	38	59	73
Less closing inventory	(6)	(9)	(4)
Goods transferred	32	50	69

If you selected option A or B you did not include the costs brought forward from processes 1 and 2. In option B, you also omitted to deduct the value of process 3 closing inventory. If you selected option D you omitted to deduct the values of closing inventory in all three processes.

2   B   An equivalent unit calculation is used in process costing to value any **incomplete units** within **work in progress and losses**.

Option A describes the output from any process, where all completed units are **identical**.

Option C describes a cost unit, and D describes a **standard hour**.

3   C   **Step 1**   **Determine output and losses**

Input Units	Output	Total Units	Materials Units	Materials %	Labour and overhead Units	Labour and overhead %
	Finished units (balance)	400	400	100	400	100
500	Closing inventory	100	100	100	80	80
500		500	500		480	

Step 2   **Calculate the cost per equivalent unit**

Input	Cost $	Equivalent production in units	Cost per unit $
Materials	9,000	500	18
Labour and overhead	11,520	480	24
			42

Step 3   **Calculate total cost of output**

Cost of completed units = $42 × 400 units = $16,800

If you selected option A you omitted the absorption of overhead at the rate of 200 per cent of direct wages. If you selected option B you did not allow for the fact that the work in progress was incomplete. Option D is the total process cost for the period, some of which must be allocated to the work in progress.

4   B   Using the data from answer 3 above, extend **step 3** to calculate the value of the work in progress.

	Cost element	Number of equivalent units	Cost per equivalent unit	Total
			$	$
Work in progress:	Materials	100	18	1,800
	Labour & overhead	80	24	1,920
				3,720

If you selected option A you omitted the absorption of overhead into the process costs. If you selected option C you did not allow for the fact that the work in progress was incomplete. Option D is the total process cost for the period, some of which must be allocated to the completed output.

5   C   Cost per unit in closing inventory = $(4.50 + 1.25 + 2.50) = $8.25
Number of units in closing inventory = 13,500 – 11,750 = 1,750 units
∴ Value of closing inventory = 1,750 units × $8.25 = $14,437.50

Option A applies a unit rate of $3.75, ie omitting the cost of the raw material transferred into the process. Option B applies a unit rate of $7, omitting the additional material added. Option D applies a unit rate of $14.50, ie all of the unit rates supplied in the question. The work in progress should be valued at the **rate per incomplete unit** in respect of labour and overheads.

6   D   **Step 1**   **Determine output and losses**

			Equivalent units of production			
Input	Output	Total	Process X		Conversion costs	
Units		Units	Units	%	Units	%
2,000	Finished units	1,600	1,600	100	1,600	100
	Normal loss	200				
	Abnormal loss (balance)	100	100	100	100	100
	Closing inventory	100	100	100	50	50
2,000		2,000	1,800		1,750	

Step 2   **Calculate cost per unit of output, losses and WIP**

Input	Cost	Equivalent units	Cost per equivalent unit
	$		$
Process X material ($8,000 – $800)	7,200	1,800	4
Conversion costs	12,250	1,750	7
			11

Step 3   **Calculate total cost of output**

Cost of completed production = $11 × 1,600 litres = $17,600

If you selected option A you included the normal loss in your equivalent units calculation, but these units do not carry any of the process costs. If you selected option B you did not allow for the fact that the work in progress units were incomplete as regards conversion costs. If you selected option C you reduced the process costs by the scrap value of all lost units, instead of the normal loss units only.

BPP)))
LEARNING MEDIA

7   C   Using the unit rates from answer 6 step 2, we can proceed again to step 3.

Calculate the total cost of work in progress

	Cost element	Number of equivalent units	Cost per equivalent unit $	Total $
Work in progress	Process X material	100	4	400
	Conversion costs	50	7	350
				750

If you selected option A you included the normal loss in your equivalent units calculation. If you selected option B you reduced the process costs by the scrap value of all lost units, instead of the normal loss units only. Option D does not allow for the fact that the work in progress (WIP) is incomplete when calculating the total cost of WIP.

8   B   Total loss = Opening inventory plus input minus (output plus closing inventory)
            = 2,000 + 24,000 – (19,500 + 3,000)
            = 3,500

Abnormal loss = Total loss – normal loss
              = 3,500 – (24,000 × 10%)
              = 1,100

STATEMENT OF EQUIVALENT UNITS

	Total units	Equivalent units Materials	Conversion costs
Output to next process	19,500	19,500	19,500
Normal loss	2,400	0	0
Closing inventory	3,000	3,000	(45%) 1,350
	24,900	22,500	20,850
Abnormal loss	1,100	1,100	1,100
Equivalent units	26,000	23,600	21,950

If you selected option A you excluded the abnormal loss units from your calculations; only the normal loss units are excluded from the equivalent units calculation. Option C does not take account of the fact that the closing inventory is incomplete. Option D includes the normal loss units in the equivalent units calculations; they should be excluded because they do not carry any process costs.

9   B   *CIMA Terminology* defines joint products as 'Two or more products produced by the same process and separated in processing, each having a sufficiently high saleable value to merit recognition as a main product'.

A joint product may be subject to further processing, as implied in option A, but this is not the case for all joint products.

10   D   *CIMA Terminology* defines a by-product as 'Output of some value produced incidentally while manufacturing the main product'.

Option A is incorrect because a by-product has some value.

Option B is incorrect because this description could also apply to a joint product.

Option C is incorrect because the value of the product described could be relatively high, even though the output volume is relatively low.

---

33 Process costing II

1   The quantity of good production achieved was [2,625] kg.

Good production   = input – normal loss – abnormal loss
                   = 3,000 – (10% × 3,000) – 75
                   = 3,000 – 300 – 75
                   = 2,625 kg

2   [✓]   At the same rate as good production

3   [✓]   A notional whole unit representing incomplete work

The concept of equivalent units is used when assessing the amount of work represented by the incomplete units in work-in-progress.

4   [1,250]   equivalent units

STATEMENT OF EQUIVALENT UNITS

	Total Units		Material		Labour		Equivalent units Production overhead
Completed output	800*	(100%)	800	(100%)	800	(100%)	800
Closing WIP	500	(100%)	500	(90%)	450	(40%)	200
	1,300		1,300		1,250		1,000

* Opening WIP 400 + units added 900 – closing WIP 500.

5   The value of completed output for the period was $ [322,400] (to the nearest $)

Step 1

STATEMENT OF EQUIVALENT UNITS

	Total units		Material		Labour		Equivalent units Production overhead
Completed output	800*	(100%)	800	(100%)	800	(100%)	800
Closing WIP	500	(100%)	500	(90%)	450	(40%)	200
	1,300		1,300		1,250		1,000

*Opening WIP 400 + units added 900 – WIP 500

Step 2

STATEMENT OF COSTS PER EQUIVALENT UNIT

	Total	Material $	Labour $	Production overhead $
Opening inventory		49,000	23,000	3,800
Costs incurred		198,000	139,500	79,200
		247,000	162,500	83,000
Equivalent units		1,300	1,250	1,000
Cost per equivalent unit	$403	$190	$130	$83

∴ Value of completed output = $403 × 800 units = $322,400

6 The value credited to the process account for the scrap value of the normal loss for the period will be

$ 200 to the nearest $10.

Normal loss = 10% × input
= 10% × 10,000 kg
= 1,000 kg

When scrap has a value, normal loss is valued at the value of the scrap ie 20c per kg.

Normal loss = $0.20 × 1,000 kg
= $200

7 The value of the abnormal loss for the period is $ 520 to the nearest $10

	kg
Input	10,000
Normal loss (10% × 10,000 kg)	(1,000)
Abnormal loss	(600)
Output	8,400

$$\text{Cost per kg} = \frac{\text{Input costs} - \text{scrap value of normal loss}}{\text{Expected output}}$$

$$= \frac{\$8,000^* - \$200}{10,000 - 1,000} \text{ (from question 6 above)}$$

$$= \frac{\$7,800}{9,000} = \$0.87$$

Value of abnormal loss = 600 × $0.87 = $520

	$
*Materials (10,000 kg × 0.5)	5,000
Labour	1,000
Production overhead	2,000
	8,000

8   The value of the closing work in progress for the period was $ | 9,396 |

Step 1   Determine output

STATEMENT OF EQUIVALENT UNITS

	Total units	Materials Equivalent units		Labour and overhead Equivalent units	
Completed output	16,000	(100%)	16,000	(100%)	16,000
Normal loss	2,000	(0%)	–	(0%)	–
Abnormal loss	200	(100%)	200	(100%)	200
Closing WIP	1,800	(100%)	1,800	(75%)	1,350
	20,000		18,000		17,550

Step 2   Calculate the cost per equivalent unit

STATEMENT OF COST PER EQUIVALENT UNIT

	Materials	Labour and overhead
Total costs	*$81,000	$16,848
Equivalent units	18,000	17,550
Cost per equivalent unit	$4.50	$0.96

* $81,600 less scrap value of normal loss ($2,000 × $0.30 = $600) = $81,000

Value of work in progress:

	$
Materials 1,800 equivalent units × $4.50	8,100
Labour and overhead 1,350 equivalent units × $0.96	1,296
	9,396

9   The full production cost of completed units during November was $ | 16,800 |

Step 1   **Determine output**

				Equivalent units			
Input Units	Output	Total Units	Materials Units	%	Labour and overhead Units	%
	Finished units (balance)	400	400	100	400	100
500	Closing stock	100	100	100	80	80
500		500	500		480	

Step 2   **Calculate the cost per equivalent unit**

Input	Cost	Equivalent production in units	Cost per unit
	$		$
Materials	9,000	500	18
Labour and overhead	11,520	480	24
			42

Step 3 Calculate total cost of output

Cost of completed units = $42 × 400 units = $16,800

If you selected option A you omitted the absorption of overhead at the rate of 200 per cent of direct wages. If you selected option B you did not allow for the fact that the work in progress was incomplete. Option D is the total process cost for the period, some of which must be allocated to the work in progress.

10 The value of closing work in progress on 30 November is $ | 3,720 |

Using the data from answer 2 above, extend **step 3** to calculate the value of the work in progress.

Cost element	Number of equivalent units	Cost per equivalent unit $	Total $
Work in progress: Materials	100	18	1,800
Labour and overhead	80	24	1,920
			3,720

If you selected option A you omitted the absorption of overhead into the process costs. If you selected option C you did not allow for the fact that the work in progress was incomplete. Option D is the total process cost for the period, some of which must be allocated to the completed output.

34 Process costing III

1 The value credited to the process account for the scrap value of the normal loss for the period will be
$ | 100 | (to the nearest $)

Normal loss = 10% × input
= 10% × 5,000 kg
= 500 kg

When scrap has a value, normal loss is valued at the value of the scrap ie 20 cents per kg.

Normal loss = $0.20 × 500 kg
= $100

2 The value of the abnormal loss for the period is $ | 300 | (to the nearest $)

	kg
Input	5,000
Normal (10% × 5,000 kg)	(500)
Abnormal loss	(300)
Output	4,200

$$\text{Cost per unit} = \frac{\text{Input costs} - \text{scrap value of normal loss}}{\text{Expected output}}$$

$$= \frac{\$4,600^* - \$100}{5,000 - 500}$$

$$= \frac{\$4,500}{4,500} = \$1.00$$

Value of abnormal loss = 300 × $1.00 = $300

	$
*Materials (5,000 kg × 0.5)	2,500
Labour	700
Production overhead	1,400
	4,600

3 The value of the output for the period is $ ⟨4,200⟩ (to the nearest $)

Output = 4,200 kg

Cost per kg = $1 (from previous answer)

∴ Output value = 4,200 × $1
= $4,200

4 The value of the output for the period was $ ⟨43,680⟩ (to the nearest $)

Step 1

STATEMENT OF EQUIVALENT UNITS

	Total Units		Materials Units		Labour and overhead Units
Completed output	8,000	(100%)	8,000	(100%)	8,000
Normal loss	1,000	(0%)	–	(0%)	–
Abnormal loss	100	(100%)	100	(100%)	100
Closing WIP	900	(100%)	900	(75%)	675
	10,000		9,000		8,775

Step 2

STATEMENT OF COST PER EQUIVALENT UNIT

	Materials	Labour and overhead
Total costs	*$40,500	$8,424
Equivalent units	9,000	8,775
Cost per equivalent unit	$4.50	$0.96

* $40,800 less scrap value normal loss $300 = $40,500

Total cost per unit = $(4.50 + 0.96)
= $5.46

STATEMENT OF EVALUATION

Output

8,000 kg @ $5.46 = $43,680

5   The value of abnormal loss for the period was $ [546] (to the nearest $)
     From question 5, 100 units abnormal loss × $5.46 = $546

6   The value of the closing work in progress for the period was $ [4,698] (to the nearest $)
     From question 5, costs per equivalent unit are:
     Materials $4.50
     Labour and overhead $0.96

Evaluation of work in progress:

	$
Materials 900 equivalent units × $4.50	4,050
Labour and overhead 675 equivalent units × $0.96	648
	4,698

7   The value of the normal process loss for the month is $ [0] (to the nearest $)
     There is no mention of a scrap value available for any losses, therefore the normal loss would have a zero value.

8   The value of the units transferred to finished goods was $ [24,750]

STATEMENT OF EQUIVALENT UNITS

	Total units		Materials		Labour		Overheads
Finished output*	900		900		900		900
Closing WIP	150	(100%)	150	(50%)	75	(30%)	45
	1,050		1,050		975		945

* 750 units input + opening WIP 300 units – closing WIP 150 units

STATEMENT OF COSTS PER EQUIVALENT UNIT

	Materials $	Labour $	Overheads $	Total
Opening inventory	3,600	1,600	400	
Added during period	11,625	6,200	4,325	
Total cost	15,225	7,800	4,725	
Equivalent units	1,050	975	945	
Cost per equivalent unit	$14.50	$8	$5	$27.50

Value of units transferred to finished goods = $27.50 × 900 units = $24,750

9   The number of equivalent units to be used when calculating the cost per unit in relation to labour is

        | 975 | units.

STATEMENT OF EQUIVALENT UNITS

	Total units		Materials		*Equivalent units* Labour		Overheads
Finished output*	900		900		900		900
Closing WIP	150	(100%)	150	(50%)	75	(30%)	45
	1,050		1,050		975		945

* 750 units input + opening WIP 300 units – closing WIP 150 units

10   Material | 30 | equivalent litres

      Conversion costs | 15 | equivalent litres

      Work in progress   = 300 litres input – 250 litres to finished goods
                         – 15 litres normal loss – 5 litres abnormal loss

                 = 30 litres

Equivalent litres for each cost element in progress are as follows:

	Material %	Equiv. litres	Conversion costs %	Equiv. litres
30 litres in progress	100	30	50	15

35 Job, batch and contract costing I

1   The profit to be recognised on the contract to date is $ | 2,508,800 |

    Total contract cost, to completion   = $3,763,200 + $2,956,800
                                    = $6,720,000

    Approximate degree of completion   = $\dfrac{\$3,763,200}{\$6,720,000}$ = 56%

Since the contract is 56% complete and no difficulties are foreseen, a profit can reasonably be taken.

    Profit to be taken   = 56% × final contract profit
                      = 56% × $(11,200,000 – 6,720,000)
                      = $2,508,800

2 | ✓ | Contract costing

Each hotel would be a separately identifiable unit, therefore either job costing or contract costing would be appropriate. Since each hotel would represent a job of long duration, contract costing would be the most likely method to be used.

BPP
LEARNING MEDIA

3 The profit to be recognised on the contract to date is $ [0] (to the nearest $)

Since the contract is in its early stages, no profit should be recognised. Profit should only be taken when the outcome of the contract can be assessed with reasonable accuracy.

4 [✓] Production of the product can be completed in a single accounting period
   [✓] Production relates to a single special order

Job costing is appropriate where each cost unit is **separately identifiable** and is of relatively **short duration**.

5 The depreciation to be charged to contract number 145 for the year ending 31 December is $ [73]

Depreciation:

	$'000
On plant delivered 1 March $420,000 × 0.2 × 10/12	70
On plant delivered 1 July $30,000 × 0.2 × 6/12	3
	73

6 [✓] Actual material cost
   [✓] Absorbed manufacturing overheads
   [✓] Actual labour cost

The actual manufacturing overheads cannot usually be determined for a specific job. Therefore overheads are charged to individual jobs through the use of a predetermined overhead full rate.

7 [✓] Customer-driven production
   [✓] Complete production possible within a single accounting period

Each job is separately identifiable, according to a customer's requirements. Therefore the first characteristic is correct.

Jobs are usually of comparatively short duration, compared to situations where contract costing is applied. Therefore the second characteristic is correct.

The third characteristic is incorrect because each job is separately identifiable.

8 [✓] Customer-driven production
   [✓] Work is often undertaken on the customer's premises
   [✓] Work is often constructional in nature

Each contract is separately identifiable and is completed according to customer's specific requirements. Therefore the first characteristic is correct.

Contract costing often applies to projects which are constructional in nature and the work is frequently based on site, at the customer's premises. Therefore the second and third characteristics are also correct.

9   The price to be quoted for job B124 is $ 124.50 (to the nearest cent)
    Production overhead absorption rate = $240,000/30,000 = $8 per labour hour
    Other overhead absorption rate = ($150,000/$750,000) × 100% = 20% of total production cost

Job B124	$
Direct materials (3 kgs × $5)	15.00
Direct labour (4 hours × $9)	36.00
Production overhead (4 hours × $8)	32.00
Total production cost	83.00
Other overhead (20% × $83)	16.60
Total cost	99.60
Profit margin: 20% of sales (× 20/80)	24.90
Price to be quoted	124.50

10 D   Statement A is correct. Job costs are identified with a particular job, whereas process costs (of units produced and work in progress) are **averages**, based on equivalent units of production.

        Statement B is correct. The direct cost of a job to date, excluding any direct expenses, can be ascertained from the documents mentioned.

        Statement C is correct, because without data about units completed and units still in process, losses and equivalent units of production cannot be calculated.

        Statement D is incorrect, because the cost of normal loss will usually be incorporated into job costs as well as into process costs. In process costing, this is commonly done by **giving normal loss no cost**, leaving costs to be shared between output, closing inventories and abnormal loss/gain. In job costing, it can be done by adjusting direct materials costs to allow for **normal wastage**, and direct labour costs for **normal reworking** of items or **normal spoilage.**

36 Job, batch and contract costing II

1   A   Job costing is a costing method applied where work is **undertaken to customers' special requirements.** Option B describes process costing, C describes service costing and D describes absorption costing.

2   C   Statement (i) is correct. The materials requisition note **specifies the job number to be charged** with the cost of the materials issued.

        Statement (ii) is incorrect. A job cost will contain actual costs for material and labour, and non-production overheads are often added as a percentage of total production cost. However, **production overheads are usually charged to jobs using a pre-determined overhead absorption rate** because it is not possible to identify the actual overhead cost of each job.

        Statement (iii) is correct. The **cost of each batch can be determined using job costing methods.** The cost per item within the batch can then be calculated by dividing the total cost of the batch by the number of items in the batch.

        Therefore the correct answer is C.

3   D

	Dept A $	Dept B $	Total $
Direct materials	5,000	3,000	8,000
Direct labour	1,600	1,000	2,600
Production overhead	1,600	800	2,400
Absorption production cost			13,000
Other overheads (20%)			2,600
Cost of the job			15,600
Profit (25% of sales = 33% of cost)			5,200
Sales price			20,800

If you selected option C you calculated the profit margin as 25 per cent of total cost, instead of 25 per cent of selling price.

If you selected option B you forgot to add administration overhead, and option A contains the same error with the profit calculated incorrectly as 25 per cent of cost.

4   C   The most logical basis for absorbing the overhead job costs is to use a percentage of direct labour cost.

$$\text{Overhead} = \frac{24,600}{(14,500+3,500+24,600)} \times \$126,000$$

$$= \frac{24,600}{42,600} \times \$126,000$$

$$= \$72,761$$

If you selected option A you used the materials cost as the basis for overhead absorption. This would not be equitable because job number BB15 incurred no material cost and would therefore absorb no overhead. Option B is based on the prime cost of each job (material plus labour) and therefore suffers from the same disadvantage as option A. Option D is the total overhead for the period, but some of this cost should be charged to the other two jobs.

5   C

	Job BB15 $
Opening WIP	42,790
Labour for period	3,500
Overheads ($\frac{3,500}{42,600} \times 126,000$)	10,352
Total costs	56,642
Profit (33 $\frac{1}{3}$% on sales = 50% costs)	28,321
	84,963

If you selected option A you forgot to add on overhead cost. If you selected option B you calculated the profit as 33% on cost, instead of 33% on sales. If you selected option D you charged all of the overhead to job BBI5, but some of the overhead should be charged to the other two jobs.

6   C   *Job number*   *WIP*
                                                                                                    $

AA10 (26,800 + 17,275 + 14,500) + ($\frac{14,500}{42,600}$ × 126,000)   101,462

CC20 (18,500 + 24,600 + 72,761)   115,861
                                                                                                    217,323

Option A is the direct cost of job AA10, with no addition for overhead. Option B is the direct cost of both jobs in progress, but with no addition for overhead. Option D is the result of charging all of the overhead to the jobs in progress, but some of the overhead must be absorbed by the completed job BBI5.

7   C   Total labour cost = $12,500 + $23,000 + $4,500 = $40,000

Overhead absorption rate = $\frac{\$140,000}{\$40,000}$ × 100% = 350% of direct labour cost

Closing work in progress valuation

	Job 1		*Job 2*	*Total*
	$		$	$
Costs given in question	38,150		52,025	90,175
Overhead absorbed				
($12,500 × 350%)	43,750	($23,000 × 350%)	80,500	124,250
				214,425

Option A is the costs given in the question, with no overhead absorbed. If you selected option B you calculated the correct amount for overhead absorbed, but forgot to add the costs given in the question. If you selected option D you added all of the overhead to the jobs in progress, but some of the overhead must be absorbed by the completed job 3.

8   C $
         Opening WIP   46,000
         Labour for period   4,500
         Overhead absorbed ($4,500 × 350%)   15,750
         Total production cost   66,250
         50% mark up   33,125
         Sales value of job 3   99,375

         Selling price per circuit board = $99,375 ÷ 2,400 $41.41

Option B is the selling price without the inclusion of any overhead absorbed. If you selected option D you calculated a 50 per cent margin based on the selling price, instead of a 50% mark up on cost.

9   A   3,300 hours represent 75% of the total time for the job. Therefore the total time must be 3,300 ÷ 0.75 = 4,400 hours.

Labour cost per hour = $\frac{\$36,300}{4,400}$ = $8.25

If you selected option B you **added 25 per cent** to the productive hours to derive the total time taken.

Option C is the hourly rate without any allowance for the idle time, and if you selected option D you **deducted 25 per cent** from the productive time to derive the total time taken.

10   C   Since wages are paid on a piecework basis they are a variable cost which will increase in line with the number of binders. The machine set-up cost and design costs are fixed costs for each batch which will not be affected by the number of binders in the batch.

For a batch of 300 binders:

	$
Direct materials (30 × 3)	90.00
Direct wages (10 × 3)	30.00
Machine set up	3.00
Design and artwork	15.00
Production overhead (30 × 20%)	6.00
Total production cost	144.00
Selling, distribution and administration overhead (+ 5%)	7.20
Total cost	151.20
Profit (25% margin = 33⅓% of cost)	50.40
Selling price for a batch of 300	201.60

If you selected option A you calculated the cost correctly, but added a profit mark up of 25% of cost, instead of a margin of 25% of selling price.

If you selected option B you failed to absorb the appropriate amount of fixed overhead. If you selected option D you treated all of the costs as variable costs.

37 Job, batch and contract costing III

1   B

	$
Selling price of job	1,690
Less profit margin (30/130)	390
Total cost of job	1,300
Less overhead	694
Prime cost	606

If you selected option A you deducted 30 per cent from the selling price to derive the total cost of the job. Option C is the result of deducting the overhead from the selling price, but omitting to deduct the profit margin. Option D is the total cost of the job; you needed to deduct the overhead to derive the prime cost.

2   C

		$
Salary costs:	senior consultant (86 × $20)	1,720
	junior time (220 × $15)	3,300
Overhead absorbed (306 hours × $12.50)		3,825
Total cost		8,845
Mark up (40%)		3,538
Selling price		12,383

If you selected option A you did not include any absorbed overhead in your total cost. Option B is the total cost with no addition for profit, and if you selected option D you calculated a 40 per cent **margin** on the selling price, rather than a 40 per cent **mark-up** on total cost.

3   A

			$
Salary costs:	senior hours (3,000 × 1/4 × $20)		15,000
	junior hours (3,000 × 3/4 × $15)		33,750
Overhead absorbed (3,000 hours × $12.50)			37,500
Total cost			86,250
Mark up (40%)			34,500

If you selected option B you calculated a 40 per cent margin based on the sales value, rather than on the cost. Option C is the total cost for the period and D is the total sales revenue for the period.

4   D

	Hours
Active hours required	380
Add idle time (5/95)	20
Total hours to be paid	400 @ $6 per hour
Total labour cost	$2,400

If you selected option A you reduced the active hours by five per cent. However, the hours to be paid must be **greater than** the active hours, therefore the idle hours must be added. If you selected option B you made no allowance for the idle hours, which must also be paid for. If you selected option C you added five per cent to the active hours, but note that the idle time is quoted as a **percentage of the total time to be paid for.**

5   D

Hours for job 34679	= 400 hours
Production overhead cost	$4,000
∴ Overhead absorption rate ($4,000 ÷ 400)	$10 per direct labour hour
Budgeted direct labour hours	45,000
∴ Total budgeted production overheads	$450,000
Budgeted direct wages cost	$180,000
∴ Absorption rate as % of wages cost	= $450,000/$180,000 × 100%
	= 250%

Cost of job 34679

	$
Direct materials	2,000
Direct labour, including overtime premium *	2,500
Overhead (250% × $2,500)	6,250
Total production cost	10,750

* The overtime premium is a direct labour cost because the overtime was worked specifically for this job.

If you selected option A you got your calculation of the overhead absorption rate 'upside down' and derived a percentage rate of 40 per cent in error. If you selected option B you did not include the overtime premium and the corresponding overhead. If you selected option C you did not include the overtime premium in the direct labour costs.

6   B   Statement (i) is correct. Each contract is **separately identifiable** and is completed according to **customers' specific requirements**.

Statement (ii) is not correct. Contract costing often applies to projects which are **constructional in nature** and the work is frequently based **on site** away from the contractor's premises.

Statement (iii) is correct. Many contracts to which contract costing is applied **span more than one accounting period**.

Therefore the correct answer is B.

7   A

	$	$
Equipment delivered to site		
Plant	380,000	
Tools	4,000	
		384,000
Plant transferred from site		(120,000)
Equipment remaining on site, 31 December:		
Plant	(180,000)	
Tools	(2,500)	
		(182,500)
Depreciation cost of equipment for year 3		81,500

Option B is the written down value of the equipment on site at the end of the year. If you selected option C you omitted to deduct the written down value of the plant removed from the site. Option D is the beginning of year written down values of the equipment that was remaining on site at the end of the year.

8   C   Notional profit = Value of work certified to date – the cost of the work certified
Notional profit = $(1,300,000 – 1,000,000)
Notional profit = $300,000

Option A is the difference between the cash received and the costs incurred. Option B is the difference between the cash received and the cost of the work certified. Option D is the contract price minus the value certified.

9   A   Since the contract is in its early stages, **no profit should be taken**. Profit should only be taken when the outcome of the contract can be **assessed with reasonable accuracy**.

The other options are all derived from the data available but none is correct in view of the early stage of the contract.

10   B   The contract is forecast to make a loss and the **total expected loss should be taken into account as soon as it is recognised**.

	$
Expected loss on contract ($86,250 – ($65,625 + $29,375)	8,750
Loss incurred to date ($57,900 – $65,625)	7,725
Anticipated future loss	1,025
Cost incurred to date	65,625
Cost of sales	66,650

The correct turnover figure is the **value of the work certified**, $57,900.

If you decided that the correct cost of sales was $65,625 (options A and C) you failed to allow for the anticipated future loss.

If you selected option D you determined the correct 'net' result of a loss of $8,750, but you allocated the data incorrectly between turnover and cost of sales.

38 Service costing

1 B   In service costing it is difficult to identify many attributable direct costs. Many costs must be **shared over several cost units**, therefore characteristic (i) does apply. Composite cost units such as tonne-mile or room-night are often used, therefore characteristic (ii) does apply. Equivalent units are more often used in **costing for tangible products**, therefore characteristic (iii) does not apply, and the correct answer is B.

2 C   Cost per tonne – kilometre (i) is appropriate for cost control purposes because it **combines** the distance travelled and the load carried, **both of which affect cost.**

The fixed cost per kilometre (ii) is not particularly useful for control purposes because it **varies with the number of kilometres travelled**.

The maintenance cost of each vehicle per kilometre (iii) can be useful for control purposes because it **focuses on a particular aspect** of the cost of operating each vehicle. Therefore the correct answer is C.

3 D   All of the activities identified would use service costing, except the light engineering company which will be providing **products not services**.

4 B   The most appropriate cost unit is the **tonne-mile**. Therefore the cost per unit =

$$\frac{\$562,800}{375,200} = \$1.50$$

Option A is the cost per mile travelled. This is not as useful as the cost per tonne-mile, which **combines** the distance travelled and the load carried, **both of which affect cost**.

Option C is the cost per hour worked by drivers and D is the cost per driver employed. Costs are more likely to be incurred in relation to the distance travelled and the load carried.

5 | ✓ | High levels of indirect costs as a proportion of total cost

| ✓ | Cost units are often intangible

| ✓ | Use of composite cost units

In service costing it is difficult to identify many attributable direct costs. Many costs must be treated as **indirect costs** and **shared over several cost units**, therefore the first characteristic does apply. Many services are **intangible**, for example a haircut or a cleaning service provide no physical, tangible product. Therefore the second characteristic does apply. **Composite cost units** such as passenger-mile or bed-night are often used in service costing, therefore the third characteristic does apply. The fourth characteristic does not apply because equivalent units are more often used in **costing for tangible products.**

6   ☑ Vehicle cost per passenger – kilometre

      ☑ Maintenance cost per vehicle per kilometre

      ☑ Fuel cost per kilometre

The vehicle cost per passenger – kilometre is appropriate for cost control purposes because it **combines** the distance travelled and the number of passengers carried, **both of which affect cost**.

The maintenance cost for each vehicle per kilometre can be useful for control purposes because it **focuses on a particular aspect** of the cost of operating each vehicle.

The fixed cost per passenger is not particularly useful for control purposes because it **varies with the number of passengers carried**.

The fuel cost per kilometre can be useful for control purposes because it **focuses on a particular aspect** of resource consumption.

7   ☑ Patient/day

      ☑ Operating theatre hour

      ☑ Outpatient visit

All of the above would be **measurable** and would be **useful for control purposes.** A ward and an x-ray department are more likely to be used as **cost centres** for the purpose of cost collection and analysis.

8   A | Total costs for period |

    B | Number of service units in the period |

9

Service	Cost unit
Hotels	D
Education	C
Hospitals	B
Catering organisations	A

10 | Intangibility |

       | Heterogeneity |

       | Perishability |

       | Simultaneity |

39 Mixed bank I

1   B

	$
Total cost for 200,000 units	60,000
Less fixed cost	10,000
Variable cost for 200,000 units	50,000

Variable cost per unit = $\dfrac{\$50,000}{200,000}$ = $0.25

Alternatively you could have calculated the correct answer using the high-low method based on the cost data for 80,000 units and 200,000 units.

If you selected option A you calculated the fixed cost per unit for a level of activity of 200,000 units. Option C is the total cost per unit at this level of activity and option D is the total cost per unit for a level of activity of 80,000 units.

2   C   Statement (i) is not correct. A major disadvantage of the high/low method is that **only two historical cost records from previous periods are used** in the cost estimation.

Statement (ii) is correct. The line of best fit is drawn by visual judgement and so is a subjective approximation.

Statement (iii) is not correct. The cost behaviour pattern observed applies only to the range of activity covered by the data available. Although managers are often forced to use this data as a basis for prediction outside this range, the results may be inaccurate.

Therefore the correct answer is C.

3   C   **Standard cost of production of product F**

	$ per unit	$ per unit
Material M 6kg × $2	12	
Material N 5kg × $3	15	
		27
Skilled labour 3 hours × $8	24	
Semi-skilled labour 1 hour × $6	6	
		30
Production overhead 4 labour hours × $4		16
Standard production cost		73

If you selected option A you did not include any production overhead, which is a part of production cost. Option B bases the absorption on the skilled labour hours only. Option D includes the absorption of administration overhead; however, the question asks for the standard cost of production; **always read the question carefully**!

4   D   Performance standards would be taken into account when estimating **material usage**, they would not have a direct effect on material price. Therefore the correct answer is D.

All of the other factors would be used to estimate standard material prices for a forthcoming period.

5   B   An attainable standard assumes efficient levels of operation, but includes **allowances** for normal loss, waste and machine downtime.

Option A describes an **ideal standard**
Option C describes a **current standard**
Option D describes a **basic standard**

6

	Debit	Credit	No entry in this account
Labour efficiency variance account		✓	
Wages control account			✓
Work in progress control account	✓		

7   ✓   Debit wages control account
    ✓   Credit labour rate variance account

The actual hourly rate is less than the standard hourly rate, therefore the labour rate variance is favourable and the variance account is credited. The debit entry is made in the wages control account.

8   The volume of closing WIP is [1,800] litres.

Workings

	Litres
Normal loss (5% × 12,000)	600
Abnormal loss	100
Completed production	9,500
Closing WIP	1,800 *
	12,000

* Closing WIP = Input − normal loss − abnormal loss − completed production
              = 12,000 − 600 − 100 − 9,500 = 1,800

9   Debit   [scrap]   account
    Credit   [process] account

10 Basic hourly rate = (1 × $14) + (3 × $10) + (1 × $6) = $50.

Output per day Units	Increase %	Hourly group remuneration $
Up to 200	–	50.00
201 to 250	10	55.00
251 to 280	12	56.00
281 to 300	15	57.50

40 Mixed bank II

1   The number of units produced in the period was $\boxed{1,600}$

Labour efficiency variance (in $)   =   \$27,000

∴ Labour efficiency variance (in hours)   =   \$27,000 ÷ \$6 per hour

                                      =   4,500 hours

Let x = number of units actually produced

	Hours
Actual hours worked	52,500
x units should have taken (30 × x)	30x
Labour efficiency variance (in hours)	4,500 (A)

Actual hours worked were therefore 4,500 more than expected (due to an adverse labour efficiency variance).

∴ x units should have taken   =   (52,500 – 4,500) hours

                                =   48,000 hours

               30x   =   48,000 hours

                   x   = $\dfrac{48,000 \text{ hours}}{30}$

                       =   1,600 units

2   The number of labour hours actually worked was $\boxed{24,780}$

4,920 units should have taken (× 6.5 hrs)   31,980

but did take   x

The variance in hours is therefore (31,980 – x) hrs × standard rate (\$5)

Labour efficiency variance   =   159,900 – 5x

          or 36,000   =   159,900 – 5x

                5x   =   159,900 – 36,000

                 x   = $\dfrac{123,900}{5}$

                   =   24,780

3   Labour hours actually worked were $\boxed{9,650}$ hours

	Hours
Should have taken (850 × 12 hrs)	10,200
Favourable efficiency variance (4,400 ÷ 8)	550
∴ Did take	9,650

4   ☑ Useful for monitoring output in a standard costing system

     ☑ The quantity of work achievable at standard performance in an hour

     ☑ A basis for measuring output when dissimilar products are manufactured

A standard hour is the quantity of work achievable at standard performance, expressed in terms of a standard unit of work done in a standard period of time. It is a useful measure since it can be used to monitor output in a budgeting or standard costing system. It also overcomes the problem of how to measure output when a number of dissimilar products are manufactured.

5

		Favourable	Adverse
The variable overhead expenditure variance	$90	☐	✓
The variable overhead efficiency variance	$60	✓	☐

(i)

760 hours of variable overhead should cost (× $1.50)	1,140	
but did cost	1,230	
Variable overhead expenditure variance	90	(A)

(ii)

400 units should take (× 2 hours)	800	hrs
but did take (active hours)	760	hrs
Variance in hours	40	hrs (F)
× standard rate per hour	× $1.50	
Variable overhead efficiency variance in $	$60	(F)

6

$

✓ Debit work-in-progress account	60,000
✓ Credit material stores account	60,000

Inventories of material are recorded at standard price therefore the material price variance would have been transferred to the variance account at the time of purchase. The transfer from inventory of 20,000 kg issued to work-in-progress on 28 June is made at the standard price of $3 per kg.

7 The ranking of the two products in order of their contribution per labour hour in the grinding process is:

1st Baker

2nd Able

Workings

	Able		Baker	
	$/unit	$/unit	$/unit	$/unit
Selling price		206.5		168.0
Direct materials	10.0		30.0	
Direct labour: grinding	35.0		25.0	
finishing	112.5		67.5	
		157.5		122.5
Contribution per unit		49.0		45.5
Grinding labour hours		7		5
Contribution per hour		$7.00		$9.10

8   The deficiency in machine hours for the next period is ┌ 13,000 ┐ hours

Workings

	Product A	Product B	Product C	Total
Machine hours required per unit	6	4	7	
Maximum demand (units)	3,000	2,500	5,000	
Total machine hours required	18,000	10,000	35,000	63,000
Machine hours available				50,000
Deficiency in machine hours for next period				13,000

9   The cost per equivalent kg for the period was:

Materials $ ┌ 2.80 ┐ per equivalent kg

Conversion costs $ ┌ 2.50 ┐ per equivalent kg

Step 1

STATEMENT OF EQUIVALENT KG

	Total kg	Equivalent kg Direct material		Conversion costs
Output completed	87,100	87,100		87,100
Closing WIP	28,200	28,200	(50%)	14,100
Normal loss (10% × 105,600)	10,560	0		0
Abnormal loss	1,440	1,440		1,440
	127,300	116,740		102,640

Step 2

STATEMENT OF COST PER EQUIVALENT KG

	Direct material $	Conversion costs $
Opening WIP	56,420	30,405
Added in period	291,572	226,195
Less scrap value of normal loss	(21,120)	
	326,872	256,600
Equivalent kg	116,740	102,640
Cost per equivalent kg	$2.80	$2.50

10   ┌ ✓ ┐ Graph 1

41 Mixed bank III

1　The mark-up which needs to be added to marginal cost to allow the product to break even is $166^2/_3\%$

Breakeven point occurs when total contribution equals fixed costs.

At breakeven point, $10,000 = 400 units × unit contribution = 400 × (price – $15)
So $10,000/400 = price – $15
So $25 + $15 = $40 = price

Mark-up = $(40 – 15) = $25
Marginal cost = $15
Mark-up = (25/15) × 100% = 166 $^2/_3$%

2　✓　A pint of milk produced by a dairy

　　✓　A call taken at a call centre

　　✓　One of a bank's business customers

　　✓　The home delivery service of a department store

A cost object is any 'product, service, centre, activity, customer or distribution channel in relation to which costs are ascertained' (CIMA *Official Terminology*).

3　The sales price variance is $ 64,000 ~~favourable~~/adverse

	$'000
Revenue from 3,200 units should have been (× $140)	448
But was (× $120)	384
Sales price variance	64　(A)

4　The sales volume variance is $ 16,800 favourable/~~adverse~~

	$'000	
Budgeted sales volume	3,000	units
Actual sales volume	3,200	units
Sales volume variance	200	units (F)
× standard contribution per unit ($(140 – 56) = $84)	× $84	
Sales volume contribution variance	$16,800	(F)

5　B　Objective classification indicates the purpose of expenditure, responsibility classification indicates who is responsible for the expenditure. Cost classification is a general term for the overall process.

6　A　Objective classification indicates the cost unit or cost centre to be charged.

7   ☑   A favourable sales volume variance

☑   A favourable labour efficiency variance

☑   A favourable material usage variance

☑   A favourable sales price variance

The improvement in quality may mean that more units are sold, leading to a favourable sales volume variance.

The more expensive material may be easier to work with, leading to a favourable labour efficiency variance.

There may be less waste with the more expensive material, leading to a favourable material usage variance.

The improvement in quality may mean that a higher price can be charged, leading to a favourable sales price variance.

8   D   The economic cost is the marginal historical cost plus the lost contribution of $10,000 from choosing customer X instead of customer Y.

9   The value added by L Company during February was $ ⬛ 34,000 ⬛.

		$'000	$'000
Sales			100
Materials:	direct	60	
	indirect (1 + 5)	6	
			66
Value added			34

10   The gross margin of FOB Co is ⬛ 36.25 ⬛ % in year 1 and ⬛ 41.67 ⬛ % in year 0.

The **pure trading activities of a business can be analysed** using the gross profit margin, which is calculated as **(gross profit ÷ turnover) × 100%**. Non-production overheads are not included.

The gross profit margin would be ((16,000 + 42,000)/160,000) × 100% = 36.25% in Year 1 and ((15,000 + 35,000)/120,000) × 100% = 41.67% in Year 0.

---

42 Mixed bank IV

1   ⬛ ✓ ⬛   A step cost

The cost described will increase in **steps**, remaining fixed at each step until another supervisor is required. Such a cost is known as a **step cost.**

2   (iii)   They are based on actual data for each period   ✓

(iv)   They are used to control overhead costs   ✓

Overhead absorption rates are determined in advance for each period, usually based on budgeted data. Therefore statement (i) is true and statement (iii) is not true. Overhead absorption rates are used in the final stage of overhead analysis, to absorb overheads into product costs. Therefore statement (ii) is true. Statement (iv) is not true because overheads are controlled using budgets and other management information.

BPP
LEARNING MEDIA

3   The total production overhead cost of unit X128 is $ [171.37]

Overhead cost absorbed by unit X128

	$
Extrusion department (5 hours × $13.31)	66.55
Machining department (7 hours × $10.50)	73.50
Finishing department (6 hours × $5.22)	31.32
	171.37

4   The total overhead for the Residential cost centre will be $ [135,318]

	Resi-dential $	Catering $	House-keeping $	Main-tenance $	Total $
Initial allocation and apportionment	85,333	68,287	50,370	23,010	227,000
Reapportion maintenance (50:30:20)	11,505	6,903	4,602	(23,010)	–
	96,838	75,190	54,972	–	227,000
Reapportion housekeeping (70:30)	38,480	16,492	(54,972)		–
	135,318	91,682	–		227,000

5   (a)   The overhead absorption rate for the Casting department was $ [30] per production hour.

Workings

	Casting department
$\dfrac{\text{Production overheads}}{\text{Expected production hours}}$	$225,000
	7,500
Predetermined overhead absorption rate	= $30/hr

(b)   The overhead in the Dressing department in period 3 was [under] absorbed by $ [875]

Workings

Dressing department overhead absorption rate = $\dfrac{\$175,000}{7,000}$ = $25 per hour

	$
Overhead absorbed (7,280 hours × $25)	182,000
Overhead incurred	182,875
(Under) absorption of overhead	(875)

6   The profit reported for period 1 using marginal costing principles is $ ⟨62,300⟩

Income statement for period 1 under marginal costing

		Period 1	
		$	$
Sales:	Alpha (2,300 × $90)		207,000
	Beta (1,600 × $75)		120,000
			327,000
Opening inventory	Alpha	0	
	Beta	0	
		0	
Variable costs:	Alpha (2,500 × $45)	112,500	
	Beta (1,750 × $32)	56,000	
		168,500	
Less:			
Closing inventory	Alpha (200 × $45)	(9,000)	
	Beta (150 × $32)	(4,800)	
Variable cost of goods sold			154,700
Contribution			172,300
Fixed costs			(110,000)
Profit			62,300

7   B

	$ per unit
Material	15.00
Labour	52.05
Production overhead (7 hrs × $9.44)	66.08
Total production cost	133.13
General overhead (8% × $133.13)	10.65
Total cost	143.78
Required return from product R	
per unit ($36,200 × 0.14)/9,530	0.53
Required selling price	144.31

8   The total cost is $ ⟨276.60⟩

	$ per unit
Material	57.50
Labour	17.90
Production overhead (11 hrs × $14.10)	155.10
Total production cost	230.50
General overhead (20% × $230.50)	46.10
Total cost	276.60

9   D

	Cost centre A $ per unit	Cost centre B $ per unit	Total $ per unit
Direct material	60.00	30.30	90.30
Direct labour	60.00	15.20	75.20
Production overhead	36.72	14.94	51.66
Total production cost			217.16
General overhead cost at 10%			21.72
Total cost			238.88
Profit margin (× 20/80)			59.72
Required selling price per unit			298.60

10   The total production cost is $ [830.10]

	Cost centre 1 $ per unit	Cost centre 2 $ per unit	Total $ per unit
Direct material	171.00	67.50	238.50
Direct labour	75.00	374.00	449.00
Production overhead	97.50	45.10	142.60
Total production cost			830.10

43 Mixed bank V

1   Charge for each hour of writing (to the nearest cent) should be $ [28.94]

Weeks worked per year = 52 – 4 = 48

Hours worked per year = 48 × 40 hrs
                       = 1,920

Hours chargeable to clients = 1,920 × 90% = 1,728

Total expenses = $10,000 + $40,000 = $50,000

Hourly rate = $\dfrac{\$50,000}{1,728}$ = $28.94 per hour

2   The price that should be charged for assignment number 3036 is $ [47,763]

	$
Salary costs: Senior consultant (172 × $40)	6,880
Junior time (440 × $30)	13,200
Overhead absorbed (612 × $25)	15,300
Total cost	35,380
Mark up (35%)	12,383
Selling price	47,763

3   The depreciation cost of the equipment to be charged to contract 3830 for 20X1 is $ | 163,000 |

	$	$
Equipment delivered to site		
Plant	760,000	
Tools	8,000	
		768,000
Plant transferred from site		(240,000)
Equipment remaining on site, 31 December		
Plant	(360,000)	
Tools	(5,000)	
		(365,000)
Depreciation cost of equipment for 20X1		163,000

4   B   Cost per tonne-kilometre (i) is appropriate for cost control purposes because it **combines** the distance travelled with the load carried, **both of which affect cost.**

The fixed cost per kilometre (ii) is not particularly useful for control purposes because it varies with the number of kilometres travelled. This cost unit would therefore be inappropriate for a transport business.

The maintenance cost of each vehicle per kilometre (iii) can be useful for control purposes because it focuses on a particular aspect of the cost of operating each vehicle.

5   C   Statement (i) is incorrect. Units of normal loss are valued at their scrap value (which may be nil).

Statement (ii) is incorrect. Units of abnormal loss are valued at the same rate as good units.

Statement (iii) is incorrect. Abnormal loss units are an addition to the equivalent units produced, abnormal gain units are subtracted.

Therefore the correct answer is C, statements (i), (ii) and (iii) being incorrect.

6   B   Statement (i) is not correct; an **expected loss is a normal loss**. Statement (iv) is not correct; normal loss could be less than actual loss if an abnormal loss occurred. Therefore the correct answer is B.

7   A   The abnormal gain units are **valued at the same unit rate as good production** so that the occurrence of the abnormal gain does not affect the cost of the good units. Therefore the correct answer is A. If you selected option C you were thinking of normal loss units, which are credited to the process account at their scrap value.

8   D   Expected output = 2,000 units **less** normal loss (5%) 100 units = 1,900 units

In situation (i) there is an **abnormal loss** of 1,900 – 1,800 = 100 units
In situation (ii) there is an **abnormal gain** of 1,950 – 1,900 = 50 units
In situation (iii) there is an **abnormal gain** of 2,000 – 1,900 = 100 units

Therefore the correct answer is D.

9   D   The abnormal loss units are valued at their **absorption production cost** and **credited** to the process account, so that their occurrence does not affect the cost of good production. Therefore the correct answer is D.

Options A and C are incorrect because the scrap value of the abnormal loss is debited to the **scrap account** and credited to the **abnormal loss account**, it has no impact on the process account.

10   C   The main process account is debited with an abnormal gain to **'cancel out' part of the normal loss entry**. The abnormal gain account therefore carries the 'other side' of the entry, being the **credit for the normal production cost**. This credit is **offset by the scrap value forgone**, which is debited to the abnormal gain account and credited to the scrap account.

Mock Assessments

CIMA

Paper C1 (Certificate)

Fundamentals of Management Accounting

Mock Assessment 1

Question Paper	
Time allowed	**2 hours**
Answer ALL fifty questions	

DO NOT OPEN THIS PAPER UNTIL YOU ARE READY TO START UNDER EXAMINATION CONDITIONS

Answer ALL 50 questions

1   A wholesaler had an opening inventory of 330 units of product T valued at $168 each on 1st February.

The following receipts and sales were recorded during February.

			Units	Av cost	Total cost
			330	1.68	55,440
4 February	Received 180 units at a cost of	$174 per unit	510	170.1	86,760
18 February	Received 90 units at a cost of	$186 per unit	600	172.5	103500
24 February	Sold 432 units at a price of	$220 per unit			

Using the weighted average cost method of valuation, what was the cost of the units sold on 24 February?

- A $72,600
- B $74,520
- C $78,875
- D $80,250

2   In a period, 28,644 kg of material were used at a total standard cost of $114,576. The material usage variance was $1,140 favourable.

4   285 6,5

What was the standard allowed weight of material for the period? Write your answer here.

 kg   RTQ

3   The following data relate to Product D.

Material cost per unit	$20.00	20
Labour cost per unit	$69.40	+69.40 = 89.4
Production overhead cost per machine hour	$12.58	+176.12 = 266.02
Machine hours per unit	14	
General overhead absorption rate	8% of total production cost	

What is the total cost per unit of Product D, to the nearest $0.01?

- A $176.12
- B $265.52
- C $286.76
- D $300.12

4   Product S is produced in two production cost centres. Budgeted data for Product S are as follows.

	Cost centre Alpha	Cost centre Beta
Direct material cost per unit	$20.00 20	$10.10 10.10
Direct labour hours per unit	1.5 11.63	1 7.35
Direct labour rate per hour	$7.75	$7.35 4.98 × 1.1
Production overhead absorption rate per direct labour hour	$4.08 6.12	$4.98

General overhead costs are absorbed into product costs at a rate of ten per cent of production cost.

41.53   RTQ

production cost per unit of $40.913

The total **production cost** per unit of Product S is, to the nearest $0.01:

A $30.10
B $60.18
Ⓒ $68.10
D $70.12

---

5   Which of the following are characteristics of job costing?

✓	Customer-driven production.
✓	Complete production possible within a single accounting period.
	Homogeneous products.

---

6   In a situation where there are no production resource limitations, which of the following must be available for the material usage budget to be completed?

✓	Standard material usage per unit
✓	Budgeted production volume
	The budgeted average lead time for delivery of materials
	Budgeted change in materials inventory

---

7   The budget committee is responsible for the following task(s):

✓	Co-ordinating the preparation of budgets
✓	Issuing the budget manual
✓	Allocating responsibility for the budget preparation
	Preparing the functional budgets
✓	Monitoring the budgetary planning process

Roles of the budget Committee

---

8   Which of the following is/are classified as direct materials?

	Cleaning materials used to clean the factory floor
✓	Component parts ordered for a specific job
✓	Part finished goods transferred into a process from an earlier process
	Maintenance materials used to repair machines

NB/ Part finished goods do count as direct costs here.

---

9   Which of the following is/are classified as indirect labour?

✓	Idle time payments to direct workers
	Overtime premium paid at the specific request of a customer
✓	Payments made to workers installing and testing new production machinery

NB/ Installing and testing new machinery is a capital costs.

10   The standard selling price of product X is $15. Actual sales in the year were 2,000 units at $15.30 per unit.

Calculate the selling price variance for the year: *shald ; 30,000*
                                                       30,600

	Favourable	Adverse
Selling price variance 600	✓	

11   Which of the following is/are functional budgets?

✓	Purchasing budget
✗	Cash budget
✓	Sales budget
✗	Income statement budget
✓	Marketing cost budget

12   Which of the following is/are descriptions of a semi-variable cost?

	Rental of a photocopier; the rent cost is $250 per month if the number of copies taken is less than 8,000. If the number of copies exceeds 8,000 the monthly rental increases to $300
✓	Hire of a delivery vehicle: the hire cost is $800 per month, plus $0.07 per mile travelled
✓	A piecework scheme with a guaranteed day rate *NB – A semi-variable cost.*

13   Product J is produced in two production cost centres. Budgeted data for Product J are as follows.

	Cost centre B	Cost centre C
Direct material cost per unit	$20.00 *20*	$10.10 *10.10*
Direct labour hours per unit	1.5 *11.63*	1
Direct labour rate per hour	$7.75	$7.35 *7.35*
Production overhead absorption rate per direct labour hour	$4.08 *6.12*	$4.98 *4.98*
	41.56	*24.67*

General overhead costs are absorbed into product costs at a rate of ten per cent of production cost.

If a 20 per cent return on sales is required from Product J, its selling price per unit should be, to the nearest $0.01:

80 = 66.23

A $66.20

100 = x

B $68.96
C $79.44
Ⓓ $82.75

The following information relates to questions 14 – 16

X Co makes one product, which passes through a single process.

Details of the process are as follows:

Materials	5,000 kg at 50c per kg
Labour	$800
Production overheads	200% of labour

Normal losses are 20% of input in the process, and without further processing any losses can be sold as scrap for 30c per kg.

The output for the period was 3,800 kg from the process.

There was no work in progress at the beginning or end of the period.

14 The value of the normal loss is $ `200`   *NB Nd loss a naual loss*

15 The value of the abnormal `loss` is $ `40`. This value will be: *NB A loss is debited to the income statement.*

☐ debited to the income statement   *NB For abnamal loss use cost per unit formula*

☑ credited to the income statement

16 The value of the output from the process is $ `4,300`   *NB Include cost of all input.*

4900   *74,1000*

The following information relates to questions 17 – 19

WCP Co manufactures three products W, C and P, for which the following data are available for the next period.

	W	C	P
	$ per unit	$ per unit	$ per unit
Selling price	38	24	57
Material cost ($2 per kg)	6	8	12
Labour cost ($8 per hour)	12	4	16
Other variable cost	2	5	6
Demand (units)	1,000	800	1,300
Fixed costs		$31,000 per period	

The supply of material and labour for the next period will be limited to 20,000 kg and 4,000 hours respectively.

17 The limiting factor for the next period will be: *Contribution*   18   7   23

per labour hour   12   14   11.5

☐ material supply   38,000   19,200   59,850

☑ labour hours   (6,000)   (6400)   (12600)

(12,000)   (3200)   (16800)

(2,000)   (4000)   (6300)

P= 18,000   P= 5,600   P= 24150

− 31,000

400 + 1500 = 1900
2100 kg.

BPP
LEARNING MEDIA

18   The ranking of the products for the next period, in order to maximise profit, will be:

         Product

    1st   C

    2nd   W

    3rd   P

19   The maximum profit achievable for the next period is $ 16750

The following information relates to questions 20 and 21

PP Co has prepared the following standard cost information for one unit of product X.

Direct materials	2kg @ $13/kg	$26.00
Direct labour	3.3 hours @ $4/hour	$13.20
Fixed overheads	4 hours @ $2.50	$10.00

Actual results for the period were recorded as follows:

Production	12,000 units = 24,000 kg
Materials – 26,400 kg	$336,600
Labour – 40,200 hours	$168,840
Fixed overheads	$160,000

All of the materials were purchased and used during the period.

20   The direct material cost variances are:

shald : 343,200
drd : 336,600

		Favourable	Adverse
material price	6,600	✓	
material usage	31,200		✓

21   The direct labour cost variances are:

		Favourable	Adverse
labour rate	80x0		✓
labour efficiency	2400		✓

22   Product X has a standard direct material cost as follows.

    10 kilograms of material Y at $10 per kilogram = $100 per unit of X.

    During period 4, 1,000 units of X were manufactured, using 11,700 kilograms of material Y which cost $98,600.

Direct material price variance
Direct material usage variance.

Required

Calculate the following variances.

		Favourable	Adverse
The direct material price variance	18,400	✓	
The direct material usage variance	17,000		✓

---

23 AB Co is currently preparing its production budget for product Z for the forthcoming year. The sales director has confirmed that he requires 120,000 units of product Z. Opening inventory is estimated to be 13,000 units and the company wishes to reduce inventory at the end of the year by 50%.   - 6,500

113,500 units of product Z will need to be produced.

---

24 The laundry operation of a major hospital wishes to develop a model to predict its total costs in a period. The following costs have been recorded at two activity levels in the past.

	Number of items laundered (L)	Total cost (TC) $
Period 1	10,400	4,880
Period 2	11,650 × 1,250	5,130 +250

2.5p/u

The total cost model for a period could be represented as:

TC = $ 2800 + $ 0.2 L

FC= 2800

---

25 An extract from a stores ledger account is as follows.

	Receipts			Issues			Inventory balance		
	Qty	Price $	Value $	Qty	Price $	Value $	Qty	Price $	Value $
1 April							100	2.00	200
							100	2.00	200
3 April	300	2.20	660				300	2.20	660
							400		860
4 April				50	2.00	100	50	2.00	100
							300	2.20	660
							350		760

The FIFO method of inventory valuation is used, and the issue cost of 150 units issued from inventory on 5 April is $ 320

50× 2 = 100
+ 100×2.2 =220

---

26 A material price standard has been set at an average price for the forthcoming period. Assuming inflation, the material price variances reported during the earlier part of the period are likely to be:

[ ] adverse

[✓] favourable

The following data are given for questions 27 and 28 below

The standard direct labour cost of product X is as follows.

2 hours of grade Z labour at $5 per hour = $10 per unit of product X.

During period 4, 1,000 units of product X were made, and the direct labour cost of grade Z labour was $8,900 for 2,300 hours of work.

27

		Favourable	Adverse
The direct labour rate variance is	$ 2,600	✓	

28

		Favourable	Adverse
The direct labour efficiency variance is $ 1,500			✓

---

29 During a period of rising prices, inventory valuations using LIFO will be _____lower_____ than those with a system of FIFO, and reported profits will be _____lower_____

---

30 The number of employees in each of the cost centres of Company X is as follows.

	Machining	Assembly	Stores	Canteen
Number of employees	50	35	15	5

The canteen costs of $10,500 are to be apportioned to the other three cost centres on the basis of the number of employees in each cost centre. The amount apportioned to the machining cost centre will be

$ 5,250 .

---

31 KH Co operates an integrated accounting system. An extract from the production overhead control account for the last period is as follows.

PRODUCTION OVERHEAD CONTROL

	$'000		$'000
Payables	48	Work in progress	58
Wages and salaries	12		
Provision for depreciation	4		
	64		

The production overhead for the last period was:

✓	under absorbed
	over absorbed

---

32 In a machine-intensive environment, the most appropriate overhead absorption basis is:

	direct labour hour rate
✓	machine hour rate

---

33 JW Co uses a flexible budgeting system to control costs. The total cost figures from the budgetary control report for the latest period are as follows.

	$
Fixed budget total	3,400
Flexible budget total	4,200
Actual results	4,050

	Favourable	Adverse
The volume variance for the latest period is ☐ 800		✓
The expenditure variance for the latest period is ☐ 150	✓	

34 A contract to build a new leisure centre began on 1 March 20X2. Details of plant and machinery used on the site are as follows.

10 years, *0.5 = 6 marks*

	$
Plant delivered to site at cost, 1 March	80,000
Plant returned from site at cost, 1 September	20,000

The contractor's year end is 31 December. The depreciation policy is to charge straight line depreciation, assuming a ten year life for plant and machinery, with no residual value.

The charge to the leisure centre contract for depreciation of plant and machinery for the year ending

31 December 20X2 is $ ☐ 4,000

35 In an integrated cost and financial accounting system, the accounting entries at the end of the period for production overhead under-absorbed would be (tick the correct boxes):

	Debit	Credit	No entry in this a/c
Overhead control account	☐	☐	☐
Work in progress account	☐	☐	☐
Income statement	☐	☐	☐

36 In a typical cost ledger, the double entry for indirect labour cost incurred is:

☐	DR	Wages control	CR	Overhead control
☐	DR	Admin overhead control	CR	Wages control
✓	DR	Overhead control	CR	Wages control
☐	DR	Wages control	CR	Admin overhead control

The following information relates to questions 37 and 38.

Harry Hall Co operates a haulage business with three vehicles. During June it is expected that all three vehicles will be used at a total cost of $10,390; 3,950 kilometres will be travelled (including return journeys when empty) as shown in the following table.

TC = 10,390

NB / Tonne-KM

B tonne × km.

Journey	Tonnes carried (one way)		Kilometres (one way)
1	34	×	180
2	28	×	265
3	40	×	390
4	32	×	115
5	26	×	220
6	40	×	480
7	29	×	90
8	26	×	100
9	25		135
	280		1,975

37 The total of tonne-kilometres in June = ☐

38 The average cost per tonne-kilometre for June = $ 4.61 per tonne-kilometre (to the nearest cent).

39 A company manufactures product A, in a single process. At the start of the month there was no work in progress. During the month 600 litres of raw material were input into the process at a total cost of $12,000. Conversion costs during the month amounted to $9,000. At the end of the month 500 litres of product A were transferred to finished goods inventory. Normal process loss is 5% of input, abnormal loss was 10 litres and the remaining work in progress was 100% complete with respect to materials and 50% complete with respect to conversion costs.

The equivalent units for closing work in progress at the end of the month would have been:

600 ($12,000)
+ (9,000)

NL = 30L
AL = 10L
WIP = 60

Material   60 equivalent litres

Conversion costs   30 equivalent litres

1200 + 540

40 A company makes a product, which passes through a single process.

Details of the process for the last period are as follows:

Materials	1,000 kg at 50c per kg
Labour	$140
Production overheads	200% of labour

Normal losses are 10% of input in the process, and without further processing any losses can be sold as scrap for 20c per kg.

NL = 100kg

proceeds = 20

The output from the process for the period was 840 kg.

The cost per kg of output is $1.

There was no work in progress at the beginning or end of the period.

The value of the output for the period is $ ☐ 860

---

41   HP Co operates a job costing system. The company's standard net profit margin is 20 per cent of sales value.

The estimated costs for job B200 are as follows.   *NB/*

Direct materials   3 kg @ $4 per kg

Direct labour   4 hours @ $8 per hour

Production overheads are budgeted to be $120,000 for the period, to be recovered on the basis of a total of 12,000 labour hours.

Other overheads, related to selling, distribution and administration, are budgeted to be $100,000 for the period. They are to be recovered on the basis of the total budgeted production cost of $500,000 for the period.

The price to be quoted for job B200 is $ ☐ 750,000   126

---

42   Which of the following are advantages of job costing for service department costs?

☐ ✓   Realistic apportionment of expenses to responsible department

☐ ✓   Improved information for the budget process

☐   Formal contracts must be drawn up by service users

---

43   340 litres of Chemical X were produced in a period. There is a normal loss of 10% of the material input into the process. There was an abnormal loss in the period of 5% of the material input.

☐ 400   litres of material were input into the process during the period.

---

44   Which ONE of the following would be classified as direct labour?

☐   Personnel manager in a company servicing cars

☐ ✓   Bricklayer in a construction company

☐   General manager of a DIY shop

☐   Maintenance manager in a company producing cameras

---

45   Which of the following would NOT be included in a cash budget?

☐ ✓   Depreciation

☐ ✓   Provision for doubtful debts

☐   Wages and salaries

---

46 A product is made in two consecutive processes. Data for the latest period are as follows:

	Process 1	Process 2
Input (kg)	47,000	42,000
Normal loss (% of input)	8	5
Output (kg)	42,000	38,915

No work in progress is held at any time in either process.

The abnormal loss or abnormal gain arising in each process during the period was:

	Process 1	Process 2
A	Abnormal loss	Abnormal loss
B	Abnormal loss	Abnormal gain
C	Abnormal gain	Abnormal loss
D	Abnormal gain	Abnormal gain

47 A chain of beauty salons finds that the cost of power consumed varies with the number of clients visiting the salon in a period

Budgets are set at the head office for each salon. An extract from the budget records is as follows:

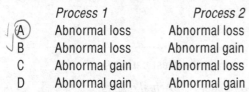

Number of clients in period	Flexible budget cost allowance for power $
1,950	2,565
2,550	2,985

The flexible budget cost allowance for electricity for the Leighton salon, in a period when 2,300 clients visit the salon is closest to:

A $1,610
B $2,110
C $2,810
D $3,210

48 A company manufactures a single product. An extract from their flexed budget is as follows.

	Activity level		
	60%	64	70%
	$		$
Direct material	4,788		5,586
Direct labour	3,700		3,950
Production overhead	11,082		11,804
Total production cost	19,570		21,340

The budget cost allowance for total production cost at the 64% activity level is closest to:

A $19,889
B $20,278
C $20,861
D $20,875

49   A company budgeted to produce 15,200 units in 20X7. The standard direct labour cost per unit is $31.

Actual production of 13,180 units in 20X7 incurred a total direct labour cost of $434,940.

In a flexible budget control statement, which two figures would be compared for the purposes of control of the expenditure on direct labour cost?

	Actual	Budget
A	$408,580	$471,200
B	$434,940	$408,580
C	$434,940	$471,200
D	$516,800	$408,580

50   The following information is available for the Flat Spot Company in the latest period.

	Original budget	Flexed budget	Actual results
Sales and production (units)	11,200	9,500	9,500
	$'000	$'000	$'000
Sales revenue	224.0	190.0	209.0
Direct material	56.0	47.5	57.0
Direct labour	66.0	57.5	56.1
Overhead	27.4	24.0	28.0
Profit	74.6	61.0	67.9

5.89/unit.

Direct labour 66.0 5.89

Which of the following statements is correct?

A   Budgeted production volumes were achieved during the period.
B   Direct labour is a variable cost
C   The actual selling price per unit exceeded the standard selling price per unit
D   Direct material cost savings were achieved against the budget cost allowance.

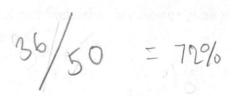

$36/50 = 72\%$

Mock assessment 1
Answers

DO NOT TURN THIS PAGE UNTIL YOU HAVE
COMPLETED MOCK ASSESSMENT 1

1   B   The weighted average cost per unit:

	$
330 units at $168 each	55,440
180 units at $174 each	31,320
90 units at $186 each	16,720
600	103,500

Weighted average cost per unit   = $103,500/600
                                        = $172.50

So cost of units sold on 24 February   = $172.50 × 432 units
                                                       = $74,520

2   The standard allowed weight of material for the period was $\boxed{28,929}$ kg

Standard price per kg of material $= \dfrac{\$114,576}{28,644} = \$4$ per kg

∴ Material usage variance in kg $= \dfrac{\$1,140}{\$4} = 285$ kg (F)

Standard allowed weight of material for period   = (28,644 + 285) kg
                                                              = 28,929 kg

3   C

	$ per unit
Material	20.00
Labour	69.40
Production overhead (14 hours × $12.58)	176.12
Total production cost	265.52
General overhead (8% × $265.52)	21.24
	286.76

4   B

	Cost centre Alpha $ per unit	Cost centre Beta $ per unit	Total $ per unit
Direct material	20.00	10.10	30.10
Direct labour	11.63	7.35	18.98
Production overhead	6.12	4.98	11.10
Total production cost			60.18

5   ☑ Customer-driven production.

     ☑ Complete production possible within a single accounting period.

6   ☑ Standard material usage per unit

    ☑ Budgeted production volume

Since there are no production resource limitations, the production budget would be prepared before the material usage budget. The budgeted material usage would then be calculated as:

budgeted production volume × standard material usage per unit

The budgeted change in materials inventory is relevant when preparing the **materials purchases budget.**

The budgeted average lead time for delivery of materials is relevant when determining **inventory control levels**. It does not affect the budgeted material usage.

7   ☑ Co-ordinating the preparation of budgets

    ☑ Issuing the budget manual

    ☑ Allocating responsibility for the budget preparation

    ☑ Monitoring the budgetary planning process

The preparation of the functional budgets is undertaken by the individual budget holders, not by the budget committee.

8   ☑ Component parts ordered for a specific job

    ☑ Part finished goods transferred into a process from an earlier process

The component parts can be identified with a **specific cost unit** therefore they are a direct materials cost. The input from a previous process is classified as direct materials **in the subsequent process.**

Cleaning materials and maintenance materials are classified as **indirect materials costs,** to be absorbed into product costs as a part of the overhead absorption rate.

9   ☑ Idle time payments to direct workers

The overtime premium can be identified with a specific order or cost unit, therefore it would be treated as a **direct labour cost** of that order or unit.

Payments made to workers installing new machinery would be classified as a **capital cost** of that machinery.

		Favourable	Adverse
10 Selling price variance	$600	☑	

	$
Sales revenue from 2,000 should be (× $15)	30,000
but was (× $15.30)	30,600
Selling price variance	600 (F)

The variance is favourable because the price was higher than expected.

11   ☑ Purchasing budget

      ☑ Sales budget

      ☑ Marketing cost budget

A functional budget is a budget of income and/or expenditure for a particular department or process. A cash budget and an income statement budget do not relate to a specific function.

12   ☑ Hire of a delivery vehicle

      ☑ A piecework scheme with a guaranteed day rate

Both of these costs contain a **fixed element which is incurred regardless of the level of activity.** In addition a variable element is incurred which **fluctuates with the level of activity.**

The rental scheme described for the photocopier is a **step cost**.

13   D

	Cost centre B $ per unit	Cost centre C $ per unit	Total $ per unit
Direct material	20.00	10.10	30.10
Direct labour	11.63	7.35	18.98
Production overhead	6.12	4.98	11.10
Total production cost			60.18
General overhead cost at 10 per cent			6.02
Total cost			66.20
Profit margin (× 20/80)			16.55
Required selling price per unit			82.75

14   The value of the normal loss is $ [300]

Normal loss = 20% × input
             = 20% × 5,000 kg
             = 1,000 kg

When scrap has a value, normal loss is valued at the value of the scrap ie 30c per kg.

Normal loss = $0.30 × 1,000 kg
             = $300

15   The value of the abnormal [loss] is $ [230]. This value will be [☑] debited to the income statement.

	kg
Input	5,000
Normal loss (20% × 5,000 kg)	(1,000)
Abnormal loss	(200)
Output	3,800

$$\text{Cost per kg} = \frac{\text{Input costs} - \text{scrap value of normal loss}}{\text{Expected output}}$$

$$= \frac{\$4,900^* - \$300}{5,000 - 1,000}$$

$$= \frac{\$4,600}{4,000}$$

$$= \$1.15$$

		$
*	Materials (5,000 kg × $0.5)	2,500
	Labour	800
	Production overhead	1,600
		4,900

Abnormal loss = $1.15 × 200 = $230

16 The value of the output from the process is $ | 4,370 |

Output	= 3,800 kg
Cost per unit	= $1.15 (see workings)
∴ Output	= 3,800 × $1.15
	= $4,370

Workings

$$\text{Cost per unit} = \frac{\text{Input costs} - \text{input costs scrap value of normal loss}}{\text{Expected output}}$$

$$= \frac{\$4,900^* - \$300}{5,000 - 1,000}$$

$$= \frac{\$4,600}{400}$$

$$= \$1.15$$

		$
*	Materials (5,000 kg × $0.5)	2,500
	Labour	800
	Production overhead	1,600
		4,900

17 | ✓ | labour hours

	W	C	P	Total
Demand (units)	1,000	800	1,300	
Material per unit (kg)	3	4	6	
Total material required (kg)	3,000	3,200	7,800	14,000
Labour hours per unit	1.5	0.5	2.0	
Total labour hours required	1,500	400	2,600	4,500

Therefore there is a shortfall of 500 labour hours, but ample material is available for next period.

18 *Product*

1st [C]

2nd [W]

3rd [P]

	W	*C*	*P*
	$ per unit	*$ per unit*	*$ per unit*
Selling price	38	24	57
Variable cost	20	17	34
Contribution	18	7	23
Labour hours per unit	1.5	0.5	2.0
Contribution per hour	$12.00	$14.00	$11.50
Ranking	2	1	3

19 The maximum profit achievable for the next period is $ [16,750]

Optimum production plan:

Product	Units	*Labour hours used*		*Contribution*
				$
C	800 (× 0.5 hr)	400	(× $14)	5,600
W	1,000 (× 1.5 hr)	1,500	(× $12)	18,000
P	1,050 (× 2.0 hr)	2,100	(× $11.50)	24,150
		4,000		47,750
			Fixed costs	31,000
			Profit	16,750

20

		Favourable	*Adverse*
Material price	$6,600	✓	
Material usage	$31,200		✓

Direct materials price variance

	$
26,400 kg should have cost (× $13)	343,200
but did cost	336,600
	6,600 (F)

Direct materials usage variance

12,000 units should have used (× 2kg)	24,000 kg
but did use	26,400 kg
Materials usage variance in kg	2,400 kg (A)
× standard price per kg	$13
Materials usage variance (in $)	$31,200 (A)

21

		Favourable	Adverse
Labour rate	$8,040		✓
Labour efficiency	$2,400		✓

Direct labour rate variance

	$
40,200 hrs of labour should have cost (× $4)	160,800
but did cost	168,840
	8,040 (A)

Labour efficiency variance

12,000 units should have taken (× 3.3 hrs)	39,600 hrs
but did take	40,200 hrs
Labour efficiency variance in hrs	600 hrs
× standard rate per hour	× $4
Labour efficiency variance in $	2,400 (A)

22

		Favourable	Adverse
Direct material price variance	$18,400	✓	
Direct material usage variance	$17,000		✓

The direct material price variance

This is the difference between what 11,700 kgs should have cost and what 11,700 kgs did cost.

	$
11,700 kgs of Y should have cost (× $10)	117,000
but did cost	98,600
Material Y price variance	18,400 (F)

The variance is favourable because the material cost less than it should have.

The direct material usage variance

This is the difference between how many kilograms of Y should have been used to produce 1,000 units of X and how many kilograms were used, valued at the standard cost per kilogram.

1,000 units should have used (× 10 kgs)	10,000 kgs
but did use	11,700 kgs
Usage variance in kgs	1,700 kgs (A)
× standard cost per kilogram	× $10
Usage variance in $	$17,000 (A)

The variance is adverse because more material than should have been used was used.

23 ☐ 113,500 units of product Z will need to be produced.

Let x = production

	Product Z units
Opening inventory	13,000
Production	x
Closing inventory (50% × 13,000)	6,500
Required sales of product Z	120,000

$$13,000 + x - 6,500 = 120,000$$
$$x = 120,000 - 13,000 + 6,500$$
$$= 113,500 \text{ units}$$

24 TC = $☐ 2,800 + $☐ 0.20 L

	Items laundered L	Total cost $
Period 2	11,650	5,130
Period 1	10,400	4,880
	1,250	250

∴ Variable cost per item laundered = $250/1,250
= $0.20

Substituting in period 2,

Fixed cost = $5,130 − (11,650 × $0.20) = $2,800

25 The ☐ FIFO method of inventory valuation is used, and the issue cost of 150 units issued from inventory

on 5 April is $☐ 320 .

	$
50 units @ $2.00	100
100 units @ $2.20	220
150	320

26 ☐ ✓ favourable

Assuming inflation, the actual material price is likely to be lower than average during the earlier part of the period.

27

	Favourable	Adverse
The direct labour rate variance is $ ☐ 2,600	☐ ✓	☐

This is the difference between what 2,300 hours should have cost and what 2,300 hours did cost.

	$
2,300 hours of work should have cost (× $5 per hr)	11,500
but did cost	8,900
Direct labour rate variance	2,600 (F)

The variance is favourable because the labour cost less than it should have cost.

28

	Favourable	Adverse
The direct labour efficiency variance is $ 1,500		✓

1,000 units of X should have taken (× 2 hrs)	2,000 hrs
but did take	2,300 hrs
Efficiency variance in hours	300 hrs (A)
× standard rate per hour	×$5
Efficiency variance in $	$1,500 (A)

The variance is adverse because more hours were worked than should have been worked.

29   During a period of rising prices, inventory valuations using LIFO will be lower than those with a system of FIFO, and reported profits will be lower

30   The amount apportioned to the machining cost centre will be $ 5,250

Total number of employees to be used as absorption base = 50 + 35 + 15

= 100

∴Amount apportioned to machining $= \dfrac{50}{100} \times \$10,500$

= $5,250

31   ✓ under absorbed

Production overhead incurred of $64,000 was $6,000 higher than the $58,000 absorbed into work in progress.

32   ✓ machine hour rate

A direct labour hour rate would be more appropriate in a labour-intensive environment.

33

	Favourable	Adverse
The volume variance for the latest period is $800		✓
The expenditure variance for the latest period is $150	✓	

Volume variance = fixed budget $3,400 – flexible budget $4,200
= $800 (A)

Expenditure variance = flexible budget $4,200 – actual results $4,050
= $150 (F)

34    $ 4,000

	Depreciation $
Plant on site from 1 March to 1 September = $80,000	
Six months depreciation = $80,000/10 years × 6/12	4,000

35

	Debit $	Credit $	No entry in this a/c $
Overhead control account		✓	
Work in progress account			✓
Income statement	✓		

Under-absorbed overhead means that the overhead charged to production was too low and so there must be a debit to the income statement.

36   [✓] DR   Overhead control   CR   Wages control

Indirect wages are 'collected' in the overhead control account, for subsequent absorption into work in progress.

37   [66,325]

Working

Calculation of tonne-km

Journey	Tonnes	Km	Tonne-km
1	34	180	6,120
2	28	265	7,420
3	40	390	15,600
4	32	115	3,680
5	26	220	5,720
6	40	480	19,200
7	29	90	2,610
8	26	100	2,600
9	25	135	3,375
	280	1,975	66,325

38    $ [0.16] per tonne-kilometre (to the nearest cent).

Working

Average cost per tonne-kilometre $= \dfrac{\text{Total cost}}{\text{Total tonne-kilometres}}$

$= \dfrac{\$10,390}{66,325}$

= $0.16 per tonne-kilometre (to the nearest cent)

39 The equivalent units for closing work in progress at the end of the month would have been:

Material | 60 | equivalent litres

Conversion costs | 30 | equivalent litres

Using the steps in your textbook.

Determine output and losses

STATEMENT OF EQUIVALENT UNITS

	Total Units	Completion		Equivalent Units	
		Materials	Labour	Materials	Labour
Closing WIP	60	100%	50%	60	30
Transferred to finished goods	500	100%	100%	500	500
Normal loss (600 × 5%)	30	–	–	–	–
Abnormal loss	10	100%	100%	10	10
	600				

Therefore closing work in progress at the month end

	Material		Conversion costs	
	%	Equiv. litres	%	Equiv. litres
Work in progress	100	60	50	30

40 The value of the output for the period is $ | 840 |

Output = 840 kg

Cost per kg = $1 (from the question)

∴ Output value = 840 × $1
                = $840

41 The price to be quoted for job B200 is $ | 126.00 |

Production overhead absorption rate = $120,000/12,000 = $10 per labour hour

Other overhead absorption rate = ($100,000/$500,000) × 100% = 20% of total production cost

Job B200	$
Direct materials (3 kgs × $4)	12.00
Direct labour (4 hours × $8)	32.00
Production overhead (4 hours × $10)	40.00
Total production cost	84.00
Other overhead (20% × $84)	16.80
Total cost	100.80
Profit margin: 20% of sales ($\times \, ^{20}/_{80}$)	25.20
Price to be quoted	126.00

42 ☑ Realistic apportionment of expenses to responsible departments

☑ Improved information for the budget process

Refer to your Study Text for more information on this area.

43 Let   x = material input to process

     0.1x = normal loss

     0.05x = abnormal loss

∴ Output = x − 0.1x − 0.05x

340 litres = x − 0.15x

340 litres = 0.85x

$$x = \frac{340 \text{ litres}}{0.85}$$

= ☐ 400 ☐ litres

44 ☑ Bricklayer in a construction company

Remember, direct labour means labour hours worked on the product itself

45 ☑ Depreciation

☑ Provision for doubtful debts

Depreciation and provision for doubtful debts do not result in a cash payment or income.

46 A

		Process 1		Process 2
		kg		kg
Input		47,000		42,000
Normal loss	(× 8%)	3,760	(× 5%)	2,100
Expected output		43,240		39,900
Actual output		42,000		38,915
Abnormal loss		1,240		985

47 C

	Number of clients	Flexible budget cost allowance
		$
	1,950	2,565
	2,550	2,985
Change	600	420

Variable cost per client = $420/600 = $0.70

Fixed cost = $2,565 − (1,950 × $0.70)

         = $1,200

Flexible budget cost allowance for 2,300 clients = $1,200 + (2,300 × $0.70)

                                  = $2,810

48   B   Direct material cost per 1% of activity = $79.80

The direct labour and production overhead appear to be semi-variable costs so we need to use the high–low method.

Direct labour and production overhead:

Activity	$
70%	15,754
60%	14,782
10%	972

Variable cost per 1% of activity = $972/10% = $97.20

Fixed cost of labour and production overhead = $15,754 – (70 × $97.20)

= $8,950

Flexible budget cost allowance at 64% activity:

	$
Variable cost ($79.80 + $97.20) × 64	11,328
Fixed cost	8,950
	20,278

49   B   Budget cost allowance for 13,180 units produced = 13,180 × $31

= $408,580

This is the correct budget figure that should be compared with the actual expenditure of $434,940.

50   C   The actual sales revenue is higher than the flexed budget sales revenue. Since the effect of a sales volume change has been removed from this comparison the higher revenue must be caused by a higher than standard selling price.

A comparison of the original budget volume with the volume shown in the flexed budget and actual result shows that option A is incorrect.

The direct labour cost per unit is different in the two budget figures for labour, therefore option B is incorrect.

The actual material cost ($57,000) was higher than the flexed budget cost allowance ($47,500), therefore option D is incorrect.

CIMA

Paper C1 (Certificate)

Fundamentals of Management Accounting

Mock Assessment 2

Question Paper	
Time allowed	**2 hours**
Answer ALL fifty questions	

DO NOT OPEN THIS PAPER UNTIL YOU ARE READY TO START UNDER EXAMINATION CONDITIONS

Answer ALL 50 questions

1   The principal budget factor is the

☐ factor which limits the activities of the organisation and is often the starting point in budget preparation

☐ budgeted revenue expected in a forthcoming period

☐ main budget into which all subsidiary budgets are consolidated

☐ overestimation of revenue budgets and underestimation of cost budgets, which operates as a safety factor against risk

---

2   R Co absorbs overheads based on units produced. In one period 110,000 units were produced and the actual overheads were $500,000. Overheads were $50,000 over absorbed in the period.

The overhead absorption rate was $ ☐ (to 2 decimal places).

---

3   X Co operates an integrated cost accounting system. The Work-in-Progress Account at the end of the period showed the following information:

WORK-IN-PROGRESS ACCOUNT

	$		$
Stores ledger a/c	100,000	?	200,000
Wages control a/c	75,000		
Factory overhead a/c	50,000	Balance c/d	25,000
	225,000		225,000

The $200,000 credit entry represents the value of the transfer to the

☐ Cost of sales account

☐ Material control account

☐ Sales account

☐ Finished goods inventory account

---

4   X Co operates a standard costing system and absorbs overheads on the basis of standard machine hours. Details of budgeted and actual figures are as follows.

	Budget	Actual
Overheads	$1,250,000	$1,005,000
Output	250,000 units	220,000 units
Machine hours	500,000 hours	450,000 hours

Overheads were ☐ absorbed by $ ☐

The following information is required for Questions 5 and 6

P Co uses the FIFO system for valuing material issues from stores to production.

The materials account had an opening value of $12,000 on 1 April 20X2:

      1,000 units @ $5.80 – Purchased 22 March 20X2
      1,000 units @ $6.20 – Purchased 23 March 20X2

The following receipts and issues were recorded during April:

2 April 20X2	Receipts	5,000 units	$6.30 per unit
15 April 20X2	Receipts	8,000 units	$6.25 per unit
30 April 20X2	Issues	9,000 units	

---

5   Using the FIFO method, the value of the closing inventory on 30 April was $ ☐

---

6   If P Co had used LIFO, instead of FIFO, the value of the material issued would have been $ ☐
higher/lower (delete as appropriate)

---

7   In an integrated bookkeeping system, when the actual production overheads exceed the absorbed production overheads, the accounting entries to close off the production overhead account at the end of the period would be

    ☐ debit the production overhead account and credit the work-in-progress account

    ☐ debit the work-in-progress account and credit the production overhead account

    ☐ debit the production overhead account and credit the income statement

    ☐ debit the income statement and credit the production overhead account

---

8   A company operates a differential piece-rate system and the following weekly rates have been set:

1 – 500 units	$0.20 per unit in this band
501 – 600 units	$0.25 per unit in this band
601 units and above	$0.55 per unit in this band

Details relating to employee A are shown below:

Employee A

| Actual output achieved | 800 units |
| Actual hours worked | 45 hours |

There is a guaranteed minimum wage of $5 per hour for a 40-hour week paid to all employees.

The amount payable (to the nearest $) to employee A is $ ☐

---

9   Overtime premium is

☐ the additional amount paid for hours worked in excess of the basic working week

☐ the additional amount paid over and above the normal hourly rate for hours worked in excess of the basic working week

☐ the additional amount paid over and above the overtime rate for hours worked in excess of the basic working week

☐ the overtime rate

10 R Co has been asked to quote for a job. The company aims to make a profit margin of 20% on sales. The estimated total variable production cost for the job is $125.

Fixed production overheads for the company are budgeted to be $250,000 and are recovered on the basis of labour hours. There are 12,500 budgeted labour hours and this job is expected to take 3 labour hours.

Other costs in relation to selling and distribution, and administration are recovered at the rate of $15 per job.

The company quote for the job should be $ ☐

The following information is required for Questions 11 and 12

X Co is preparing its budgets for the forthcoming year.

The estimated sales for the first four months of the forthcoming year are as follows:

Month 1	6,000 units
Month 2	7,000 units
Month 3	5,500 units
Month 4	6,000 units

40% of each month's sales units are to be produced in the month of sale and the balance is to be produced in the previous month.

50% of the direct materials required for each month's production will be purchased in the previous month and the balance in the month of production.

The direct material cost is budgeted to be $5 per unit.

11 The production budget in units for Month 1 will be ☐ units

12 The material cost budget for Month 2 will be $ ☐

13   When calculating the material purchases budget, the quantity to be purchased equals

☐ material usage + materials closing inventory – materials opening inventory

☐ material usage – materials closing inventory + materials opening inventory

☐ material usage – materials closing inventory – materials opening inventory

☐ material usage + materials closing inventory + materials opening inventory

---

14   The following extract is taken from the overhead budget of X Co:

Budgeted activity	50%	75%
Budgeted overhead	$100,000	$112,500

The overhead budget for an activity level of 80% would be $ ☐

---

15   Which of the following would be included in the cash budget, but would not be included in the budgeted income statement?

☐ Repayment of a bank loan

☐ Proceeds from the sale of a non-current asset

☐ Bad debts write off

16

This graph is known as a

☐ semi-variable cost chart

☐ conventional breakeven chart

☐ contribution breakeven chart

☐ profit volume chart

17   The following details have been extracted from the payables' records of X Co:

Invoices paid in the month of purchase   25%
Invoices paid in the first month after purchase   70%
Invoices paid in the second month after purchase   5%

Purchases for July to September are budgeted as follows:

July $250,000
August $300,000
September $280,000

For suppliers paid in the month of purchase, a settlement discount of 5% is received. The amount budgeted

to be paid to suppliers in September is $ ⬚

The following information relates to Questions 18 and 19

A cleansing detergent is manufactured by passing raw material through two processes. The details of the process costs for Process 1 for April 20X2 were as follows:

Opening work-in-progress	5,000 litres valued as follows:	
	Material cost	$2,925
	Conversion costs	$6,600
Raw material input	50,000 litres valued at cost of	$37,500
Conversion costs		$62,385

Normal loss is 3% of the input during the period and has a scrap value of $0.20 per litre. It is company policy to deduct the income from the sale of normal loss from that period's materials cost.

Actual output to Process 2   49,000 litres
Closing work-in-progress   4,000 litres, which were 100% complete for materials and 40% complete for conversion costs.

A template that could be used to calculate the cost of the output from Process 1 is shown below. The template has been partially completed.

	Costs	Equivalent litres	Cost per equivalent litre
	OWIP + period cost = total	Transfers in + abnormal loss + CWIP = total	
Materials	$2,925 + A =	+ 500 + =	$0.75
Conversion	$6,600 + $62,385 = $68,985	+ + = 51,100	$1.35

OWIP = Opening work-in-progress
CWIP = Closing work-in-progress

18   The value to be inserted in the table at **A** is $ ⬚

19   The total value of the transfers to Process 2 is $ ⬚

The following information relates to Questions 20 and 21

BB Co, a fast food restaurant, prepares and sells a meal called 'Yum Yum'. The meal consists of a burger, fries and a cold drink. BB Co uses a standard marginal costing system.

The budgeted meal sales for the quarter ended 31 March 2002 were 100,000 meals with a selling price of $5 per meal. The standard labour cost for preparing each meal was $0.60. The standard labour time per meal was 6 minutes. The standard food and drink cost for each meal was $1.50. The budgeted fixed overheads for the year were estimated to be $500,000 and these are expected to be incurred evenly throughout the year.

For the quarter under review, the actual results were as follows:

Sales of 'Yum Yum'	90,000 meals
Selling price per meal	$4.75
Labour cost incurred for 8,250 hours	$48,675
Food and drink cost incurred	$112,500
Fixed overhead incurred	$120,000

There was no inventory of food or drink at the beginning or end of the quarter.

---

20 The budgeted profit for the quarter ending 31 March 20X2 was $ ☐

---

21 The total sales margin contribution variance for the quarter ending 31 March 20X2 was $ ☐ adverse/favourable. (Delete as appropriate).

---

22 Which of the following are functional budgets?

I   Purchasing budget
II Cash budget
III Sales budget
IV Marketing cost budget

A   I and II
B   None of the above
C   All of the above
D   I, III and IV

---

23 Shown below is an extract from the stores ledger card for material X.

		Receipts			Issues			Balance	
Date	Quantity	Value	Total	Quantity	Value	Total	Quantity	Value	Total
		$	$		$	$		$	$
April 1							8		84.40
April 12	10	10.50	105.00				18		189.40
April 15	12	10.29	123.48				30		312.88
April 20				4		A			
April 21				15		B			C

The values that would be entered on the stores ledger card for A and B in a FIFO pricing system would be:

BPP))))
LEARNING MEDIA

A [   ] (to 2 decimal places)

B [   ] (to 2 decimal places)

The value that would be entered on the stores ledger card for C in a LIFO pricing system would be:

C [   ] (to 2 decimal places)

---

24 An employee is paid according to the following schedule.

No of units produced	Rate of pay per unit in this band
	$
Up to and including 50	4.10
51 to 60	4.30
61 to 70	4.40
71 and above	4.50

This type of remuneration is known as [   ]

The employee's remuneration for an output of 68 units in a period would be $ [   ].

---

25 The following information relates to Diesel plc's main cost centres.

	Machining	Assembly	Maintenance	Stores	Total
Total overheads	$130,000	$122,000	$39,150	$42,000	$333,150

The maintenance cost centre overhead is to be reapportioned to the other three cost centres on the basis of the number of maintenance hours.

The stores cost centre overhead is to be apportioned to the two production cost centres on the basis of the number of stores requisitions.

	Machining	Assembly	Maintenance	Stores
Number of employees	25	32	8	4
Number of stores requisitions	22,100	8,000	7,525	–
Area occupied (sq m)	5,000	3,000	1,000	800
Maintenance hours	9,200	2,800	1,450	1,050
Machine hours	31,000	9,000	1,000	1,000
Direct labour hours	8,000	15,000		

To the nearest cent, the overhead absorption rate for the machining department was $ [   ] for each [   ]

---

26 Solo Co makes and sells a single product. The following data relate to periods 1 to 4.

	$
Variable cost per unit	30
Selling price per unit	55
Fixed costs per period	6,000

Normal activity is 500 units and production and sales for the four periods are as follows:

	Period 1 units	Period 2 units	Period 3 units	Period 4 units
Sales	500	400	550	450
Production	500	500	450	500

There were no opening inventories at the start of period 1.

(a)   The value of closing inventory carried forward in period 2 = $ ☐

(b)   The (under)-/over-absorbed overhead in period 3 = $ ☐

27   Jetprint Co specialises in printing advertising leaflets and is in the process of preparing its price list. The most popular requirement is for a folded leaflet made from a single sheet of A4 paper. From past records and budgeted figures, the following data have been estimated for a typical batch of 10,000 leaflets.

Artwork	$65
Machine setting	4 hours @ $22 per hour
Paper	$12.50 per 1,000 sheets
Ink and consumables	$40
Printers' wages	4 hours @ $8 per hour

Note. Printers' wages vary with volume.

General fixed overheads are $15,000 per period during which a total of 600 labour hours are expected to be worked.

The firm wishes to achieve 30% profit on sales.

The selling price (to the nearest $) per thousand leaflets, for quantities of 20,000 leaflets is $ ☐

28   The management accountant of Paul Waring Co has used the following data to draw the contribution breakeven chart shown.

Fixed costs of sale = $10,000
Variable costs of sale = $0.50 per $ of sale
Variable selling costs = $0.10 per $ of sale
Sales revenue = $90,000
Fixed administration cost = $15,000

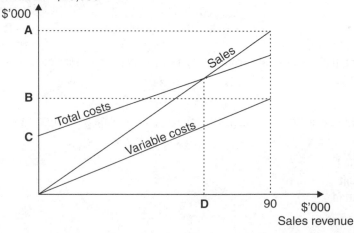

The monetary values indicated by A, B, C and D on the contribution breakeven chart shown above are:

A $ _____

B $ _____

C $ _____

D $ _____

---

29   A company has the following summary results for two trading periods.

	Period 1	Period 2
	$'000	$'000
Sales	742.7	794.1
Variable costs	408.3	409.0
Contribution	334.4	385.1
Fixed costs	297.8	312.7
Net profit	36.6	72.4

Selling prices were 10% higher in period 2 than period 1. Cost inflation was 5%.

(a)   The change in profit between the two periods resulting from the selling price increase was

$ _____

(b)   The change in profit between the two periods resulting from cost inflation was $ _____

---

30   An ice cream manufacturer is in the process of preparing budgets for the next few months, and the following draft figures are available.

Sales forecast	Cases
June	6,000
July	7,500
August	8,500
September	7,000
October	6,500

There are 750 cases of finished ice cream in inventory on 1 June and it is policy to have inventories at the end of each month to cover 10% of the next month's sales.

The production budget (in cases) for the months of June, July, August and September are:

June   _____

July   _____

August   _____

September   _____

The following information relates to questions 31 and 32

JJ Co manufactures a product which has a selling price of $14 and a variable cost of $6 per unit. The company incurs annual fixed costs of $24,400. Annual sales demand is 8,000 units.

New production methods are under consideration, which would cause a 30% increase in fixed costs and a reduction in variable cost to $5 per unit. The new production methods would result in a superior product and would enable sales to be increased to 8,500 units per annum at a price of $15 each.

31 If the change in production methods were to take place, the breakeven output level would [   ] by [   ] units.

32 If the organisation implements the new production methods and wishes to achieve the same profit as that under the existing method, the number of units that would need to be produced and sold annually to achieve this is [   ].

33 XYZ Co is planning to make 120,000 units per period of a new product. The following standards have been set for direct materials.

	Per unit
Direct material A	1.2 kgs at $11 per kg
Direct material B	4.7 kgs at $6 per kg

Actual results for the period were:

Production	126,000 units
Material A	cost $1.65m for 150,000 kgs
Material B	cost $3.6m for 590,000 kgs

The material cost variances for the period are:

	Material price variance	Material usage variance
Material A	$ [ ]	$ [ ]
Material B	$ [ ]	$ [ ]

34 Of what does the master budget comprise?

A   The budgeted income statement
B   The budgeted cash flow, budgeted income statement and budgeted balance sheet
C   The entire set of budgets prepared
D   The budgeted cash flow

35 Which of the following is a feature of job costing?

A   Production is carried out in accordance with the wishes of the customer
B   Associated with continuous production of large volumes of low-cost items
C   Establishes the cost of services rendered
D   Costs are charged over the units produced in the period

BPP
LEARNING MEDIA

36   A firm uses job costing and recovers overheads as a percentage of direct labour cost.

Three jobs were worked on during a period, the details of which are as follows.

	Job 1	Job 2	Job 3
	$	$	$
Opening work in progress	8,500	0	46,000
Material in period	17,150	29,025	0
Labour for period	12,500	23,000	4,500

The overheads for the period were exactly as budgeted, $140,000.

Job 3 was completed during the period and consisted of 2,400 identical circuit boards. The firm adds 50% to total production costs to arrive at a selling price.

What is the selling price of a circuit board?

A   It cannot be calculated without more information
B $31.56
C $41.41
D $55.21

---

37   P Co manufactures ring binders which are embossed with the customer's own logo. A customer has ordered a batch of 300 binders. The following data illustrate the cost for a typical batch of 100 binders.

	$
Direct materials	30
Direct wages	10
Machine set up	3
Design and artwork	15
	58

Direct employees are paid on a piecework basis.

P Co absorbs production overhead at a rate of 20 per cent of direct wages cost. Five per cent is added to the total production cost of each batch to allow for selling, distribution and administration overhead.

P Co requires a profit margin of 25 per cent of sales value.

The selling price for a batch of 300 binders (to the nearest cent) will be

A $189.00
B $193.20
C $201.60
D $252.00

38   The following data relate to a process for the previous period.

Opening work in progress   240 units
Input   2,180 units
Normal loss   10% of input
Abnormal gain   20 units
Closing work in progress   200 units

All material is input at the start of the process.

The number of good units produced during the period was:

A   1,804
B   2,022
C   2,042
D   2,240

39   The following information relates to a company's polishing process for the previous period.

Output to finished goods   5,408 units valued at $29,744
Normal loss   276 units
Actual loss   112 units

All losses have a scrap value of $2.50 per unit and there was no opening or closing work in progress.

The value of the input during the period was:

A $28,842
B $29,532
C $29,744
D $30,434

40   In process costing the 'Point of separation' is relevant to which of the following?

A   Abnormal losses
B   Normal losses
C   Joint products
D   Abnormal gains

41   A company discovers, at the end of a process, that abnormal losses had occurred.

At what value would a unit of abnormal loss be recorded in the process account?

A   The total cost per unit of normal output
B   Scrap value
C   The direct cost per unit of normal output
D   Nil value

BPP)))
LEARNING MEDIA

42   What are conversion costs?

☐   Rework costs

☐   Direct costs only

☐   Indirect costs only

☐   Production costs excluding direct materials

43   The material stores control account for J Co for March looks like this:

MATERIAL STORES CONTROL ACCOUNT

	$		$
Balance b/d	12,000	Work in progress	40,000
Suppliers	49,000	Overhead control	12,000
Work in progress	18,000	Balance c/d	27,000
	79,000		79,000
Balance b/d	27,000		

Which of the following statements are correct?

(i)   Issues of direct materials during March were $18,000
(ii)   Issues of direct materials during March were $40,000
(iii)   Issues of indirect materials during March were $12,000
(iv)   Purchases of materials during March were $49,000

A   (i) and (iv) only
B   (ii) and (iv) only
C   (ii), (iii) and (iv) only
D   All of them

44   Standard costing is used to control the material costs of product A. No material inventories are held.

The following data are available for product A during June.

	Budget	Actual
Production units	4,000	4,200
Material usage	32,000 kg	35,200 kg
Material cost	$384,000	$380,000

The material usage variance for May is:

A $19,200 (A)
B $20,900 (F)
C $23,100 (A)
D $38,400 (A)

45   Which of the following would NOT be classified as a direct cost of the organisation concerned?

A   The cost of hops used in a brewery
B   The rental cost of a telephone line installed on a construction site
C   The salary of an in-house lawyer in a FTSE 100 company
D   The cost of food served on an aeroplane flight

46   A wholesaler had an opening inventory of 330 units of product T valued at $42 each on 1 March.

The following receipts and sales were recorded during March.

4 March	Received 180 units at a cost of	$43 per unit
10 March	Received 90 units at a cost of	$46 per unit
24 March	Sold 432 units at a price of	$55 per unit

Using the FIFO valuation method, what was the cost of the units sold on 24 March?

A $14,400
B $18,144
C $18,246
D $18,533

47   A wholesaler had an opening inventory of 330 units of product T valued at $57 each on 1 May.

The following receipts and sales were recorded during May.

1 May	Received 80 units at a cost of	$51 per unit
17 May	Received 250 units at a cost of	$59 per unit
27 May	Sold 560 units at a price of	$71 per unit

Using the LIFO valuation method the gross profit earned from the units sold on 27 May would be

$ _____ .

48   The following data is available for the paint department for the latest period.

Budgeted production overhead	$150,000
Actual production overhead	$150,000
Budgeted machine hours	60,000
Actual machine hours	55,000

Which of the following statements is correct?

A   There was no under or over absorption of overhead
B   Overhead was $13,636 over absorbed
C   Overhead was $12,500 over absorbed
D   Overhead was $12,500 under absorbed

49   Which of the following statements is/are correct?

(i)   Using FIFO, the cost of issues from inventory approximates to economic cost because closing inventory is valued at the most recent prices.

(ii)   FIFO is essentially an historical cost method of inventory valuation because issues are priced at the oldest prices of items held in inventory.

(iii)   The use of AVCO method of inventory valuation helps to smooth out fluctuations in the purchase price of inventory items

A   Statement (i) only
B   Statements (i) and (ii) only
C   Statements (ii) and (iii) only
D   All of them

50   A internet service provider operates a customer service centre to deal with domestic and industrial customers' enquiries about their internet connection.

A standard time is allowed for dealing with each enquiry and employees are paid a bonus for any time saved compared with the standard allowance

The following data relates to the bonus scheme.

Basic daily pay for each employee	8 hours @ $15 per hour
Standard time allowed to deal with one enquiry	10 minutes
Bonus payable at basic hourly rate	30% of time saved

The bonus payable to an employee who deals with 60 enquiries in a single day would be $ ☐ .

Mock assessment 2
Answers

1 ☑ factor which limits the activities of the organisation and is often the starting point in budget preparation.

2 The overhead absorption rate was $ 5.00 (to 2 decimal places)

Workings

Actual overheads = $500,000

∴ Absorbed overheads = $500,000 + $50,000
= $550,000

Absorbed overheads = actual production × overhead absorption rate (OAR)

$550,000 = 110,000 units × $OAR

∴ OAR = $\dfrac{\$550,000}{110,000 \text{ units}}$

= $5.00 per unit

3 ☑ Finished goods inventory account

4 Overheads were over absorbed by $ 95,000

Workings

Overhead absorption rate = $\dfrac{\$1,250,000}{500,000 \text{ machine hours}}$

= $2.50 per machine hour

Standard machine hours per unit = $\dfrac{500,000 \text{ hours}}{250,000 \text{ units}}$

= 2 machine hours

Standard machine hours produced = 220,000 × 2 machine hours
= 440,000 machine hours

	$
Overhead absorbed (440,000 standard hours × $2.50)	1,100,000
Actual overheads incurred	1,005,000
Over-absorbed overhead	95,000

5 Using the FIFO method, the value of the closing inventory on 30 April was $ 37,500

Workings

	Units
Opening inventory	2,000
2 April receipt	5,000
15 April receipt	8,000
30 April issue	(9,000)
Closing inventory	6,000

Using the FIFO method, all 6,000 units in inventory on 30 April were valued at $6.25 per unit.

Therefore, closing value = 6,000 units × $6.25
= $37,500

6   If P Co had used LIFO, instead of FIFO , the value of the material issued would have been $ [300] higher/~~lower~~

Workings

LIFO – Material issues

	$
8,000 units × $6.25	50,000
1,000 units × $6.30	6,300
	56,300

FIFO – Material issues

	$
1,000 units × $5.80	5,800
1,000 units × $6.20	6,200
5,000 units × $6.30	31,500
2,000 units × $6.25	12,500
	56,000

	$
Value using LIFO	56,300
Value using FIFO	56,000
Difference	300

7   [✓] debit the income statement and credit the production overhead account

If actual overheads are greater than absorbed overheads, then overheads are **under-absorbed**. Under-absorbed overheads are debited to the income statement in order to make up for the 'shortfall' ie debit income statement and credit production overhead account.

8   The amount payable (to the nearest $) to employee A is $ [235]

Workings

	$
500 units at $0.20	100
100 units at $0.25	25
200 units at $0.55	110
	235

9   Overtime premium is

[✓] the additional amount paid over and above the normal hourly rate for hours worked in excess of the basic working week.

10   The company quote for the job should be $ 250

Workings

	$
Variable production cost	125
Fixed overheads $\left(\dfrac{\$250,000}{12,500} \times 3 \right)$	60
Other costs	15
Total costs	200
Profit (20/80 × $200)	50
Quote for job	250

11   The production budget in units for Month 1 will be 6,600 units

Workings

	12	Month 1	2	3	4
	Units	Units	Units	Units	Units
Production – month 1	3,600	2,400			
Production – month 2		4,200	2,800		
Production – month 3			3,300	2,200	
Production – month 4				3,600	2,400
	3,600	6,600	6,100	5,800	2,400

12   The material cost budget for Month 2 will be $ 30,500

Workings

6,100 units at $5 per unit = $30,500

Note that the question asks for the **material cost** budget for Month 2 and not the **material purchases** budget.

13   ☑ material usage + materials closing inventory – materials opening inventory

14   The overhead budget for an activity level of 80% would be $ 115,000

Workings

Using the high-low method:

	Activity %	Overhead $
Low	50	100,000
High	75	112,500
	25	12,500

Variable cost per 1% of activity

25% = $12,500

$1\% \ = \dfrac{\$12,500}{25}$

= $500

Fixed costs

Substitute at 50% level:

Variable costs at 50%	=	50 × $500
	=	$25,000

Total costs	=	fixed costs + variable costs
$100,000	=	fixed costs + $25,000

Fixed costs	=	$100,000 − $25,000
	=	$75,000

Therefore at 80% activity:

Total costs	=	Fixed costs + variable costs
	=	$75,000 + (80 × $500)
	=	$75,000 + $40,000
	=	$115,000

15
    [✓] Repayment of a bank loan

    [✓] Proceeds from the sale of a non-current asset

Bad debts written off would not be included in the cash budget but would be shown in the budgeted income statement

16
    [✓] conventional breakeven chart

17 The amount budgeted to be paid to suppliers in September is $ [289,000]

Workings

			Paid in Month		
	July	*August*	*September*	*October*	*November*
Purchases	$	$	$	$	$
July $250,000	59,375[1]	175,000[2]	12,500[3]		
August $300,000		71,250[4]	210,000[5]	15,000[6]	
September $280,000			66,500[7]	196,000[8]	14,000[9]
			289,000		

1	$250,000 × 25% × 0.95	=	$59,375
2	$250,000 × 70%	=	$175,000
3	$250,000 × 5%	=	$12,500
4	$300,000 × 25% × 0.95	=	$71,250

5	$300,000 × 70%	= $210,000
6	$300,000 × 5%	= $15,000
7	$280,000 × 25% × 0.95	= $66,500
8	$280,000 × 70%	= $196,000
9	$280,000 × 5%	= $14,000

18   The value to be inserted in the table at A is $ [37,200]

Workings

	$
Raw material input	37,500
Less: Scrap proceeds of normal loss (see below)	(300)
Material cost for period	37,200

Normal loss   = 3% × input
              = 3% × 50,000 litres
              = 1,500 litres

Each litre is sold for $0.20 and this revenue is used to reduce the cost of raw materials input. 1,500 litres × $0.20 = $300

19   The total value of the transfers to Process 2 is $ [102,900]

Workings

Cost per equivalent litre = $0.75 + $1.35
                           = $2.10

Actual output to process 2 = 49,000 litres

∴ Value of transfer to Process 2   = 49,000 litres × $2.10
                                   = $102,900

20   The budgeted profit for the quarter ending 31 March 20X2 was $ [165,000]

Workings

Budgeted profit

	$	$
Selling price per meal		5.00
Variable costs		
Labour costs	0.60	
Food and drink costs	1.50	
Budgeted contribution		2.10
		2.90

Budgeted meals = 100,000

Budgeted contribution = 100,000 × $2.90   = $290,000

Budgeted fixed overheads for the year   = $500,000

∴ Budgeted fixed overheads per quarter $= \dfrac{\$500,000}{4}$

$= \$125,000$

∴ Budgeted profit for quarter = budgeted contribution – budgeted fixed overheads
= $290,000 – $125,000
= $165,000

21 The total sales margin contribution variance for the quarter ending 31 March 20X2 was $ $\boxed{51,500}$ adverse/~~favourable~~

Workings

Total sales margin contribution variance

	$	$
Actual sales revenue (90,000 × $4.75)	427,500	
Actual standard cost of sales (90,000 × $2.10)	189,000	
Actual margin based on standard unit costs		238,500
Budgeted margin (100,000 × $2.90)		290,000
Total sales margin variance		51,500 (A)

22 D A functional budget is a budget of income and/or expenditure for a particular department or process. A cash budget does not relate to a function.

23 A $\boxed{\$42.20}$ (to 2 decimal places)

B $\boxed{\$157.49}$ (to 2 decimal places)

Workings

FIFO

		Issues		Closing inventory balance		
	Quantity	Value	Total	Quantity	Value	Total
		$	$		$	$
April 20	4	10.55	42.20	4	10.55	42.20
				10	10.50	105.00
				12	10.29	123.48
				26		270.68
April 21	4	10.55	42.20			
	10	10.50	105.00			
	1	10.29	10.29			
			157.49	11	10.29	113.19

C $\boxed{\$115.90}$ (to 2 decimal places)

Workings

LIFO

		Issues			*Closing inventory balance*	
	Quantity	Value $	Total $	Quantity	Value $	Total $
April 20	4	10.29	41.16	8	10.29	82.32
				10	10.50	105.00
				8	10.55	84.40
				26		271.72
April 21	8	10.29	82.32	3	10.50	31.50
	7	10.50	73.50	8	10.55	84.40
			155.82			115.90

24 This type of remuneration is known as ⟨ a differential piecework scheme ⟩

The employee's remuneration for an output of 68 units in a period would be $ ⟨ 283.20 ⟩

Workings

			$
First 50 units =	50	× $4.10	205.00
Units 51 to 60 =	10	× $4.30	43.00
Units 61 to 68 =	8	× $4.40	35.20
	68		283.20

25 $ ⟨ 6.15 ⟩ for each ⟨ machine hour ⟩

Workings

	Machining $	Assembly $	Main-tenance $	Stores $	Total $
Total overhead	130,000	122,000	39,150	42,000	333,150
Apportion maintenance*	27,600	8,400	(39,150)	3,150	–
Apportion stores	33,150	12,000		(45,150)	–
	190,750	142,400	–	–	333,150

Overhead absorption rate for machining department = $190,750/31,000

= $6.15 per machine hour

* The total maintenance hours for the cost centres receiving a charge = 9,200 + 2,800 + 1,050 = 13,050.
Therefore, charge to machining department = 9,200/13,050 × $39,150 = $27,600.

26 (a) The value of closing inventory carried forward in period 2 is $ [4,200]

Workings

Period 2 closing inventory = 100 units (500 – 400)

The absorption rate for fixed costs is $\dfrac{\$6,000}{500 \text{ units}}$ = $12 per unit

Inventory is valued at $30 + $12 = $42 per unit

100 units at $42 per unit = $4,200

(b) The (under)-/over-absorbed overhead in period 3 is $ [(600)]

Workings

Absorbed overhead= $12 × 450 units = $5,400

Actual overhead = $6,000

∴ under –absorbed overhead = $5,400 – $6,000 = $600

27 The selling price (to the nearest $) per thousand leaflets for quantities of 20,000 leaflets is $ [53]

		20,000 leaflets
		$
Artwork		65
Machine setting	(4 × $22)	88
Paper	($12.50 × 20)	250
Ink and consumables	($40 × 2)	80
Printers' wages	(4 hrs × $8 × 2)	64
General fixed overheads	($15,000/600 × $8 × 2)	200
Total cost		747
Mark up	(see workings)	320
Selling price		1,067
Selling price per 1,000 leaflets	(÷ 20)	$53

Workings

20,000 leaflets

Let x = mark up on cost

30% × (747 + x) = x

224 +0.3x   = x

$$x = \frac{224}{0.7}$$

  = $320

BPP
LEARNING MEDIA

28   A $ 90,000

     B $ 54,000

     C $ 25,000

     D $ 62,500

Workings

A: sales revenue = $90,000

B: variable cost for sales of $90,000 = $90,000 × $(0.50 + 0.10) = $54,000

C: fixed cost   = $10,000 cost of sales + $15,000 administration
                   = $25,000

D: **Contribution per $ of sales**

	$
Sales price	1.00
Cost of sales	(0.50)
Selling and distribution costs	(0.10)
Contribution per $ (C/S ratio)	0.40

Monthly sales breakeven point $= \dfrac{\text{Fixed costs}}{\text{C/S ratio}}$

$= \dfrac{25{,}000}{0.4}$

$= \$62{,}500$

29   (a)   The change in profit between the two periods resulting from the selling price increase was $ 74,300

Working

With no other changes, the profit that would be expected in period 2 as a result of a 10% selling price increase is:

	Period 2 $'000
Sales ($742.7 × 1.1)	817.0
Variable costs	408.3
Contribution	408.7
Fixed costs	297.8
Net profit	110.9

Therefore the change in profit due to selling price increases = 110.9k – 36.6k = $74.3k

(b) The change in profit between the two periods resulting from cost inflation was $ (35,300)

Working

With no other changes, the profit that would be expected in period 2 as a result of 5% cost inflation is:

	Period 2
	$'000
Sales	742.7
Variable costs (408.3 × 1.05)	428.7
Contribution	314.0
Fixed costs (297.8 × 1.05)	312.7
Net profit	1.3

Therefore the reduction in profit due to cost inflation = 1.3k – 36.6k = $(35.3)k

30 June   6,000

   July   7,600

   August   8,350

   September   6,950

	Production budget			
	June	July	August	September
	Cases	Cases	Cases	Cases
Sales quantity	6,000	7,500	8,500	7,000
Closing inventories	750	850	700	650
	6,750	8,350	9,200	7,650
Less opening inventories	(750)	(750)	(850)	(700)
Budgeted production	6,000	7,600	8,350	6,950

31 The breakeven output level would increase by 122 units

	Current	Revised	Difference
	$	$	
Selling price	14	15	
Variable costs	6	5	
Contribution per unit	8	10	
Fixed costs	$24,400	*$31,720	
Breakeven point (units) (see working)	3,050	3,172	**122 higher**

*$24,400 × 130% = $31,720

Working

$$\text{Breakeven point (BEP)} = \frac{\text{Total fixed costs}}{\text{Contribution per unit}}$$

$$\textbf{Current BEP} = \frac{\$24,400}{\$8} = 3,050 \text{ units}$$

$$\textbf{Revised BEP} = \frac{\$31,720}{\$10} = 3,172 \text{ units}$$

32 The number of units required to be produced and sold annually to achieve this is $\boxed{7,132}$ units

Current profit	= total contribution – fixed costs
	= (8,000 × $8) – $24,400
	= $39,600
∴ **Required profit**	= $39,600

If the new production methods are implemented the required contribution will be:

Required contribution	= revised fixed costs + required profit
	= $31,720 + $39,600
	= $71,320

Required sales $= \dfrac{\text{Contribution required}}{\text{Contribution per unit (revised)}}$

$= \dfrac{\$71,320}{\$10}$

= 7,132 units

33

	Material price variance	Material usage variance
Material A	$ $\boxed{0}$	$ $\boxed{13,200 \text{ (F)}}$
Material B	$ $\boxed{60,000 \text{ (A)}}$	$ $\boxed{13,200 \text{ (F)}}$

Workings

Material A	$
150,000 kg should cost (× $11)	1,650,000
but did cost	1,650,000
Price variance	0

126,000 units should use (× 1.2 kgs)	151,200	kgs
but did use	150,000	kgs
	1,200	kgs (F)
× standard price per kg	× $11	
Usage variance	$13,200	(F)

Material B	$
590,000 kgs should cost (× $6)	3,540,000
but did cost	3,600,000
Price variance	60,000	(A)

126,000 units should use (× 4.7 kgs)	592,200	kgs
but did use	590,000	kgs
	2,200	kgs (F)
× standard price per kg	× $6	
Usage variance	$13,200	(F)

34   B   Basic knowledge. There's no excuse for getting this wrong.

35   A   Job costing is a costing method applied where work is **undertaken to customers' special requirements.** Option B describes process costing, C describes service costing and D describes absorption costing.

36   C   *Workings*

Total labour cost incurred during period   = $(12,500 + 23,000 + 4,500)$
                                             = \$40,000

∴ Overhead absorption rate   = $(\$140,000/\$40,000) \times 100\%$
                                             = 350% of labour cost

	$
Opening WIP	46,000
Labour for period	4,500
Overhead absorbed ($4,500 × 350%)	15,750
Total production cost	66,250
50% mark up	33,125
Sales value of job 3	99,375

Selling price per circuit board = $99,375 ÷ 2,400 $41.41

Option B is the selling price without the inclusion of any overhead absorbed. If you selected option D you calculated a 50 per cent margin based on the selling price, instead of a 50% mark up on cost.

37   C   Since wages are paid on a piecework basis they are a variable cost which will increase in line with the number of binders. The machine set-up cost and design costs are fixed costs for each batch which will not be affected by the number of binders in the batch.

For a batch of 300 binders:

	$
Direct materials (30 × 3)	90.00
Direct wages (10 × 3)	30.00
Machine set up	3.00
Design and artwork	15.00
Production overhead (30 × 20%)	6.00
Total production cost	144.00
Selling, distribution and administration overhead (+ 5%)	7.20
Total cost	151.20
Profit (25% margin = $33^1/_3$% of cost)	50.40
Selling price for a batch of 300	201.60

If you selected option A you calculated the cost correctly, but added a profit mark up of 25% of cost, instead of a margin of 25% of selling price.

If you selected option B you failed to absorb the appropriate amount of fixed overhead. If you selected option D you treated all of the costs as variable costs.

38 B

Input	Units	Output	Units
Opening work in progress	240	Normal loss (10% × 2,180)	218
Additional input	2,180	Good units (bal fig)	2,022
Abnormal gain	20	Closing work in progress	200
	2,440		2,440

39 B Abnormal gain = 276 units − 112 units = 164 units

Cost per unit of good production = $29,744/5,408 = $5.50

∴ Value of abnormal gain = 164 units × $5.50 = $902

The value of the input can be found as the balancing figure in the value columns of the process account.

Polishing process account

	$		$
Input (balancing figure)	29,532	Output	29,744
Abnormal gain	902	Normal loss (276 × $2.50)	690
	30,434		30,434

40 C The **point of separation,** also referred to as the split-off point, is the point in a process where **joint products** become separately identifiable. Costs incurred prior to this point are common or **joint costs**.

41 A Abnormal loss units are valued at the same cost per unit as completed output. The cost per unit of output and the cost per unit of abnormal loss are based on expected output.

42 [✓] Production costs excluding direct materials

43 C Statement (i) is not correct. A debit to stores with a corresponding credit to work in progress (WIP) indicates that **direct materials returned** from production were $18,000.

Statement (ii) is correct. **Direct costs of production** are 'collected' in the WIP account.

Statement (iii) is correct. **Indirect costs of production or overhead** are 'collected' in the overhead control account.

Statement (iv) is correct. The purchases of materials on credit are credited to the creditors account and debited to the material stores control account.

Therefore the correct answer is C.

44 A Standard price per kg of material = $384,000/32,000 = $12

Standard material usage per unit = 32,000 kg/4,000 = 8 kg per unit

4,200 units should have used (× 8 kg)	33,600 kg
but did use	35,200 kg
Usage variance in kg	1,600 kg (A)
× standard price per kg	× $12
Material usage variance	$19,200 (A)

45   C   The lawyer's salary is an indirect cost because it cannot be traced to a specific cost unit. It would be classified as an administration overhead.

All of the other costs can be traced to a specific cost unit. The cost of hops (A) would be a direct ingredients cost of a specific batch of beer. The telephone rental cost (B) would be a direct cost of a construction contract. The cost of food served (D) would be a direct cost of a particular flight.

46   C   The FIFO method uses the cost of older batches first.

Cost of units sold on 24 March:	$
330 units at $42 each	13,860
102 units at $43 each	4,386
432 units	18,246

47   The gross profit would be $ | 7,820 |

The LIFO method values issues using the cost of the most recent batches first.

Cost of units sold on 27 May:	$
250 units at $59 each	14,750
80 units at $51 each	4,080
230 units at $57 each	13,110
560 units	31,940

	$
Sales revenue = 560 units × $71 =	39,760
Less cost of units sold	31,940
	7,820

48   D

$$\text{Production overhead absorption rate} = \$150,000/60,000$$
$$= \$2.50 \text{ per machine hour}$$

$$\text{Production overhead absorbed} = \$2.50 \times 55,000 \text{ hours}$$
$$= \$137,500$$

$$\text{Production overhead incurred} = \underline{\$150,000}$$

$$\text{Production overhead under absorbed} = \underline{\$ \ 12,500}$$

49   C   Statement (i) is incorrect. Although closing inventory is valued at the most recent prices, the issues from inventory are valued at the earliest delivery remaining in stock. Therefore the first part of the statement is not correct.

50   The bonus would be $ | 9.00 |.

Standard time allowed for 60 enquiries = 60 × 10/60
                                       = 10 hours

Time saved = 10 hours − 8 hours = 2 hours

Bonus payable = 2 hours × 30% × $15
              = $9.00

BPP
LEARNING MEDIA

Review Form & Free Prize Draw – Paper C1 Fundamentals of Management Accounting (12/07)

All original review forms from the entire BPP range, completed with genuine comments, will be entered into one of two draws on 31 July 2008 and 31 January 2009. The names on the first four forms picked out on each occasion will be sent a cheque for £50.

Name: _____   Address: _____

_____

_____

How have you used this Kit?
(Tick one box only)

☐ Home study (book only)

☐ On a course: college _____

☐ With 'correspondence' package

☐ Other _____

Why did you decide to purchase this Kit?
(Tick one box only)

☐ Have used the complementary Study text

☐ Have used other BPP products in the past

☐ Recommendation by friend/colleague

☐ Recommendation by a lecturer at college

☐ Saw advertising

☐ Other _____

During the past six months do you recall seeing/receiving any of the following?
(Tick as many boxes as are relevant)

☐ Our advertisement in *CIMA Insider*

☐ Our advertisement in *Financial Management*

☐ Our advertisement in *Pass*

☐ Our brochure with a letter through the post

☐ Our website www.bpp.com

Which (if any) aspects of our advertising do you find useful?
(Tick as many boxes as are relevant)

☐ Prices and publication dates of new editions

☐ Information on product content

☐ Facility to order books off-the-page

☐ None of the above

Which BPP products have you used?

Text	☐	CD	☐	i-Learn	☐
Passcards	☐	Virtual Campus	☐	MCQ cards	☐
Kit	☑	i-Pass	☐		

Your ratings, comments and suggestions would be appreciated on the following areas.

	Very useful	Useful	Not useful
Effective revision	☐	☐	☐
Exam guidance	☐	☐	☐
Multiple choice questions	☐	☐	☐
Objective test questions	☐	☐	☐
Guidance in answers	☐	☐	☐
Content and structure of answers	☐	☐	☐
Mock assessments	☐	☐	☐
Mock assessment answers	☐	☐	☐

Overall opinion of this Kit   Excellent ☐   Good ☐   Adequate ☐   Poor ☐

Do you intend to continue using BPP products?   Yes ☐   No ☐

The BPP author of this edition can be e-mailed at: heatherfreer@bpp.com

Please return this form to: Janice Ross, CIMA Certificate Publishing Manager, BPP Learning Media Ltd, FREEPOST, London, W12 8BR

Review Form & Free Prize Draw (continued)

TELL US WHAT YOU THINK

Please note any comments and suggestions/errors below

Free Prize Draw Rules

1   Closing date for 31 July 2008 draw is 30 June 2008. Closing date for 31 January 2009 draw is 31 December 2008.

2   Restricted to entries with UK and Eire addresses only. BPP employees, their families and business associates are excluded.

3   No purchase necessary. Entry forms are available upon request from BPP Learning Media Ltd. No more than one entry per title, per person. Draw restricted to persons aged 16 and over.

4   Winners will be notified by post and receive their cheques not later than 6 weeks after the relevant draw date.

5   The decision of the promoter in all matters is final and binding. No correspondence will be entered into.